Editor Frank Bechhofer

POPULATION GROWTH AND

THE BRAIN DRAIN

This book is an expression of the new interest
in Demography, and a vindication of it. As
the vast problems of the population explosion
increasingly demand long-range and internationally co-ordinated action, it is the exact
science of Demography that provides the data
and the classifications, the corpus of information, without which such planning is little
more than guesswork.

This stimulating collection of papers by
international authorities dealing with fertility
and death rates, the structure of migration,
the 'Brain Drain', and with techniques and
methods of study, derives from the Edinburgh
conference on Demography, 1967.

In the fields of international co-operation, of
civil administration, of public health and social
medicine, of biology, cytogenetics, and ecology,
the Demographer has been restored to his
rightful place ; and exponents in all these
fields will find much interest and stimulus in
this present work.

The editor, Mr Frank Bechhofer, is lecturer
in Sociology, University of Edinburgh, and
author of The Affluent Worker : Industrial
Attitudes and Behaviour (1968), and of The
Affluent Worker : Political Attitudes and
Behaviour (1968).

EDINBURGH UNIVERSITY PRESS
22 George Square Edinburgh
North America
ALDINE PUBLISHING COMPANY
529 South Wabash Avenue
Chicago 60605

Proceedings of the Edinburgh Conference
on Demography

Population Growth and the Brain Drain

edited by F. BECHHOFER

at the University Press
Edinburgh

© Edinburgh University Press 1969
EDINBURGH UNIVERSITY PRESS
22 George Square, Edinburgh
North America
Aldine Publishing Company
529 South Wabash Avenue, Chicago
Australia and New Zealand
Hodder and Stoughton Ltd
Africa, Oxford University Press
India, P.C.Manaktala & Sons
Far East, M.Graham Brash & Son
85224 066 x
Library of Congress
Catalog Card Number 7577159

Printed in Great Britain by
The Kynoch Press, Birmingham

Preface

Demography as a branch of the social sciences was long neglected in Great Britain. After a good start academic attention shifted to other fields, so that the landmarks of British demography are few and far between – notably the work of D. V. Glass and A. M. Carr-Saunders. During the last ten years, however, there have been signs of a re-awakening. Historical demography has taken firm root in Cambridge. University sociology departments now expect to employ at least one demographer. And medical demography is in a flourishing state. The object of the seminar, for which the papers in this book were prepared, was to give demography a further boost in British universities by attracting attention to just what demographers in Britain and abroad were doing.

The idea of holding such a seminar originated with Tom Burns, Professor of Sociology in Edinburgh, who also undertook the considerable task of compiling an initial list of representative speakers. The holding of the seminar, in Edinburgh, May 1967, was made possible by a generous donation from the Joseph Rowntree Trust. The detailed arrangements were handled by a committee under the chairmanship of J. N. Wolfe, Professor of Economics. And the work of preparing and editing the papers was undertaken by Frank Bechhofer, Lecturer in Sociology. To all of them, the speakers and the chairmen of the various sessions, the Board of Research of the Faculty of Social Sciences of the University of Edinburgh wishes to express its gratitude.

H. J. Hanham *Convener, Board of Research*
Faculty of Social Sciences, Edinburgh.

Contents

List of Participants

S. van Bath, Agricultural University, Wageningen.
G. Beijer, Research Group for European Migration Problems, The Hague.
W. Brand, Leiden.
W. Brass, Department of Medical Statistics, London School of Hygiene.
T. Burns, Department of Sociology, University of Edinburgh.
N. Carrier, London School of Economics.
G. M. Carstairs, Department of Psychiatry, University of Edinburgh.
C. Clark, Agricultural Economics Research Institute, Oxford.
H. J. D. Cole, Department of Economic Affairs, London.
K. H. Connell, Department of Economic and Social History, University of Belfast.
P. R. Cox, Government Actuary's Department, London.
M. Drake, University of Kent.
D. C. Eversley, University of Sussex.
E. Grebenik, Department of Social Studies, University of Leeds.
H. J. Habakkuk, Jesus College, Oxford.
G. F. Hammersley, Department of History, University of Edinburgh.
T. H. Hollingsworth, University of Glasgow.
R. Illsley, Department of Sociology, University of Aberdeen.
P. Johnson-Marshall, Department of Urban Design and Regional Planning, University of Edinburgh.
P. Laslett, Trinity College, Cambridge.
J. M. Last, Department of Social Medicine, University of Edinburgh.
A. Sauvy, Institut Nationale d'études Demographiques, Paris.
S. A. Sklaroff, Department of Social Medicine, University of Edinburgh.
W. Steigenga, Department of Planning and Demography, University of Amsterdam.
L. Tabah, Institut Nationale d'études Demographiques, Paris.
J. N. Wolfe, Department of Economics, University of Edinburgh.
E. A. Wrigley, Cambridge Group for the History of Population and Social Structure, Cambridge.

Introduction

Editing the proceedings of this seminar has proved a rather curious experience. As a sociologist – and not even a sociologist with strong leanings towards demography – I have felt very much outside the papers and discussions; a social scientist peering into little known and perhaps rather murky waters! This has had disadvantages on occasion, and I should like here to acknowledge the assistance of my colleague, Mr Peter Nelstrop, who is a sociologist with very strong leanings towards demography! He helped me out from time to time when I became lost, and read the reports of some of the discussions.

The seminar consisted of groups of papers, in the main circulated in advance and introduced rather than read by their authors; prepared comments by invited discussants; and general discussion. My task as editor has consisted firstly of persuading the authors and prepared discussants to revise their contributions where necessary and return them to me within a reasonable time. The material contained in these sections of the book is exactly as they wrote it with the exception of a little editorial work (particularly in the case of the papers by foreign contributors) which has been agreed to by the authors. The reports of the discussions have been prepared from tapes recorded in the sessions and are entirely my own responsibility. Only in the case of very extended verbatim quotations has the approval of the participant been secured. I should like to apologize to anyone who feels they may have been misrepresented, and to those whose comments have disappeared for ever under the editorial pencil. I have attempted to sharpen and re-arrange the contributions to the discussion while at the same time trying to keep the flavour of an on-going debate which was such a noticeable feature of the seminar. As Professor Burns remarked in his closing comments, no-one expects conferences to provide all the answers – or perhaps even many answers – but there was some lively discussion, and it is to be hoped that in studying the accounts of what was said the reader may chance upon ideas which stimulate further thought and research. To an outsider it certainly seemed that many hares were set running which merit chasing.

To attempt to summarize the proceedings of a seminar which ranged as widely as this one is clearly an impossible task and one which I have no intention of attempting. Nevertheless, my position as a sociological outsider tempts me to make a few, perhaps provocative observations. I should make it clear right at the beginning that these remarks are largely stimulated by the papers and discussions, although I think they have some general reference and also that they are certainly more true of European than of American demography.

It became more and more apparent to me as I listened to the proceedings, and then re-read and re-heard them several times, that demography as a single unified discipline no longer exists, if indeed it ever did. There are, of course, still demographers concerned with the detailed examination of the statistics of population description and change, and the development of the techniques of demographic analysis. Some of these appear to be concerned with the development of demography as a *service* discipline, rather as some statisticians see their role. In increasing numbers, however, demographers seem to be economists, economic and social historians, or sociologists who choose to become expert in the use of demographic material, rather than demographers first and foremost. Admittedly a good deal of effort is still being devoted to the building of purely demographic models; the idea of 'making bricks not only without straw but also without clay', as it has been described, is still a large part of the demographer's activities. In the case of the historical demography sessions it was quite clear that the unravelling of data about the past is an immense task and one which we are only just beginning to tackle seriously and methodically, despite the considerable strides which have already been made. If we turn, however, to the papers on the 'brain drain', it becomes clear that there the problems facing the demographer are somewhat different. The relevant demographic material is again in many cases simply not available, statistics on migration are inadequate, incomplete and often misleading. But this is to a considerable extent highlighted by the shift of emphasis which, while not unanticipated in the past, I am suggesting is occurring increasingly in the present. Data has not been collected, or has been collected badly, because the problems are new, and they are new because they spring from a different source than hitherto. Thus again and again in the conference there was discussion not only of the reliability of the data, but more importantly of the *interpretations* which the data would sustain. This occurs, it appears to me, at least partly because the fundamental *problem* which most demographers are attacking is no longer one of establishing the demographic facts as an end in itself. The problems stem essentially from one of the other disciplines which I have mentioned, and the demographic material is being brought to bear on these problems.

With this shift in emphasis comes an increasing concern to assess the part played by demographic changes in the *explanation* of socio - economic phenonema, and to *explain* the demographic changes or situations themselves in terms of the socio-economic system. Now, the linking of the demographic facts to the social and economic environment in which they are embedded appears to have brought demographers face to face with a number of problems which have a familiar ring to social scientists in general.

Firstly, the search for explanation rather than description is now a central problem in the social sciences. In order to explain in a scientific way it is necessary to develop models and theories, and this is proving a difficult and at times frustrating task. Yet it is a task which must be tackled. To say that I was struck by the paucity of such models in this conference is not to point an accusing finger; it would be a particularly dangerous procedure for a sociologist as well as presumptuous for an outsider. Yet it seemed to me that while demo - graphy has a long history of the building of models of population change and description, these are closed system models in which popu - lation parameters and *only* population parameters appear. Models which include socio - economic variables appear to be largely lacking. Developing such models clearly presents tremendous problems but a start will not be made on them until it is accepted that this *is* an aim, that the development and testing of such models is *the problem.* I am not sure to what extent it has so far been perceived as such among the practitioners of what I shall call, conveniently but I know unjustifiably, modern demography.

Secondly, the debate between those who would like to *predict* population structure and change in the future and those who believe that demography must restrict itself to describing and explaining population in the *past* is paralleled elsewhere. Here there seem to be two strands worthy of brief mention. If demographic material can be related to socio - economic phenomena in a meaningful and dynamic way, then the problem of prediction is in a sense pushed one stage further back. Predicting population patterns will depend on predicting socio - economic change, although it is also true that our models will have to provide us with the means of estimating the dynamic effects of current population structure on the social system as a whole. Which variables are independent and which dependent must depend on the problem under consideration, and for some purposes we shall require feedback models which enable us to move alternately from one side of the picture to the other. Objections to the idea of prediction in social science generally take one of three forms. The first two rest largely on a misconception of the idea of prediction. One objection claims that a prediction can always be falsified by an unanticipated factor which the model does not take into account. This is clearly also so in natural science and simply requires the refinement of the model rather than the abandonment of the task. The second claims that predictions can be self-falsifying or self-fulfilling as humans are capable of purposive action and can act on the basis of the prediction. This is undoubtedly true in theory, but in practice requires the prediction to be widely known and based on processes relatively amenable to change, and also that a large majority of those cognizant of the prediction and having access to the means of change agree to act in concert. Although this can occur it is by no means necessarily so, and in any case all predictions must take the form of a statement that, given this and that, something else will happen, other things remaining constant. The objection therefore is both relatively unimportant and again based on a misconception. The third objection to prediction is a much more difficult one to deal with. This claims in essence that the actions of human beings are imbued with meanings and that they take these meanings from the social situation in which they occur. Human action, therefore, is always subject to change which cannot be directly related to the social situation but must be interpreted in the light of the meaning the actor gives to the situation. Although it is a perfectly adequate reply that in the last resort it should be possible to bring the mechanisms of this interpretation within the scope of scientific analysis, this is a counsel of perfection which may for ever elude us, and though philosphically adequate hardly helps us to deal with the problem in the here and now. I think the answer we must give at present is that all prediction will remain for a very long time, possibly for ever, uncertain; the critical question to me is the degree of uncertainty. As I have already stressed, social scientists must remain clear that their predictions are always subject to the clause 'other things being constant'. And one of the things which has to remain constant is the interpretation the actor gives to the social situation. To the extent that demography has started to move out of the closed demographic parameter model, prediction is brought a stage nearer. This model requires to remain constant so many things which we know are readily capable of change and indeed can be induced to change, that prediction is a very chancy matter indeed. If we can obtain models which explain demographic phenomena in terms of socio-economic variables we are able to make predictions with, hopefully, a slightly greater degree of certainty. To some extent social scientists are being forced to make predictions, whether they like it or not, by the demands of society, and this brings me to my last set of familiar problems.

One question raised for demographers today as well as for other social scientists is whether they *wish* to become applied social scientists. The dilemma between a knowledge that social science is very imperfect at the present time and the demands of society for action, however imperfect, is very acute and it emerged from time to time in the course of this conference although not in a very explicit way. Increasingly social scientists are being presented with problems which stem not from the theoretical structure of their discipline but from society; these are societal problems rather than sociological ones or economic-theoretical ones, and so on. Modern demography in part owes its starting points more and more often to demands for answers to societal problems, for example the 'brain drain', or population growth related to food supply. It is because members of a society wish to change something or are perturbed by something that they call in the social scientist, in this case the demographer. Increasingly, demographers in common with other social scientists are being asked how they would go about achieving or changing something rather than how they explain its occurrence. This raises the question of prediction very sharply, because any recommended action must depend on a prediction of its effects. It also raises very familiar questions of the influence of moral or political commitment on social science. I suspect modern demographers are confronted with very well-known problems in the debate on a *wertfrei* social science, and are being asked about the extent to which they can claim their findings and predictions are value-free. These arguments are so well-known that it would be fatuous to repeat them here but I shall make just one observation which brings me back to my first major point. Unless models of the kind I have suggested can be developed, 'modern demography' cannot possibly hope to be value-free, and without such models it will never be possible to recommend courses of action which are more than the judgement of an expert, but probably biased, and partial observer.

The impression which this seminar gave me is of rapidly growing areas of interest, research and knowledge within several disciplines, with demographic data and phenomena as a linking theme but with no common theoretical framework. Perhaps heretically (an outsider is allowed to be a heretic) I wonder whether the position is not that most modern demographers have much more in common with the practitioners of the disciplines from which their problems spring, than with each other. If this is so, then it is very striking and disturbing to see how little reference was made to theories, models or even concepts drawn from these disciplines. To put the position very extremely, not only does there seem to be a lack of theoretical framework for much of the work being discussed, but it remains detached from such theories and models as exist in these social sciences within which the work seems to lie.

Thus I would suggest that the demographers' dialogue has been too exclusively with each other. Given that 'classical' demography has been concerned largely with models for the generation of empirical data, it is not surprising that demographers now working in the various disciplines have concentrated on similar methods, have in the main remained resolutely empiricist and have not attempted to construct *explanatory* models for the problems they now find themselves tackling.

In the course of the seminar, however, it also became clear that most participants were very conscious of the need for further research and for greater precision. But strikingly this went beyond a wish to improve the data available or its manipulation and suggested a move towards the examination and explanation of the *processes behind the data*. And if this is their aim, then I hope it is not just a limited and partial vision which leads me to suggest that demographers may be too concerned with demography rather than economics, history, sociology, and so on.

If I may allow myself a prediction, I would hazard that in twenty years time the holding of a conference of this kind will be extremely unlikely. I suspect that by that time there will be many different kinds of demographers and they will find it more fruitful to converse with their fellow economists, historians or sociologists than with each other. And this could be very unfortunate; in 1990 there may well be a move to bring demographers together again to benefit from a study of each other's techniques and models in differing fields of applications. At this conference in any event they showed themselves well able to talk to each other and engage in brisk discussion.

In conclusion, then, I should like to thank contributors for revising their papers and comments, putting up with editorial pestering and entrusting me with the work of correcting proofs and generally preparing this volume. I have found the task stimulating and I would not wish them to regard this introduction as an attack. Nor do I offer it as something totally new. It is rather offered as a friendly if possibly completely misguided suggestion from someone who read and listened with great interest and considerable profit, but wondered why the content all seemed so familiar and yet so strange.

Frank Bechhofer, Edinburgh, July 1968.

Migration and the Brain Drain

G. BEIJER
Brain drain as a burden, a stimulus
and a challenge to European integration

J. M. LAST
International mobility in the medical profession

A. SAUVY
The economic and political consequences of
selective migrations from one country to another

with prepared comments by R. Illsley

CHAIRMAN
A. J. Youngson

B

G. BEIJER

Brain Drain as a Burden, a Stimulus and a Challenge to European Integration

For a long time the flow of migrants from Europe to the New World was caused by political, racial, religious, and demographic pressure and differences. The migrants came from all social strata. In the nineteenth century and up to 1914, lords and beggars, adventurers and underdogs, gold-diggers and bread-winners moved on a large scale from Europe to North America, Latin America, Oceania, and South Africa.

The change to present times is evident. 'The modern pattern shows a reversal of the flow: skilled labour and scientific personnel are moving from the less prosperous countries to the four richest nations of the world, and especially the United States.'[1] This view of an English demographer and economist on the emigration of European people might be supplemented with the view of a continental demographer, Alfred Sauvy. In his address to the first European Population Conference on the 'Population Situation in Europe', he refers to the emigration of eminent intellectuals which the Americans call the 'brain drain': 'It is a phenomenon which merits our closest attention in view of its impact and its unobtrusiveness.'[2]

Sauvy draws attention to the fact that 'if an individual or a company were to steal a ton of steel or petroleum from another country the machinery of the law would be set in motion and the country concerned would complain loudly about the loss. Nothing of the sort happens when a country loses men, whose value, however, is much greater.'

The author of the first quotation, Brinley Thomas, goes so far as to state that 'if physical capital must be paid for, why should publicly financed human capital be received free?' Consequently, migrating scientists should be considered as an item in the balance of payments.[3]

Alfred Sauvy, however, sees the solution of the problem in 'deploying the scant efforts made towards adequate co-ordination, particularly by the European Communities, who are after all in a good position to take such action.' The idea that humanity is not enslaved, that the individual can freely shape his destiny, as is stated by Sauvy, runs contrary to other opinions. Hofmeijer,[4] for instance, holds that migration is no longer a concern of individuals only or, in brief, that

migration nowadays is a social problem to be handled by governments in close co-operation with employers and trade unions, with
local authorities and voluntary social agencies. Evidently, this proposal to more or less plan migratory movements of people is a result
of the European labour-market situation.

As the movement of scientists and technologists is an old and
traditional phenomenon, such proposals as mentioned by Hofmeijer
are perhaps suitable for the mass of migrants but must be rejected
for the flow of scientists. The migration of scientists both in the past
and present[5] has made a significant contribution not only to the
progress of science but also to the development of Western and world
civilization. Mobility has always been an important characteristic of
the intellectual community, which is reflected in the migration not
only of scientists and technologists but also of other scholars. 'For
every country the links created by the movement of scientists and
technologists are multi-national: its emigrants go to many countries
and its immigrants come from many. The patterns are further complicated by what seems to be a substantial amount of re-emigration as
individuals move on to third, even fourth countries. Major changes
in migration patterns may also have implications for a country not
directly involved. Such changes, for example, may make it more
difficult to recruit needed immigrants.'[6]

Generalizing roughly from the very meagre facts, the movements
of intellectuals, that is, mostly scientific and technical manpower,
make headlines. These arouse increasing interest and concern in
academic, political, and social circles, which have shone some light
on this very complicated matter, or will try to do so in the future.

In Europe the discussion has been encouraged by the report
Emigration of Scientists from the United Kingdom.[7] This report is also
a reaction to articles and letters in the popular press and the professional journals, in which it was hypothesized that British scientists
and technologists were being attracted to foreign countries (especially
the United States of America) by greater professional and economic
opportunities there. Remarkably enough the emigration figures are
given in this report, but the immigration of scientists into Great
Britain is not mentioned.

Within the OECD the problem has also been observed, and an
'*Ad hoc* Steering Group on Migration' has proposed to OECD's
Committee for Scientific and Technical Personnel that they should
try to bring about statistical investigations on the international
exchange of technical and scientific manpower (1964). Unfortunately,
in the countries concerned, the statistical basis for investigation of
this problem has been almost completely missing. In the United
States and Great Britain a few analyses have been made. However, it

has not yet been possible to compile statistics complete enough to draw definite conclusions about the net balances in any country concerned.[8]

It was felt that, since the migration statistics were imprecise both in their figures and in the definitions of the academic professions, perhaps as many as one-half or more of the migrants in these statis- tics returned to their homeland after a certain period. Premature judgements and conclusions are often brought forward (without any consideration on either side to the intellectual balance of payments[9]).

A significant aspect of the discussion around the loss of excellently trained scientists, that is, the costs of producing scientists, was diffi- cult to approach. Assuming that the costs of 'producing' those scientists and engineers amount to an average of $50,000 (irrespec- tive of all difficulties experienced in undertaking such an estimation) it is possible to arrive at an estimated value of capital impact by immigration of qualified manpower to the United States of $300 million in 1963.[10]

According to a recent article,[11] Mr Quintin Hogg, for the Opposi- tion in the House of Commons, believed that Britain could not afford to let the 'brain drain' go on for ever. 'Even from the point of view of money, it costs about £20,000 to produce a PhD, about £10,000 to produce a first degree graduate.' This total of £20,000 or £10,000 respectively is certainly also a very rough estimate. Another aspect of the discussion on 'brain drain' is that there have been some anomalies, arising from the efforts of developing countries to pro- mote the expansion of education and training by the immigration of scientific manpower on the one hand and from the growing outflow of qualified people from some such countries on the other.[12]

When highly qualified manpower migrates from a less developed country to a more developed one, the loss to the former is very great and possibly greater than the benefit of the latter.[13] The problems of the 'brain drain' from one of the highest developed Latin American countries, that is Argentina,[14] to the United States is a sample of the problems involved for other developing countries of the Western hemisphere.

Therefore a positive aspect of the exodus of scientists from Western Europe and North America to under-developed countries might be the wise use of these people and of the scientists and scholars educated there; Latin America, with its Spanish and Portuguese language, is an integrated part of Western culture and civilization. Every effort to develop the infrastructure of these countries to contribute to the economic growth process in this Continent is therefore in the interest of the Western world.[15]

Anyway, it is to be expected that international migration of

qualified persons to and from developing countries may tend to increase in the near future. Definitely not in the form of mass movements, but, as W. D. Borrie[16] has said: 'temporary movements
abroad for purposes of higher education and selective immigration
of persons with skills essential to stimulate the rate of economic
growth, with the basic solution sought through the movements of
capital and extension of international trade. These last two factors
would thus play the same role as overseas investment from Europe in
the nineteenth century.'

Against the many spontaneous statements such as the 'absurdity
that our scientists cannot work at home' and 'could a country afford
the "brain drain" to go on for ever', more logical and less emotional
opinions have been expressed by many scientists. The situation on a
large scale and seen over a longer period would be other than
expected, and European and non-European countries may have a
positive balance of exchange, so that the 'brain drain' in the longer
or shorter run may become a 'brain gain'.

In summarizing the description of the problem, both from publications and from my own studies in this field, it might be concluded
that:

(1) the exodus of scientists, especially in the field of natural sciences
and engineering, cannot be identified as a typically European
phenomenon; it is a world-wide phenomenon. Scientists and engineers are on the move from Canada, from Latin American countries,
from Asia (Israel),[17] and in Europe from one European country to
another;

(2) in contradiction to many of the rather emotional publications,
it is not possible to underline the problem with figures about the
'two-way' traffic of this movement; this is an incomplete note, but

(3) in the near future it might be possible to arrive at a clearer
identification and description of this movement, based on more
exact national statistics and studies in execution;

(4) the past and present day discussion, however, (a) is more or
less based on incomplete statistical data, mostly concerning one side
of the traffic, and (b) comes up now and then in connection with the
emigration of a well-known and qualified scientist;

(5) 'One of the consequences of the greater concentration of resources on research and development in the United States, of better
working conditions, and of the higher level of research salaries prevailing there, is the attraction for foreign scientists and engineers to
research projects in that country';[18]

(6) the discussion of the migration of scientists from Europe and
other parts of the world has had the consequence that there are some
forces making for a certain degree of concentration in scientific

research as well as for the evaluation of the benefit which education represents to the individual and its effects on the economic growth.

BRAIN DRAIN — A BURDEN, A STIMULUS AND A CHALLENGE
The analysis of the problems arising from the 'brain drain', for example the burden upon the sending country and the gain for the receiving country, is extremely difficult. Too many aspects are involved in this movement. In fact, it is only through very rough calculations that the entire scope of the 'brain drain' can possibly be measured.

The burden to the sending country
'Even some developed countries of Western Europe observe the transatlantic flow with misgivings,'[19] and in general in the sending countries 'the current interest in the migration of professional scientific and technical personnel is largely keyed to economic growth and development.'[20]

The fact that 'education is the most important contribution to economic growth' is 'based on a number of assumptions and estimates which were necessary in the absence of factual data. On this basis, however, it is possible to examine in detail the sources of economic growth in the past, ways of changing the growth rate in the future, the effect of education on the quality of labour, the relationship of international differences in education to levels of output and growth rate.'[21]

Knowledge, qualifications, and motivations of manpower are relevant to production and growth of the national economy, and are to be regarded as a factor of production, involving costs to produce, and serving for more than one period. For the whole productive life of a person the fact that the homeland has partially or wholly paid for the education of emigrating individuals (by family support, government funds, student bursaries) makes permanent emigration a burden. By emigration of such individuals the community loses the opportunity to make use of the results of such education – as a contribution to economic and social progress – and to refund the costs of education through taxpaying. If a scientist migrates permanently it can be assumed, in general, that he is not only an economic and social loss to his native land, but that he is at least a loss in so far as his continuing participation in the scientific research work of that country is concerned. Following an American source:[22] 'Many of the immigrants represent the highest levels of professional qualifications and achieve national and international fame in making their contributions to American science and technology.'

Recently, at a 'workshop and conference' in the United States, the reactions to, but particularly the advantages and disadvantages of the 'brain drain' to developing countries were pointed out.[23] In the introduction to the proceedings it has been stressed already, for example, that in contrast with the recent past, now 'this situation has changed as a consequence of the increasing recognition of the crucial part played by *education, science and technology* in the drama of national development and in the general course of economic and social progress.' This is a great problem, for the developed as well as the under-developed countries. 'In theory and praxis the burden arising from the "brain drain" points to an emphasis in the country of origin.'

Causes for migration

In connection with the refugees in Europe after 1945, the expression: 'they vote with their feet' has often been used. Generally this will also apply to emigrant scientists – but when scientists choose to vote with their feet it is invariably whatever they walk away from that is at fault. That is why it seems better to try to establish the determinant motives that induce scientists to leave their native country for ever. When these motives are known, action can be taken in order to prevent losses of talents and skill.

In the first instance the discussion – a discussion which also attracted notice in the Soviet Union – gives as the most important causes for departure that:

(1) The economic and industrial situation of the country in question is too tightly tied to traditions, or that this country has not reached the advanced state of development that is needed to provide for these scientists work which complies with their talents, in the industry, etc.

(2) In regard to universities, research and development, management, but also to equipment of institutes, laboratories, libraries, etc., many countries bear a close resemblance to medieval monasteries; or it can also be said that, indeed, they do have the best university system in the whole world, but this is still operating and teaching in the manner which in the nineteenth century was considered progressive.

Briefly, the working climate as a whole cannot always be described as modern. The better working opportunities elsewhere do not only concern the availability of the requirements for the pursuit of science (laboratories, libraries, for example) but also the non-existent language-barrier. Publishing in an internationally recognized language (for example English) offers possibilities to obtain, without great effort, international reactions and contacts, and to inform the whole world of outstanding achievements. Therefore it is not surprising that the emigration of scientists plays an important part, particularly in Great Britain. For the Germans, especially the older generation, it is already far more difficult; and also, in France, the emigration to other than French-speaking countries is insignificant because of the language handicap. For Italy and the smaller European countries, the emigration of scientists is proportionately higher because, in most of these countries, the secondary schools teach English with other languages and their mother tongue, and at the universities an adequate knowledge of the English language is considered a matter of course.

Here it is not necessary to enter into the generally known causes for emigration (economic, social, psychological, etc.); nevertheless from many publications it can be inferred that, contrary to a seemingly obvious assumption, when scientists emigrate the financial-economic motives are definitely not the predominating ones. But in this connection reference should be made to the results of an inquiry which was quite recently carried out among a group of British scientists working in the US.[24]

This inquiry aimed to find out *who* the British migrant scientists were, *why* they had left Britain, *when* they had emigrated, *where* they settled in North America, *what sort of work* they were doing at the time of the inquiry, *how satisfied* they were with their original decision to migrate, and *what their intentions* were concerning the future. The answers, besides those that apply to Great Britain in particular, generally show a considerable degree of conformity with similar statements of continental European migrants, and particularly that economic motives are not predominant. As to the quality of the persons questioned, this report deals only with those who are in possession of a good British first or higher degree.

Another, more simply formulated statement of the causes for the migration towards the United States says that the American high-school system, which does not turn out sufficiently qualified scientists, compels the American government, the American universities, and the American business community to 'buy' talent elsewhere in the world, preferably in Great Britain and Europe. This is often done via a so-called 'talent scout', who comes to Europe expressly for this purpose. Continental and English university graduates accept offers because America gives them more possibilities for scientific research and they are not obliged to do other work, such as lecturing (which keeps them from scientific research). Most emigrants state emphatically that it is not in the first instance the higher salary that makes them go to the US, although it is only natural that it is of some influence. After the Second World War the academic salaries in Europe adapted very slowly to the rapidly increasing prosperity. For many people this 'pay-pause' was one of the causes for emigration.

We shall express no opinion as to whether this formulation of causes for emigration to the US is based on facts; in all its simplicity of phrasing it is dangerous, and agrees only partly with the hitherto known results of scientific research into the motives for emigration.

The stimulus for the sending countries
It has been said in the first paragraph that it would be contradictory to all ideals, and to the tradition of the Western world, to bring up arguments against the free mobility of people in general and scientists in particular. The totalitarian representatives of modern mercanti-lism, for example, may sit down and calculate in advance the loss and profits respectively that such a migration might bring. They would find already at hand the costs of education estimated in various studies.

The fact of a 'brain drain' could become, however, an important stimulus for the sending countries, if it leads to a greater flexibility in education in general and in university training especially, and to the abolition of all the old, traditional, and sometimes parochial methods used. If it promotes the employment of scientific manpower 'under acceptable working conditions' it is possible that many will stay there or return to their homeland and contribute by research and development to the economic and social benefit. In brief, it should be stressed that to provide equality of opportunities for every scien-tist according to his ability is one of the most essential measures to overcome the losses of talents and skill by 'brain drain'.

Stimulating reactions in the 'brain drain' discussion. It is interesting that precisely in England, the country that set the problem of the 'brain drain' going in European discussion, many different tales are told also. In 'Who stays home'[25] a tolerant view of the problem is given.

Emigration from England is compensated by, for example, the immigration of physicians from Ireland, India and Pakistan. It is a good thing that young graduates show elsewhere what England has to offer in academic education. Most assuredly it is also worth while to show in England what others can offer. If this mobility remains in a state of equilibrium it will certainly be beneficial to all countries concerned. In 'Making sure there is no place home'[26] the English industrialists are advised to show a more personal interest in gra-duates-to-be and university graduates with a PhD or other degree. In the United States every pre-graduate and every graduate student is individually approached. In Great Britain there are enough positions and good careers available; the personal element in recruitment and acquaintance with the difficulties in the industry, and so on, is, how-ever, totally wanting. Should this be remedied then the emigration of scientists to the US or any other country might, in many cases, be prevented.

On the one hand the progress of science in the country of emigration benefits from the emigrating scholars or the temporary migrants after their return. On the other hand the achievements of the permanently emigrating scientists come to the knowledge of the whole scientific world, and consequently also benefit their country of emigration. Against the quantitative loss, which seems great, as a Swiss inquiry states,[27] often stands a 'brain gain', represented by the wealth of knowledge acquired for their country by the many who return to Switzerland. This study takes an optimistic view of the expected return of physicians and professors, whilst it is more pessimistic in its expectations regarding the return of those scientists who work, for instance, in industrial laboratories, especially because these can offer more and better tools for their work. The Swiss author sees a remedy in expanding the potentialities of scientific research and development in the field of nuclear physics and electrical engineering. Industry should devote much more attention to research and development, in order to give the scientists the opportunity to use their capacity and to help extend the national technical potential.

In Germany (DFR)[28] it was recommended that scientifically employed persons should be paid a salary identical to that which is earned by those that are employed in the domestic and foreign industry, in order to prevent an efflux to places abroad. They even went so far as to formulate 'Richtlinien zur forderung der Ruckkehr deutscher Wissenschaftler und wissenschaftlicher Nachwuchskrafte aus dem Ausland vom 4 Juni 1966.'[29] According to these plans the scientists who had emigrated to other countries can obtain financial aid when they return to Germany in order to meet their travelling expenses and as a transition benefit for a possible period of waiting until their employment in a new job.

In the Netherlands,[30] as well as in Switzerland, a country with a tradition of emigration by scientists and engineers, the problems of the increasing exodus of university graduates were approached very soberly. The Netherlands would not consider taking any measures against the exodus, and they hold the opinion that every country should do individually whatever is possible in order to attain better equipment – that is, the most modern apparatus, the best possible salaries – and that it should make many other arrangements towards improving the conditions for scientific research and development. Typical is the remark made by a member of the board of directors of the Netherlands Philips concern – that the technological advance of the United States is not without profit in bridging the loss and sometimes self-inflicted technological gap. To close the gap is up to

Europeans. Observation of the technological advance in the most industrialized nations opens up the possibility of making use of their experience and arriving more quickly at the same or even better production levels.

Accepting the challenge. According to many people, science in Europe is still too individualistic, the scale of salaries for scientists is not flexible enough, too little has been done for the capital-intensive equipment of education, and there is an inordinate variety of research institutes. Many signs of a challenge, however, can be noted, a challenge to invest more in scientific research and development on the national level, and to do on a broader level more towards integration and collaboration in this field.

Last but not least it should be emphasized that the creative genius of these scientists is also a valuable contribution by which the whole free world may benefit.[31]

THE CHALLENGE TO MORE INTERNATIONAL INTEGRATION

The two most advanced industrial countries in the world (the US and the USSR) have the world's biggest markets and industrial output. But, in comparison, the most voluminous European market has only one-sixth of the size of that of the United States.

It is not the lack of talent, it is the hegemony of the big industrial nations in the world that widened the technological gap and made the 'brain drain' into a serious problem. The reasons for such a development are, therefore, that in recent times Europe as a whole has not spent enough money on education, research and development, and that the European national markets are too small to apply the results of laboratory and other scientific research to industrial production. Not only are the meagre results of applying scientific research to industry a handicap, but it is also true that the whole system of small national or international units endangers the possibility (given the growing nationalism) of coming to broader multinational co-operation needed in practically every field of scientific research.

Scientific and technological manpower resources are an essential element for the economy and welfare of every nation, but investment and output in education in general, and higher education especially, are insufficient in Europe and other countries, and even in the United States.[32] As the magnitude of the research effort in particular largely depends on the flow and supply of scientific manpower, the output must be raised.

In contrast to the much larger stock and much larger supply of scientific manpower in the United States, the output is significantly lower than the demand for talent.[33] However, the technological balance of payments between the rest of the world and the United States (exact data on this subject are still scarce) is favourable and will be more favourable in the near future.[34] The European countries and Europe as a whole – notwithstanding the impressive results in theore-tical science and engineering – do not spend so much on research and development as the US or the USSR.[35] In France, for instance, the proportion of the national resources spent on research and develop-ment is probably still less than in some other industrialized countries. In 1962, research and development expenditure represented 1·5 per cent of the gross national product as against 2·2 per cent for the United Kingdom and 3·1 per cent for the United States,[36] and in Western Europe only about 20 per cent of the available scientific manpower is employed in research as against 33 per cent in the US. It would thus be a very ambitious undertaking for Western Europe to try and catch up with the US or the USSR. It might be feasible as far as research for civilian purposes is concerned, but in the field of military and space research, where the disparity is of the order of 4 to 1, it would seem to be unattainable in the foreseeable future, unless Western Europe could achieve a much greater efficiency in this field than either of the two great powers.[37]

The challenge is evident, especially in Western Europe
National governments support, more than they ever did in the past, all efforts to attain better and more systematic scientific research. New scientific bodies were created to find out where the countries concerned stood in the matter of scientific research and development, and to advise the governments in the matter of the 'brain drain', how much was to be spent, and on what projects, and so on.[38] Financial support granted to research and development varies widely from one country to another, not only in its extent, but also in its purpose (for example contributions to military advancement) and the terms on which it is granted. But within these policies, in the field of higher education, it is to be expected that 'by 1970 some countries, such as France and Sweden, envisage this percentage to be 7 or 8 per cent, and in the case of Yugoslavia the percentage of university graduates in any age group is expected to exceed 10 by the end of the present decade. Other countries seem to be content with maintaining during the 1960s the level of university graduation achieved in the early 1960s.'[39]

For European countries 'the question still remains whether such a wide variety of policies in this field is likely to reflect in each indivi-dual country an optimal solution to the problem of allocating re-sources to education. The chance of new entrants to higher education completing their studies also varies considerably from country to country.'[40] Thanks to these efforts a clear trend can be found in Western Europe towards a far more rapid increase in the output of natural scientists than of engineers. Other existing forecasts indicate that in 1970 European universities may turn out twice as many scientists as engineers, while in 1955 the number of graduates in engineering was clearly superior to that of natural science. This trend, which is not found in North America, may to some extent reflect a shift in the preferences of students and/or a more rapidly expanding demand for natural scientists.[41] Is this trend perhaps reflected in the relatively high portion of natural scientists in the 'brain drain' to the United States? However, it has also been estimated recently that engineering, which has relatively strict and sometimes very selective entry regulations in most European countries, will in the years before 1970 show a rise in the drop-out at university level.

Thanks to more investment to extend the support for general training facilities, 'the European stock of scientists and engineers has been growing at an annual rate of 4 per cent during the latter half of the 1950s and, according to existing forecasts, will grow at a higher rate – 6 to 7 per cent – in the first half of the 1960s.'[42] But, more essentially, there seems to be a clear need in European countries for a closer co-operation in education – especially higher education – and more co-operation aimed at strengthening the opportunities to work on research and development. In the framework of such co-ordination and integration of all efforts a better contribution to Europe's economic growth and welfare will be achieved.

The increasing activities in Europe to come to a better
technological balance of payments
Without neglecting the existing co-operation in the field of atomic research and so on, only proposals for such activities can be mentioned. Unfortunately for the 'brain drain', data on this subject of the technological balance of payments are still scarce. Undoubtedly the volume of the international flow of technological knowledge was, and is, favourable for the United States. There is some evidence that the loss in money is perhaps not so serious as the loss of quality.

What can Europe do to redress the balance without impairing the co-operation which is essential? Certainly intra-European co-operation, and integration of national, specialized, and other industries to come to a greater concentration of resources on research and development, to better working conditions, and so on, is on the way. The Europe of the Six, with its rich intellectual past and its 174 million inhabitants, can make up the arrears, if not completely then at least partly, only when it eventually recognizes that, in order to achieve this, co-ordination and co-operation are the first essentials. Here and there the disturbed balance is being restored, as regards technical perfection as well as fundamental research. Striking are, for example, the approximately-estimated figures which are given below for the field of controlled thermonuclear reaction, which is of great impor- tance to the use of nuclear energy: United States 25 per cent; Soviet Union 35 per cent; laboratories associated or collaborating with Euratom 19 per cent; United Kingdom 12 per cent. Consequently for the whole of Europe together: 31 per cent. This is only one of the many examples.[43]

A common European policy for scientific and technological research and development is necessary [44]

The challenges that faced the world in the 1950s, not only in space although these were considerable, but also across the entire spectrum of scientific research, required the mobilization and maximum use of national resources – particularly human resources. The sophisticated requirements of our times demand highly-skilled, well-trained, fully- educated men and women in the humanities, social, and natural sciences. The scope and enormity of the problems require a greater number of college-educated men and women than the traditional system is capable of providing, at present, with existing facilities and standard normal operating procedures. But can states be expected to discharge this new task in isolation? Research and development have been common to all societies, but so long as the world remains divi- ded into antagonistic nations or groups of nations of which the frontiers are not even clearly drawn, the question for Europe is assumed to be of special significance. According to the Paris and Rome treaties, the European communities have the duty to co- ordinate and stimulate fundamental scientific research. In the years that have gone by since the signing of these treaties, technological development has progressed enormously, which makes it a matter of necessity to extend the powers of the community. This is only natural, and it is a consequence of European integration. In the larger context of the technological development within the Common Market a general argument for common scientific management can already be found.

In the last few years it has been recognized everywhere that the continued existence of the Common Market depends on the pursuit of an *economic policy*. Flexible scientific planning will be a great help in achieving this. In the expectations and purposes of such a general programme technological development will have to be given special attention. It should also leave scope for the selective advancement of this technological development. In this way scientific policy becomes an essential link between scientific planning and economic and social policy.

The fact that the various national and intra-European initiatives are not integrated constitutes a problem and a great danger. Amongst themselves they are still not sufficiently co-ordinated, which leads to overlapping of work, frittering away, and wastage. In the first instance it is certainly not desirable to form a supranational research organization. It would be better to form a small Brains Trust to formulate the aims of a collective approach, and in which an efficient division of work between the European countries can be laid down. By mobilizing the means that Europe has at its disposal the Brains Trust could be very effective: it might stop the 'technological gap' and also prevent the 'brain drain'. But more research into the problem and a closer insight into these issues is urgently required.

In concluding, it can be said that stress should be laid on the necessity for intensive fundamental research, as the crown of a much needed alteration in higher education for the training of new generations of scholars, research workers, and engineers. On this basis, keeping an eye on the industrial developments and the essential renovations, the European scientific policy should be built up in order to conserve or re-collect irreplaceable capital, the capital of creative talent.

All these imperative common efforts should bring about a strengthening of democracy and the freedom of the nations, by enriching and building strong centres of learning across Europe and the world. They should also further the recognition that increasing the opportunities in the highly industrialized countries will automatically result in making the poor countries share more and more in the fruits of scientific discoveries.

In introducing his paper Dr Beijer expanded on a number of points and also added a good deal to his previous paper. What follows is a freely edited version of what he said, which has been approved by him as accurately representing his remarks.

Just before I left the Netherlands I received a bibliography on the 'brain drain' and 'brain gain' from a colleague in Sweden. It covers all recent publications, and lists 426 works published in the last eight or ten years. From this we can see that the phenomenon of the 'brain drain' is not just a matter under discussion today, but has been a point of contention for years and years. In fact I think it was already in question four or five hundred years ago. Thus it is commented on both by Tycho Brahe in 1570 and by Indian social scientists in 1965! It is interesting to read this comment: 'Brains go where brains are, brains go where money is, brains go where humanity and justice prevails, brains go where recognition and healthy competition is

18494

assured.' I think that in these words of an Indian colleague the whole problem of the 'brain drain' is covered. Except under exceptional conditions of forced migration, the refugees and so on, I do not be-lieve that the loss of scientists by migration to other countries con-stitutes a big drain.

I will start first of all by giving you some statistics. I shall refer to the tables given in the appendix to my paper. In Table 1 you will see figures giving the annual average number of immigrants into the US between 1956 and 1961. And you will also see those immigrants expressed as a percentage of the total 1959 output of science and engineering graduates for the relevant countries. This gives us, for instance, a figure of 15·1 for the Netherlands. We have checked this data and the total output figure and the percentage of 15·1 is correct, but these statistics include people leaving the Netherlands for two or three years but returning within five years. If we take this figure into account, thus seeing the other side of the balance, then the percentage quoted above is reduced to 1·9. Furthermore, if my information is correct, similar research is underway in Great Britain and the figures emerging are essentially lower than those quoted in Table 1. The critical point here is that in papers published all over the world it is this 14 or 15 per cent of the output going abroad that is emphasized and that this gives the material an emotional slant.

To take an example; it is true that the United States has an enor-mous shortage of scientists and engineers. In addition, if the data are reliable, in the near future the output of the universities and techni-cal colleges in the United States will still be too low to fill all the opportunities offered in the economy, especially in the armament industry and the space industry. Now if you turn to the figures men-tioned by Professor Sauvy, the 32,000 engineers and scientists, mostly natural scientists, going to the United States do not come solely from Europe. Only 50 per cent are European, the others are from Latin America, Asia, and from Africa. If I am well informed, and the statistics are very poor in this field, a lot of these people are students. They are European, African or Asiatic students who obtained their Masters degree, doctorate and so on from a university in the United States. I very much doubt whether we can regard these students who have completed their studies in the United States as a drain on the sending country. Their countries of origin did not really invest in these people; they perhaps invested in their families, in their primary and possibly secondary education, but the United States financed their university or high school education and they completed that education in the United States.

If we turn to Table 4 we see a somewhat different picture. We then find the total stock of immigrant scientists and engineers in the

C

United States in 1964 is 11,458 and not 32,000. Most of these people have already been in the United States for more than five years, because they have already applied for or obtained United States citizenship. If we used the figures of the American Science Association we would arrive at a much lower figure for European countries than this 11,000, because this total includes not only Europeans but people from other parts of the world. We can see, therefore, that the rate of returning migrants after 1957 must be relatively high. This is certainly a consequence of the economic position at this time in the United States and the better economic conditions in Europe. I believe that a lot of British engineers returned to Great Britain from the United States at the end of the fifties and in the early sixties because they had better opportunities here than over there.

Thus we come to what I think is the hub of the whole question. If we can create opportunities in Europe for our academically-trained people – opportunities in industry, in teaching, and in the universities and technical colleges – then I think that a lot of the people who are at present in the United States and Canada will return to Europe and work in industry or teaching in universities in Europe. But this is the critical question as we can see from the figures for Switzerland. Switzerland has a lot of emigration, a lot of engineers in particular leave for the United States and other countries. We are given relatively good statistics for the number of Swiss scientists and engineers in the United States in a paper by Heinz Killias of the General Electric Research and Development Centre in Zurich. He states, in his article, that he is afraid that a lot of the people working in industry in the United States – about 50 per cent of the 900 working there – will stay there longer. And he is also afraid that a lot of doctors have better opportunities in the United States and will not return to Switzerland.

Here I should emphasize that the figures generally available are in my opinion almost without any value. They show only one side of the balance. To really throw more light on the situation we need more collaboration between countries, and we need better statistics. For instance we require figures for the United States not only for a fiscal year but also for a calendar year as we have them in Europe. At present comparison with American statistics is practically impossible. So, as far as I can judge the situation for Europe, the phenomenon of the 'brain drain' exists, and it is not a new one. But we do not have any really accurate information about the size of the phenomenon, about the loss or gain of scientists *on balance*. So I think we need better statistics and also we need to know more about the causes of migration.

I was astonished by an article by Dr Wilson in *Minerva* (October

1966). He gave figures which stated there were about 550 British scientists in the United States of whom about one-third were temporarily there and the remaining two-thirds permanently; and he gives the incomes of this permanent group. About 72 of the total of 543 people in the United States had incomes over 80,000 dollars per year. This is a lot of money if we think in European terms, but in American terms it is not so much. In fact I am not very worried about these 543 people, but what is more interesting is to note that he asked all of them why they were staying in the United States and they answered, as people have done in other investigations, that they were not staying for economic reasons. They claimed to be staying because they had better opportunities for work, better possibilities for contact with other scientists and so on. This is one of the things which we forget in all our discussions. If we in Europe do not create suitable economic conditions and suitable working conditions in industry and in the academic field, what will we do if our trained people are offered better opportunities in Canada or in the United States tomorrow, or perhaps in India or in Pakistan the day after tomorrow? They will leave, and I think it is impossible to argue, as Brinley Thomas has done, that we require something like a balance of payments. He suggested that if the United States, or another country, want to have scientists from Europe then the country should pay a suitable sum – let us say £12,000 – for the educational investment and the experience of such a man. This seems to me quite impractical. And here I can see a problem. Professor Sauvy has said that we must find a way to halt the 'brain drain', but will we do so? Perhaps incorrectly I believe that the majority of history is a history of the movements of people. Most of the countries of Europe have many immigrants from other parts of Europe. If you look at the telephone book for the Hague you will be astonished how many Friesian people and Europeans from other countries are living in Holland.

I recall reading some years ago how migration from Scotland to England was growing day by day. And this is a question of opportunities in the southern part of Great Britain compared with the northern part. Well, you must create better opportunities in Scotland! To take a similar case, I can understand why people go to Glasgow or to Edinburgh to work from some of the surrounding villages, for some villages are very poor. In the modern world you cannot stop people doing this. If you cannot force people to stay in the countryside, can we force scientists to stay in their homeland? No, I think that skilled and talented people will only stay in their countries of origin if opportunities for these people exist in industries, colleges, schools, and universities. Nor is it just a question of money, because the effective difference in salaries is not as big as it seems. We should not assume for instance that all the scientists referred to by Dr Wilson were working in universities. Many of them may have been working in industry, in which case their salaries do not appear so astronomically large. But the question is whether European industry is ready to absorb scientists and engineers. Are the big industries and international concerns in Europe, such as Shell, Philips, Unilever, or British Petroleum, prepared to do more research? Is Europe as a whole prepared to absorb the output of the modern and new schools? If there are not the opportunities then people will go, and it is in this field that there is a lot of work to be done.

We do not have enough research in this area, we do not have adequate political decisions. For instance there is no agreement between the six countries of the Common Market, nor is there enough collaboration between all the countries of Europe. And it is possible that in the near future there will be opportunities for collaboration with Eastern Europe. It has recently been said that Yugoslavia has a surplus of engineers and natural scientists and if Western Europe needs them they could be sent there. So perhaps in the future we will send people to the United States and Canada, and receive the engineers and scientists our countries require from Eastern Europe.

Notes and References

1 Brinley Thomas, 'From the Other Side: A European View', *American Academy of Political and Social Science, Annals*, 367 (1966) 63.
2 Alfred Sauvy, 'The Population Situation in Europe', Address to the opening sitting of the European Population Conference, Strasbourg, Doc. CDE (66) 5/3 (30 August 1966) 9.
3 See Note 1.
4 David Hofmeijer, 'On Anticipating the Future', *Official Documents of the Conference*, Strasbourg, 2, Doc. CDE (66) C 32 (1966) 6.
5 We need mention only the study by Norman Bentwich, *The Rescue and Achievement of Refugee Scholars. The Story of Displaced Scholars and Scientists* (The Hague 1953); and the American contribution by Stephen Duggan and M.Drury, *The Rescue of Science and Learning* (New York, Macmillan Co., 1948).
6 G.Beijer, 'Selective Migration for and "Brain Drain" from Latin America', *International Migration* 1 (1966) 28. For a more sprightly discussion over the periods before World War II see: D.Dedijer, 'Why did Daedalus leave?', *Science*, 133 (1961) 204.
7 Royal Society (London 1963). 'Scientists have always been migrants and Britain has for many centuries been a migrant nation'.

8   See the samples of some statistical data in the Appendix.
9   Friedrich Edding and Hans J. Bodenhofer, 'On Movements of
    Intellectuals', in: *Official documents of the Conference*, 2 Doc. CDE
    (66) C 33 (Strasbourg 1966) 2. Edding and Bodenhofer, *op. cit.*,
    (p.1) consider in general 'migration rates as a function of educa-
    tion (and of course of age) in so far as migration probability
    rises with the level of education (in every age class)'.
10 *Ibid.*, 2.
11 'How to halt "Brain Drain". No curbs on Emigration', *The
    Times Educational Supplement* (17 February 1967) 540.
12 R. Blandy, 'Some questions concerning education and training in
    the developing countries', *International Labour Review*, 92 (1965)
    476.
13 E. Oteiza, 'Emigration of Engineers from Argentina! A Case of
    Latin-American Brain Drain', in: *International Labour Review*,
    92 (1965) 446. The 'brain drain' from Argentina, especially to
    the United States, of engineers and scientists is a post-war
    phenomenon and the author investigates the causes and
    dimensions of what is considered to be a serious loss of the
    country's resources. The loss of engineers is of particular interest
    in relation to the renewed efforts made in the field of selective
    migration. See the very interesting publication, *The International
    Migration of Talent and Skills*, in: Proceedings of a Workshop and
    Conference (Washington, 1966).
14 G. Beijer, *International Migration*, 1 (1966) 30.
15 Raoul Prebisch, 'Only one solution for the poor countries, commerce
    and aid', in: *Algemeen Handelsblad* (24 December 1965) 3.
16 Wilfrid David Borrie, 'Trends and Patterns in International
    Migration since 1945', United Nations World Population
    Conference 1965, Belgrade, (*Background paper* B 9/14/E/474) 41.
17 In the *Neue Zuricher Zeitung* (11 January 1967) it is stated in a
    short article, that 1 million 250 thousand persons immigrated
    into Israel during 1948–66. In the same period about
    165,000 persons returned to their former homeland. Among these
    returnees was a great number of qualified persons returning to
    the USA (50%), Europe (20%), and other countries because of
    the lack of economic and scientific opportunities for their
    qualifications.
18 C. Freeman and A. Young, *The Research and Development Effort
    in Western Europe, North America and the Soviet Union* (Paris,
    OECD, 1965) 57 and 61.
19 *Reviews of Data on Science Resources*, (Washington DC 1965) 5
    and E. Oteiza, 'Emigration of engineers from Argentina: a Case
    of Latin American Brain Drain', *International Labour Review*,
    92 (1965) 445.
    See also: *Migration of health personnel, scientists, and engineers
    from Latin America*, report prepared by the PAHO sub-committee
    on migration for the PAHO advisory committee on medical

research (Pan American Health Organization. Washington;
1966). P. de Suro, 'The brain drain and Latin America',
NAFSA newsletter, **5** (1967) 4–6.

20   'The new Immigration', *American Academy of Political and Social
Science, Annals*, **367** (1966) 71.

21   'The Residual Factor and Economic Growth', *The OECD
Observer*, **16** (1965) 38. (Abstract of a paper by Edward F.
Denison, presented to a meeting of high-level economists and
educators, held by the Study Group in 'the Economics of
Migration'.)

22   Thomas J. Mills, 'Scientific Personnel and the Profession', *American
Academy of Political and Social Science, Annals*, **367** (1966) 36.

23   *The International Migration of Talent and Skills* (Washington 1966)
8. (Proceedings of a Workshop and Conference sponsored by the
Council on International Affairs and Cultural Affairs of the US
Government.)

24   James A. Wilson, 'The Emigration of British Scientists', *Minerva*,
5 (1966) 1, 22 and 24–9.

25   *Nature*, **79** (1966) 1329–30.

26   A. and K. Gebbie, 'Making sure there's no place home', *New
Scientist*, **32** (1966), 503–23.
See also: S. Jonas, 'Why doctors emigrate', *Socialist Commentary*,
5 (1965) 9–11. During 1949–59, every year about 400 doctors
emigrated from Great Britain. This was about 25 per cent of the
graduates in medical sciences. The socialistic organization of
medical care was not the reason for their migration, which was
that it was impossible to find a suitable place on the hierarchic
ladder.
J. Walsh, 'Trained Manpower: British Studies call for better use of
supply', *Science* (1966) 1425–7. According to the Swann
Report, 'Manpower parameters for scientific growth', the
output of engineers in Great Britain doubled, from 10,000 to
about 20,000 in ten years. To find work in industry is very
difficult for many of them; on one side, university teaching is
not adequately directed towards the aims of practical work in
industry; and on the other side, a lot of engineers preferred
to work on research and development in American laboratories,
as working conditions are significantly better.

27   H. Killias, 'Schweizer Naturwissenschaftler und Ingenieure in
Nordamerika. Eine statistische Uebersicht', *Neue Zuricher
Zeitung*, **40** (1967) 6. (The author is a member of the General
Electric Research and Development Centre, Zurich). For the
statistics see: Appendix, table 7.

28   'Unzureichende Bezahlung fuhrt zur lautlosen Emigration',
Akademischer Dienst, **7** (1966) 579–80.

29   *Mitteilungen des Hochschulverhandes*, **5** (1966) 203–5.

30   v.d.V. 'Vergelijkend wetenschappelijk onderwijs en exodus van
geleerden', *Economisch Statistische Berichten*, **2438** (1964) 403–5.

31 *Economisch Statistische Berichten*, **2438** (1964) 405.
32 'Scientists and Engineers from Abroad, Fiscal years 1962 and
    1963' *Reviews of Data on Scientific Resources*, **1** (1965) 1.
33 E. M. Friedwald, 'The Research effort of Western Europe, the USA
    and the USSR' *OECD Observer*, Special Issue (1966) 14.
34 E. M. Friedwald, *OECD Observer*, Special Issue (1966) 12.
35 Keith Pavitt, 'Government and Technical Innovation', *OECD
    Observer*, Special Issue (1966) 16.
36 'French Science Policy', *OECD Observer*, **23** (1966) 10.
37 E. M. Friedwald, in *OECD Observer*, **23** (1966) 14.
38 'Belgium's policy for the sciences', *OECD Observer*, **20** (1966) 6.
    As in France, in Belgium measures have also been taken to
    encourage young people to take up research careers. Until
    recently in Belgium research workers who were not also teachers
    have had very little security. A research assistant in a govern-
    ment laboratory, for example, was normally engaged for two
    years and a maximum of three possible renewal periods with the
    result that after eight years he risked finding himself out of a
    job. To remedy this situation and to create a government
    research corps career posts have been established.
39 'Resources of Scientific and Technical personnel', *OECD Observer*,
    10 (1964) 36.
40 *Resources of Scientific and Technical Manpower in the OECD Area*
    (Paris 1964).
41 See notes 8 and 39.
42 *OECD Observer*, **10** (1964) 40.
43 *Draft resolution concerning a common European policy in sciences*,
    (Strasbourg 1966) 11. European Parliament, Document 107.
44 See 'European Parliament', *Proceedings* 1966, Documents 7, 97
    and 107. and: *Proceedings of the 13th combined meeting of
    members of the European Parliament and the European Assembly*,
    (Strasbourg, 23 and 24 September 1966) 207.

APPENDIX

Some statistics to illustrate the difficulties in evaluating the losses and gains of the international migration of scientists and engineers

TABLE 1 Migration of scientists and engineers to the USA

Country of last permanent residence	Immigrants into the USA (annual average 1956–61)			Immigrants as a ratio of 1959 output of science and engineering graduates percentage		
	Scientists	Engineers	Scientists and Engineers	Scientists	Engineers	Scientists and Engineers
France	26	56	82	0·5	1·2	0·9
Germany	124	301	425	6·0	9·8	8·2
Netherlands	34	102	136	7·9	21·8	15·1
United Kingdom	155	507	661	2·6	17·2	7·4
Total 'Western Europe'	339	966	1,304	2·5	8·7	5·4
Austria	23	43	67	—	10·9	7·0[1]
Greece	14	50	64	3·6	20·7	10·2
Ireland	13	32	45	4·7	15·4	9·3
Italy	29	42	71	0·9	1·7	1·3
Norway	6	72	78	3·4	23·8	16·2
Sweden	8	97	106	1·3	16·3	8·8
Switzerland	38	96	134	10·6	22·4	17·0
All Europe, *including others.*	549	1,684	2,233	—	—	—
Canada	212	1,027	1,240	12·5	48·0	32·3
All countries	1,114	3,755	4,868	—	—	—

Sources: Scientific Manpower from Abroad, NSF 62–24, Washington, and *Resources of Scientific and Technical Personnel in the OECD Area* (OECD 3rd International Survey, Paris, 1963).

C. Freeman and A. Young, *The Research and Development Effort in Western Europe, North America, and the Soviet Union* (Paris, OECD, 1965) 73.

[1] Estimated.

TABLE 2   Natural scientists and engineers[1] admitted to the
United States as immigrants, by year of entry and broad
occupational group,[2] fiscal years 1957–63

				Percentage distribution[4]		
Fiscal year	Total	Engineers[3]	Natural scientists[3]	Total	Engineers	Natural scientists
1957	5,892	4,547	1,345	100·0	77·2	22·8
1958	5,244	4,032	1,212	100·0	76·9	23·1
1959	5,138	3,950	1,188	100·0	76·9	23·1
1960	4,397	3,354	1,043	100·0	76·3	23·7
1961	3,992	2,890	1,102	100·0	72·4	27·6
1962	4,105	2,940	1,165	100·0	71·6	28·4
1963	5,702	4,014	1,688	100·0	70·4	29·6
1964	5,479	3,725	1,754	100·0	67·7	32·6

Source: National Science Foundation, based on tabulations prepared by the
Immigration and Naturalization Service, United States Department of Justice.
[1] Does not include social scientists.
[2] The occupational classification is based on the visa-application information.
As professional classifications vary between countries, the occupations do not
necessarily all represent university-trained persons.
[3] Includes professors and instructors.
[4] Percentage may not add to 100 because of rounding.

TABLE 3   Country of origin of natural scientists and engineers immigrated
into the United States, 1957–64

	1957	1958	1959	1960	1961	1962	1963	1964	Total 1957–64
United Kingdom	842	790	485	614	575	925	1,153	1,097	5,906
Germany (DFR)	659	423	428	324	291	356	428	435	3,344
France	101	82	90	80	58	43	77	50	581
Netherlands	270	65	86	150	108	110	82	84	945
Austria	100	63	97	47	26	37	46	38	454
Switzerland	187	140	110	131	102	89	129	107	995
All Europe, *including the other European countries.*									
	2,959	2,271	2,412	1,916	1,608	2,431	3,002	2,669	19,268
All Europe, and other parts of the world.									
	5,825	5,190	5,081	4,326	3,922	4,297	5,933	5,056	39,630

Source: Various US statistics, especially from the US Department of Justice,
Immigration and Naturalization Service.

Table 3 only serves as an indication of the trend of the volume p.a. of immigration into the United States. The figures do not exactly correspond with the figures given in Table 2.

For 1957-64, the total of admitted immigrants of both professional groups is 39,949 in Table 2, and 39,630 in Table 3 – only a slight difference.

As Table 4 shows, only 11,458 scientists and engineers in the immigrant group have already applied or are applying for us citizenship. That is only 28·1 per cent of the total figure of 39,949 in Table 2.

TABLE 4   US stocks of immigrant scientists and engineers, 1964

Country of origin	Immigrants who have US citizenship or have applied for it		Immigrants as a ratio of 1963 stocks of science and engineering graduates within the different countries[1]	
		Percentage	Percentage	Rank
Germany	1,803	15·7	0·6 [2]	5
Canada	1,674	14·6	1·8	2
Austria and Switzerland	962	8·4	2·2	1
United Kingdom	874	7·6	0·3	6
Benelux	386	3·4	0·8	3
Italy	328	2·9	0·2	8
Scandinavian peninsula	320	2·8	0·7	4
Greece, Cyprus, Yugoslavia	317	2·8	0·3	6
France	191	1·7	0·1	9
Japan	95	0·8	—	—
Turkey	92	0·8	0·1	9
Iberian peninsula	48	0·4	0·1 [2]	9
All other countries	4,363	38·1	—	—
Total	11,458	100·0	—	—

[1] Source: Resources of Scientific and Technical Personnel in the OECD Area, (OECD 3rd International Survey, Paris, 1963); and National Register of Scientists (Washington D.C., 1964).
[2] Estimated.

TABLE 5   US stocks of immigrant scientists and engineers, 1964

Country of origin	Non - nationalized immigrants Percentage of the country's supply of immigrants to USA	Absolute number
Japan	81	393
United Kingdom	50	894
Iberian peninsula	44	38
Canada	39	1,080
Turkey	36	52
Benelux	33	186
Greece, Cyprus, Yugoslavia	30	133
Scandinavian peninsula	28	123
France	23	56
Germany	21	441
Austria	20	236
Italy	18	73
All other countries	48	3,054
Total	37 (average)	6,749

Source: National Register of Scientists (Washington DC, 1964).

Table 5 gives 6,749 non-nationalized immigrants for the same occu-pational groups as in Tables 3 and 4. The totals of Tables 4 and 5 amount to 18,207 persons, or about 45·5 per cent of the total of immigrants in Table 2. All these totals in Tables 2–5, however, are in contradiction with a special tabulation prepared by the Immigration and Naturalization Service, published by the National Science Foun-dation (J. Mills, The Annals, 367 (1966) 35, Table 1). According to these tabulations, 15,754 natural scientists and 44,283 engineers–in total 60,037 persons (including professors and instructors of both professions) – were admitted as immigrants in the period 1949–64. If the figures in Tables 2 and 4 are more or less correct then of all scientists and engineers who immigrated during the period 1949–64, only 18,207, or about 30 per cent, were still residents of the US in 1964 and only 11,458, or roughly 20 per cent, of these immigrants had a US citizenship or had applied for it. In the two-way traffic, that is the outflow of about 70 per cent, the re-migrants and the migrants to countries other than that of origin cannot be statistically measured.

TABLE 6   The Netherlands net migration of engineers, 1963–4

| Country of immigration | 1963 | | | | 1964 | | | |
| | Nationals | | Foreigners | | Nationals | | Foreigners | |
	Mobility	Balance	Mobility	Balance	Mobility	Balance	Mobility	Balance
Europe total	148	−26	290	+68	173	−31	461	+109
EEC	67	−23	148	+12	91	−13	175	+39
United Kingdom	38	+2	74	+34	30	−6	159	+65
Other Europe	43	−5	68	+22	52	−12	127	+5
USA and Canada	68	−14	183	+53	65	−3	228	+66
Rep. of South Africa	8	—	7	−3	13	−5	6	+2
Oceania	14	—	16	+6	4	−2	12	−4
All other countries	248	+10	80	+2	247	+21	108	+36
Total	486	−30	576	+126	502	−20	815	+209

Table 6 shows the balance of migration of engineers for the years 1963 and 1964. According to the figures, a loss of 50 nationals occurs. There is, however, a net immigration of about 335 foreigners. Hence the Netherlands had a net gain of 280 engineers for these years.

TABLE 7   The Netherlands net migration of physicians and surgeons,[1]
1960—5

		Immigrants and re-migrants	Emigrants	Balance
1960	Nationals	142	150	−8
	Foreigners	50	49	+1
	Total	192	199	−7
1961	Nationals	136	132	+4
	Foreigners	64	56	+8
	Total	200	188	+12
1962	Nationals	146	154	−8
	Foreigners	49	40	+9
	Total	195	194	+1
1963	Nationals	148	122	+26
	Foreigners	82	53	+29
	Total	230	175	+55
1964	Nationals	132	158	−26
	Foreigners	98	43	+55
	Total	230	201	+29
1965	Nationals	111	119	−8
	Foreigners	85	53	+32
	Total	196	172	+24
1960—5	Total Nationals	815	835	−20
	Total Foreigners	428	294	+134
	Overall total	1,243	1,129	+114

Source: Based on special tabulations of the Netherlands Central Bureau of Statistics, the Hague.
[1] For 1961, 62, 64 and 65, some veterinary surgeons and dentists are included; for 1963, some pharmacists and biologists.

Against a negative balance of 20 nationals there is a positive balance of 134 foreigners. The negative balance for nationals to the United States and Canada, however, was 29 people. Certainly no reason to speak of a quantitative loss of any importance!

TABLE 8   Swiss scientists and engineers in the United States

(a) Distribution according to discipline and grade

Discipline	PhD	MS	BS	Total
Mathematics	25	2	—	27
Physics	65	8	—	73
Chemistry	142	12	25	179
Biology	40	1	—	41
Medical science	133	—	3	136
Electro -technical engineering	20	66	51	137
Mechanical engineering	9	85	85	179
Building engineering	2	34	10	46
Architecture	—	20	8	28
Agriculture, Forestry	8	15	—	23
Geology, Metereology	28	2	2	32
Economics	2	5	3	10
Unknown	2	—	—	2
Total	476	250	187	913

(b) Distribution of the 913 people according to employment

Employer	PhD	MS	BS	Total
University professor	108	5	—	113
University, other	116	35	10	161
Industry in U S or Canada	101	166	151	418
Swiss industry in U S or Canada	32	20	12	64
Government	33	12	7	52
Hospitals	49	—	1	50
Other and unknown	37	12	6	55
Total	476	250	187	913

Source: 'Schweizer Naturwissenschafter und Ingenieure in Nordamerika,' Eine statistische Ubersicht, Heinz Killias, Züricher Zeitung (27 January 1967).

Table 8 shows the distribution, according to discipline, grade and employment, of Swiss scientists, residents of the United States, based on the registration figures of the consulates and the 'Address list of Swiss Scientists and Engineers in North America.' Some shortcomings (about 10 per cent) in the figures are possible. With this restriction, the total of residents (immigrants before 1965) is about 913.

J.M. LAST

International Mobility in the Medical Profession

Bearers of professional qualifications in several technologies – engineering, architecture, physical and biological sciences, and medicine – can move easily across national and even linguistic boundaries, seeking the best market for their talents, or the environment which offers maximum personal and professional satisfaction. My data concern members of the medical profession, hereafter referred to as doctors. Similar factors may or may not determine the international movement of members of other professions; probably it is not justifiable to generalize from the facts given here. A certain type of doctor is likely to go abroad for reasons which will be mentioned; but we cannot assume that engineers or scientists will follow the same pattern of behaviour. They may, but it is equally likely that they do not.

The loss by emigration of a doctor whose basic training costs approximately £12,000[1] constitutes a serious economic setback to his homeland and a corresponding gain for the country to which he emigrates. However, if young British doctors go abroad temporarily and then return, the benefits both to the recipient country and to Britain will be considerable. There is likely to be a gain in international goodwill, and overseas experience will enrich the doctor's ultimate contribution to health services in Britain.

Estimates of the loss by emigration of British doctors vary from 500 per annum downwards, but methods of calculation used in the past have sometimes been unsatisfactory. Official lists of legally registered medical practitioners have been used to count doctors after their arrival in other countries, and allowance has not always been made for movement from one country or region of registration to another, so that multiple counting occurs.[2] In some reports it has been implied that when doctors leave Britain their move is almost always permanent and one way.

The most accurate estimates were produced by Abel-Smith and Gales[3] who sampled names on the Home List of the *Medical Register*, to arrive at a figure for loss by emigration of 22 per cent of British-trained doctors, and 11·8 per cent of those who were both British-born and British-trained. These figures were a factual statement of the whereabouts in 1962 of doctors registered in 1925–59, and some of those overseas in 1962 may only have been abroad temporarily.

Some years ago I suggested that not all young British doctors who go abroad, even as far afield as Australia, intend to remain away permanently.[4] I have since confirmed this, using official lists of registered medical practitioners. In the Australian state of Victoria, record-keeping methods facilitate most accurate measurements. Of 74 British doctors resident there in 1962, who had qualified in or since 1955, four, that is, about 5 per cent, had returned to Britain by 1965. Young British doctors evidently go abroad for short-term experience in the same way as young doctors from British Commonwealth countries come to Britain for postgraduate training, but intend ultimately to go back and settle in their homeland.

The same survey of official lists in the Australian states and territories indicated that, in the three-year period 1962–5, the number of overseas-trained doctors in Australia increased by 418, of whom 232 had trained in Britain; and because revision of current addresses does not keep pace with movement in most states, these figures are probably an overestimate by as much as 10 per cent. In the same period, net population gain by immigration was 275,843; there was therefore one overseas-trained doctor for every 660 of the immigrant population, without correcting for the probable over-estimation in the number of doctors. Even so, this is not a disproportionate intake in a country where there is one doctor for every 750 population.

How much movement is there into Britain? By sampling university graduate lists, and registers of medical practitioners in Australian states, I estimated that at least 1,000 Australian doctors will be working in Great Britain each year; anecdotal evidence suggests that they remain in Britain for an average period of about three years. These, and doctors from other Commonwealth and a few foreign countries, appear to balance the short-term overseas loss of young British doctors. About 46 per cent of hospital registrars were born (and mostly trained) outside the United Kingdom and Eire.[5]

Long-term international migration of medical practitioners also operates, at least in part, to Britain's advantage. In England and Wales 4 per cent of consultants and 5 per cent of general practitioners had their medical training outside the United Kingdom and Eire;[6] and 5 per cent of permanent university medical staff were trained outside the United Kingdom and Eire.[7]

PRESENT SURVEY

In 1966 my colleagues and I conducted a postal enquiry among 1,737 young British doctors who had already provided some sociological information about themselves when they were medical students in 1961. At that time, 94 per cent of students at most British medical schools were asked about their social background, previous educational experience, reactions to medical education and to life in the medical school, and plans for the future.[8] Questions were not asked then about ultimate place of settlement.

The follow-up enquiry in 1966 was designed to investigate experience since completing the undergraduate medical course, present situation and work, and future plans both for the nature and place of practice.

In addition to data collected by questionnaires in 1961 and 1966, information on performance in examinations was supplied by administrative staff in the universities which had been attended by the surveyed doctors. Examination procedure varies, so only a very simple classification was possible: graduation with honours, completion of the undergraduate course without any examination failures, or after failure in one, two, or three or more of the major examinations which mark the milestones in undergraduate medical education: anatomy and physiology; pathology and bacteriology; and the final qualifying or degree examinations in medicine, surgery, obstetrics, paediatrics, and so forth.

After pilot studies in February and March 1966, questionnaires were posted in May–June 1966 to a randomly selected stratified sample comprising 50 per cent of United Kingdom citizens who had been second, fourth or sixth year students when they took part in the survey in 1961, and had since completed the course and registered. Citizens of countries other than the United Kingdom who received medical education in Britain were excluded before drawing the sample, as one objective was to investigate intentions about emigration.

Results

Completed questionnaires were returned by 1,496 young doctors in time for analysis (Table 1). Information on many non-respondents was obtained from Churchill's *Medical Directory* and from records kept by the British Medical Association and the Ministry of Health. Interviewers from Marplan Limited, a market research organization, attempted to make contact with a randomly selected 25 per cent of non-respondents whose last known address had been in the United Kingdom. Of the 50 individuals selected for this approach, five were overseas, four could not be traced, and five declined to co-operate. Non-respondents did not differ in other ways from respondents.

Present whereabouts. As we might expect, the most senior cohort included the highest proportion abroad and few of the most recent graduates had left Britain at the time of the investigation (Table 2).

D

Higher proportions of non-respondents than respondents were abroad; no doubt their remoteness contributed to their lower level of co-operation.

Almost 50 per cent of the respondents who were abroad were working in the less wealthy countries of the world, such as tropical Africa and the Far and the Middle East. North America and Australia, the most affluent countries of the English-speaking world, are by no means the only places to attract young British doctors in search of overseas experience (Table 3).

Intended emigration. Intention to emigrate can be considered separately among those overseas and those still in Britain. Of respondents abroad in 1966, 19 out of 103 were in general practice, and therefore perhaps relatively permanently settled. However, the proportion in general practice was the same among the United Kingdom residents. So if it can be said that only 19 per cent of those abroad were permanently rooted there because they were in general practice, the same may also be true of those in Britain.

Almost one-third of those abroad stated that they will probably return and settle in Britain. Nearly two-fifths were more equivocal, and less than 1 in 6 have no intention of returning to live in Britain at any time in the future (Table 4).

The intentions of those in Britain in 1966 can be similarly classified. Although only 3·6 per cent definitely plan to emigrate, 12·4 per cent will probably emigrate and 25·6 per cent have not excluded the possibility (Table 5). The intentions of respondents as a whole with respect to emigration can be summarized as definite, probable, and possible emigration, and no intention of emigrating; if stated intentions are a reliable guide to future movements, nearly 1 in 5 of these young doctors can be regarded as 'definitely' or 'probably' emigrating (Table 6).

Most of those considering emigration were prepared to specify a country of destination. North America was the most popular choice: 193 named Canada and 80 the United States; Australia was named by 117 and New Zealand by 43. Places elsewhere in the world were less often mentioned: only 22 named Africa, 11 the Far East, 9 Europe, 3 South America, and 19 other places (mostly in the Middle East). The intention to go abroad permanently is most often associated with a desire to live in industrially advanced rather than developing countries.

Several hundred of the respondent doctors supplied comments, often quite lengthy, giving their reasons for considering or having decided upon emigration. These included better facilities for doing the job for which they had been trained (252); financial gain (227); more professional freedom (120); more rapid promotion (99); a kinder climate (64); better opportunities for training (57); higher social status (36); and family connections (25); the numbers in parenthesis are those who gave these reasons; many gave more than one reason, so the total exceeds the number of potential emigrants. Though materialistic motives were important, professional satisfaction – especially access to modern hospital facilities – was the most commonly stated reason for emigrating.

Short-term movement overseas. Since previous estimates of loss by emigration have usually included short-term overseas movement these estimates may have been considerably inflated. It would certainly be useful to know what proportion of young British doctors go abroad only to obtain short-term overseas experience.

There were 1,460 replies to questions about intentions to obtain some training abroad. Of these, 31 per cent intended to spend some time abroad for postgraduate training, 32 per cent did not, 26 per cent were uncertain, 6 per cent were working abroad at the time of the enquiry, and 5 per cent had already worked abroad and returned to Britain. Those who had had difficulty with undergraduate examinations significantly less often planned to obtain overseas postgraduate experience than their more successful colleagues (Table 7), and honours graduates most often planned to get short-term overseas experience in the United States, probably because they were aware that in addition to valuable specialist experience, the United States could offer the accolade 'been to America', often regarded as an important ingredient in academic pedigrees.

Career choice and place of practice

Young doctors must decide on the nature of their careers as well as the place where these will be pursued. Career choice is a complex decision and may undergo repeated changes during undergraduate education and for a few years after qualification.[9] Potential general practitioners and potential surgeons decide significantly earlier than their colleagues (Table 8), and surgeons less often change their minds once a decision has been made. This becomes important when we consider the relationship between choice of specialty and intention to emigrate. Potential surgeons include the highest, and general practitioners the lowest proportion definitely planning to emigrate (Table 9). It is understandable that the highest proportion intending to remain in Britain and the lowest proportion uncertain about their future location should be among general practitioners, because the sample population includes more actual than potential general practitioners, while potential specialists in other fields are mostly still training, and therefore less settled.

Their decisions may be influenced by other sociological factors.

In another investigation I showed that general practitioners significantly more often than consultants settled in the part of the country
where they lived in their youth, and if faced with a choice between
settling in a desired locality, or pursuing a career in a chosen field,
general practitioners more often gave a high priority to choice of
locality, specialists in other fields more often gave a high priority to
pursuit of career ambitions.[10] Watson[11] described a sociological
distinction between the 'spiralist', prepared to move around while
moving upwards in his occupational hierarchy, and the 'burgess' who
is culturally tied to a particular community. In the medical profession
a majority of specialists appear to be spiralists rather than burgesses,
and among general practitioners the proportions are reversed.

If a high proportion of potential hospital specialists are spiralists
rather than burgesses, the emigration rate among them is likely to
be relatively high since there is a considerable excess of applicants
over the available number of vacancies for hospital specialists in the
National Health Service (Table 10). In particular there are too many
applicants for the small number of annual vacancies in the specialties
of internal medicine and general surgery. The discrepancy is large
and particularly serious in surgery, for individuals who decide on a
career in surgery not only do so on average earlier in their career than
other doctors, but tend to be more determined on pursuit of this
career and less adaptable to alternative possibilities. Not only are
they less adaptable in a technological sense but their personality too
may make it more difficult for them to accept an alternative role.[12] If
potential surgeons cannot be accommodated in the National Health
Service in a role which accords with their own perception of compe-
tence and ability, they may well emigrate in order to pursue a surgical
career in a country where there is more demand for their services.
This has been happening in the past: surgeons are numerous among
British doctors in Australasia and in North America. Many are
general practitioner/surgeons in group practices and appear to find
this a satisfactory compromise. Reorganization of the health service
in Britain to permit a dual role might encourage larger proportions of
these young doctors to remain in Britain.

How much 'brain drain' is there?

Although more honours graduates than others intend to spend some
time abroad, a higher proportion of them, 70 per cent as compared
to 60 per cent of all others, intend ultimately to settle permanently in
Britain and none definitely plan to emigrate (Table 11). While
emigration of doctors from Britain undoubtedly leads to considerable
loss of professional skills, it may not, strictly speaking, constitute quite
such a serious 'brain drain' as is sometimes suggested.

Consideration of selection procedures which operate in appoint-ment of registrars and consultants in the hospital service suggests that emigrant hospital specialists may frequently be individuals who had difficulty passing examinations. Selection committees give pre-ference to applicants with distinguished academic records and a record of relevant training posts in teaching hospitals. Unsuccessful applicants are likely to have had less distinguished academic records and to have held postgraduate training posts in non-teaching hos-pitals, perhaps in inappropriate specialties, irrelevant to their future plans.[13] Among those uncertain about their future location, these unsuccessful applicants may be more likely to emigrate. They may represent the very antithesis of a 'brain drain', coming predominantly from the bottom of the class rather than from the top. However this discussion, based on future intentions rather than past events, must be treated with some reserve. Further follow-up of this population will be required to confirm the suggestions here advanced about the relationship between specialty, academic record, and emigration.

SUMMARY AND ACKNOWLEDGMENTS

Britain gains, as well as loses, by the international movement of doctors. Not all British doctors who leave Britain are emigrating. About 5 per cent of young doctors who go abroad return quite soon, and the proportion who ultimately return after obtaining short-term overseas experience could reach 30 per cent.

Although only about 4 per cent of a representative sample of young British doctors definitely intend to emigrate, almost 20 per cent are seriously considering this step, and the proportion could rise as high as 40 per cent if the 'possibles' are also included.

Potential surgeons are the most likely specialists to emigrate; potential general practitioners least likely. Rather than a 'brain drain' of doctors, those who emigrate probably come predominantly from among the less rather than the more academically distinguished.

Most of the work reported here was conducted jointly with my colleagues Dr F. M. Martin and Mrs G. R. Stanley, and financially supported by the Ministry of Health and the Royal Commission on Medical Education. I am grateful for this assistance, and for the co-operation and interest of the young doctors who returned com-pleted questionnaires.

References

1 K.R.Hill, 'Cost of Undergraduate Medical Education in Britain', *Brit. med. J.*, **1** (1964) 300.
2 See, for example, J.R.Seale, 'Emigration of British Doctors', *Brit. med. J.*, **1** (1962) 782.

3   B.Abel-Smith and K.Gales, 'British Doctors at Home and Abroad', *Occasional Papers on Social Administration*, No. 8 (London 1964).
4   J.M.Last, 'Migration of British Doctors of Australia', *Brit. med. J.*, 2 (1963) 744.
5   Ministry of Health, 'N.H.S. Medical Staff', *Lancet*, 2 (1966) 1456.
6   J.M.Last, 'Settlement of General Practitioners and Consultants in the National Health Service', *Brit. med. J.*, 2 (1967) 796.
7   J.M.Last, 'University Medical Staff', *Lancet*, 2 (1967) 1318.
8   F.M.Martin, J.M.Last and G.R.Stanley, 'British Medical Students in 1961', *London Association for Study of Medical Education* (1967).
9   J.M.Last and G.R.Stanley, 'Career Preference of Young British Doctors', *Brit. J. med. Educ.*, 2 (1968) 137.
10 See note 6.
11 W.Watson, 'Social Mobility and Social Class in Industrial communities', in M.Gluckman (Ed.), *Closed Systems and Open Minds* (Edinburgh 1964).
12 H.J.Walton, J.Drewery, and A.E.Phillip, 'Typical Medical Students', *Brit. med. J.*, 2 (1964) 744.
13 J.M.Last, F.M.Martin and G.R.Stanley, 'Academic Record and Subsequent Career', *Proc. roy. Soc. Med.*, 60 (1967), 813.

TABLE I   The survey populations

Year in 1961	Number surveyed in 1961	UK citizens completed course registered	Sample surveyed in 1966	Unco-operative, died, untraced	Non-respondents	Response (No.and per cent)
2	1,549	874	440	8	57	375 (85·2)
4	1,514	1,203	617	16	69	532 (86·2)
6	1,597	1,344	680	15	76	589 (86·6)
Total	4,660	3,421	1,737	39	202	1,496 (86·1)

Unrecorded and unusable responses have been excluded from subsequent tables, reducing the total below 1,496 in some cases.

TABLE 2   Location, 1966

Year in 1961		In UK	Dead, untraced, unknown	Abroad	Total (=100%)
2	Respondents	367		8	
	Non-respondents	57		2	
	All in year	424	6	10 (2·3%)	440
4	Respondents	489		43	
	Non-respondents	53		10	
	All in year	542	22	53 (8·6%)	617
6	Respondents	537		52	
	Non-respondents	57		23	
	All in year	594	11	75 (11·0%)	680
	All years	1660	39	138 (7·9%)	1,737

TABLE 3

Country of residence, 1966	Year in 1961 2	4	6	Total
United Kingdom	367 (97·9%)	489 (91·2%)	537 (91·2%)	1,393
US		3	8	11
Canada	2	6	14	22
Australia	1	3	5	9
New Zealand	1	1		2
Africa	3	13	10	26
South America			1	1
Europe		4		4
Far East		4	3	7
Other	1	6	9	16
No information		3	1	4
Total	375	532	589	1,496

TABLE 4   1966 location and ultimate intended location

Year	Not returning	Overseas May return	Probably returning	No response to question	Total
2	—	3	3	2	8
4	7	13	15	8	43
6	7	23	13	9	52
Total	14 (13·6%)	39 (37·9%)	31 (30·1%)	19 (18·4%)	103

TABLE 5   1966 location and ultimate intended location

			In UK			
Year	Not emigrating	Definitely emigrating	Probably emigrating	Not excluded possibility	No response to question	Total
2	208	13	39	91	16	367
4	260	20	67	119	23	489
6	295	16	67	147	12	537
Total	763	49	173	357	51	1393
	(54·8%)	(3·5%)	(12·4%)	(25·6%)	(3·7%)	

TABLE 6   Emigration

	No.	Per cent
Definite	63	4·2
Probable	121	14·2
Possible	388	25·9
Not emigrating	763	51·0
No response to question	70	4·7
Total	1496	100·0

TABLE 7   Academic record and training abroad

	Will seek to obtain some training abroad (%)		Will not seek training abroad (%)		Uncertain (%)		Working abroad (%)	Already worked abroad and returned (%)		Total
Honours at Graduation	18	33	14	26	21	39		1		54
No failures	223	32	203	29	186	27	40	45		697
One failure	86	35	73	30	63	26	12	10		244
Two failures	42	26	61	38	39	24	12	7		162
Three or more failures	84	38	113	37	75	25	21	10		303
Total	453	31	464	32	384	26	86	6	73	5	1460

$P < 0·05$

(Non-response to question not included)

TABLE 8   Career preference and stage decided

	Before graduation (%)	Pre-reg. year (%)	Since (%)	Undecided (%)	Total (=100%)
Surgery	80 45	50 28	29 16	17 10	176
General Practice	139 37	60 16	107 29	61 17	367
All other careers	198 29	169 23	250 34	126 14	743

$X^2 = 69.40$ d.f. 8
P<0·0005

TABLE 9   Career choice and ultimate location

	In UK (%)	Emigrating (%)	Uncertain (%)	No response (%)	Total (=100%)
General Practice	302 73	16 4	90 22	3 1	411
Path., Bact., Basic Science	53 67	—	26 33	—	79
Internal Medicine	104 61	5 3	61 36	—	170
Derm., ENT, Eyes	43 61	5 7	23 32	—	71
Paed., Psych.,	89 55	6 4	67 41	1 1	163
Anaes., Radiol.	63 48	9 7	59 45	1 1	132
Surgery	106 53	19 10	73 37	2 1	200
Obstet./Gynaec.	49 46	7 7	48 45	2 2	106
Other	83 51	9 5	52 32	20 12	164
Total	892 60	76 5	499 33	11 1	1,496

P<0·0005

J.M. LAST

TABLE 10   Career choice and 'Room at the Top' (Clinical specialties)

Specialty	Graduates	(%)	Establishment, 1965[1]	(%)	Prospects[1]
Anaesthetics	107	8	1,034	4	•••
Dermatology	20	1	151	0·5	••
ENT, Surgery	22	2	316	1	•••
General Practice	414	29	19,963	70	••••
Internal Medicine	176	12	1,499	5	
Obstetrics/Gynaecology	110	8	513	2	•
Ophthalmology	32	2	331	1	••
Paediatrics	98	7	251	1	••
Pathology, Bacteriology	55	4	939	3	•••
Psychiatry	64	5	914	3	•••
Radiology/Radiotherapy	25	2	704	2	••
Surgery	201	14	1,576	6	•
Other	83	6	243	1	•
Total	1,407		28,434		

[1] Source: 'Medical Staffing in the National Health Service, 1965,' Lancet, 2 (1966) 1456.

TABLE 11   Academic record and intention to settle in UK

	Intend to settle in UK	(%)	Intend to emigrate	(%)	Uncertain	(%)
Honours at Graduation	38	70			16	30
No failures	431	61	41	6	232	33
One failure	130	53	14	6	102	41
Two failures	105	64	9	5	50	30
Three or more failures	197	63	13	4	101	32
Total	901	61	77	5	501	34

(Non-response to question not included)

A. SAUVY

The Economic and Political Consequences of Selective Migrations from One Country to Another

For some time now there has been talk about how the best citizens are migrating from one country to another, and this has come to a head with the phenomenon known as the 'brain drain'. The question ought to be looked at as widely as possible and seen in conjunction with the general problems attendant upon such international migra- tions and their selective character. Certain general considerations must be taken into account before we proceed to the examination of this typical problem, which is rightly giving everybody such concern at the present time.

MIGRATION AND SELECTION

The selectivity which is an inevitable part of any migration

Leaving out of account such general expulsions as merit the title 'deportation', as, for example, was the case with the Germans who were driven out of Poland, Czechoslovakia, and East Germany by the Potsdam treaty, and the sort of large-scale exodus occasioned by famine, any migration is bound to be selective in one way or another. The people leaving a country can never be called a representative sample.

For instance, migrations within a country, from country to town, involve the young rather than the old, and people of enterprise rather than those lacking in it.

This kind of selection, or creaming off, often has a very unfavour- able effect on the particular localities or regions left behind. How- ever, there may be compensations of various kinds within any one nation, but none of this applies when it comes to migration from one country to another. Any losses suffered then are definitive and offer no return benefits.

The classic type of migration

Migrations at the present time (we can drop the term international from now on) are voluntary on the part of the individuals concerned but subject to control by the various national authorities. Thus it comes about that there are two kinds of selection : one, a natural one, at the point of departure, and the other, an artificial one, on arrival.

Natural selection

First of all, there is a kind of physical selection to be pointed out. Sick people and chronic invalids are usually prevented from going. In certain cases there may even be something genetic about it, as when their infirmities are the result of inherited disabilities.

For a long time, the question has been asked, and is still asked, what could explain the fact that the people of North America are bigger and heavier than Europeans. It may be because of environmental factors, but also because of selection at the point of departure or, again, because, when the immigrants had landed, they were weeded out by mortality. In the case of the white immigrants it seems likely that selection before they set out played no small part in it.

Such physical selection is usually, although not always, accompanied by some intellectual sifting too. The faint-hearted and the mentally-deficient are no more capable than are the sick of embarking on such enterprises.

From the point of view of character, there are two qualities migrants may have, each very different from the other. In their favour is their spirit of enterprise, the creative spirit, but on the other hand, they may not always be very moral, in the strict sense of the word : not to put too fine a point on it, they may be dishonest or unscrupulous.

Then again, there is the angle of occupation. Your classic examples of voluntary migration usually affect unskilled workers who have found it difficult to get employment in their homelands. The man who is in a good, safe job with a pension ahead has less inducement to leave home than the man with no security. So, in this case, there can be no question of positive selection.

Artificial selection

Since the 1914 – 18 war, most countries have introduced immigration restrictions where before there were hardly any. Such restrictions have been dictated by political, or racial, or economic motives. We shall, here, take no account of the first of these and very little of the second. It is the United States which was principally involved. There, in 1923, a law was passed with the aim of protecting the country against low quality immigrants. The ingenious artifice used was that of giving preference to people coming from the more advanced countries, so that coloured people found themselves, until a further law was passed in 1965, pretty well excluded.

It is, however, economic considerations which have usually weighed most heavily, and this has led to several kinds of selection being made.

Physical condition. Immigration to European countries demands a medical examination in the country of origin, and this can be very strict, the aim being to keep out those who might fall a charge on the public purse, so that the social security budget is thus eased.

Age. Actuarially speaking, a worker's economic value to the state varies with his age. Starting from nothing at birth, this value increases gradually until he reaches employable age or a little later. A certain maximum point is then reached, after which his value diminishes again to nothing and even becomes negative once the worker reaches retirement age. Then, however, he becomes a 'creditor' again and his value rises until his death, when he loses all value.

For a manual worker, the age at which he becomes valueless is from 40–5 years. And it is precisely at this age level that most immigrants are refused admission. Without any hard and fast calcu-lation, the people who pass the immigration laws or administer them have acted on guesswork and got it right.

Occupation. This factor, which has gradually taken precedence over the other two, arises from a popular fear of unemployment and an official desire to defend well-organized professions.

A system of work permits, or contracts, with a time limit makes it possible to accept foreign workers only for jobs which the local inhabitants do not want, which usually means the heavy, poorly paid ones.

Could one say this was a kind of selection? That is a debatable point : one might even say it was a selection by exclusion, since many highly skilled workers are thus kept out, but we shall be coming back to this tricky question later on.

At this juncture we must simply take note that when emigration takes place from country A to country B their two balance sheets do not necessarily equal out, because the balance sheet for the two of them together may be positive or negative, usually positive in this.

Some historic examples of high quality migration

Such migrations are no new phenomenon. Various historic pre-cedents can be cited, such as the expulsion of the Moors and Jews from Spain and, especially, of the Protestants from France in the sixteenth and then in the seventeenth centuries. Louis XIV's action in driving them out deprived his country of its leading merchants, industrialists, and progressive thinkers, who thus enriched their new homelands. The losses which France suffered thereby have often been bemoaned, but in the light of further economic and historical re-search it seems clear that, even so, they have been underestimated, particularly where their long-term consequences are concerned.

The Low Countries, on the contrary, owe their prosperity, partly, to the spirit of toleration, thanks to which these valuable exiles were received by them.

Geneva, too, drew enormous benefit from the quality of its immigrants : the first wave of Protestant refugees gave a wholly unlooked-for fillip to various trades ; hat-making, linen-weaving, the goldsmith's craft, printing, etc., but also it brought them the watch trade, an industry to which the city and surrounding region owe their prosperity and which was brought into the country in 1554. A second wave saw the introduction of lace-making, glove-making, wig-making and cotton-spinning in which 800 people were employed in 1728, but 2,000 in 1785, and whose principal market was France.

When Marmontel asked him to what the people of Geneva owed all their prosperity, Voltaire told him 'Watch-making, reading your newspapers, and profiting from your silly mistakes.'

The rise of Prussia in the eighteenth century was alike due, in large measure, to its Huguenot refugees.

To come nearer home, during the 1930s, the way in which the Nazis expelled their intellectuals and their artists did a great deal of harm to the German economy.

Before we tackle our present-day problem, there are some theories one can put forward about the general problem of selective migration.

One simple example

Let us take the case of two countries, A and B, whose level of development is pretty well equal. In these two countries the working population is divided up in a certain way according to various professions and crafts.

In every country there is some ideal balance in the working population which, allowing for trade with foreign countries, corresponds to private and public needs within the country, such as make themselves felt in a normal way. I am only touching lightly on this question which really ought to be illustrated by a rather complicated mathematical model if one is to get it right. When the working population does in fact equal up to what it ideally ought to be, then conditions of full employment and production are realised.

Thus each of these two countries A and B has an *ideal* professional structure. Each of them needs a certain proportion of butchers, cooks, doctors, dress-designers, and so on, but this proportion may well not be the same in one country as in the other. However, the actual population is often not identical with the ideal. Mostly one exceeds the other only too clearly, with unemployment or underemployment and wrong employment, and there are other shortcomings which are harder to uncover.

Supposing a certain occupation to be over-staffed in country A but not to have sufficient members in country B, then the migration of those employed in it from country A to country B is advantageous for both of them and in both of them helps, if no more, towards creating full employment.

For a long time this was true in the case of building workers who migrated from Italy to France. In the same way, surplus agricultural workers from countries with a high birth rate moved in to rural areas of France that were under-populated because of their rather barren soil.

However, in most cases, and for sociological rather than economic reasons, the same deficiencies and surpluses are to be found in any two countries at the same level of development. For example, retail trade workers are almost always under-employed, at least in the many branches outside the food trade. Never once in the course of history has any country been known to appeal outside its borders for immigrants to fill these occupations.

It follows from this that any migration from country A must be harmful to country B, whether it reduces a surplus in A, or aggra- vates a deficiency in B. The determining factor is that shortages and deficiencies should exist in the two countries. Where there are sur- pluses there are bound to be shortages in other sectors, although these are less in evidence. In that special case, never yet realised, where one of the populations might be perfectly balanced, then any kind of migration would be bound to harm it, at any rate from the short-term point of view.

It is true, actually, that certain adaptations may take place after immigration, whether by switching professions or by guiding young workers into certain jobs, and this lessens the harm done.

Absolute and relative values of migration

This straightforward and general example is an illustration of the fact that the advantage and disadvantage in migration for any one country spring from the relative scarcity of migrants, not from their particular quality. Take the case of a motor, in which some parts cost more and are more vital than others. Nevertheless, let any of its parts fail, be it a driving belt or a mere screw nut in some place, then the most valuable part is not the expensive, but the faulty one.

Here we are up against the old argument about the theory of value : exchange value or value in terms of labour ?

This means that a man has no particular value in himself, but only in relation to his workmates. It is possible to imagine a man who might be particularly gifted for some job but whose value to society would be nil.

A marginalist concept of this kind is, of course, too rigid since all the various functions to be fulfilled in any society are much less clear cut than are the functions of a car part or a living organism. No able-bodied man can ever be quite without use but, as he expects a wage for the work he does, it may happen that his value in terms of production is not as great as the money he needs for his normal consumption, especially if these needs are defined in terms of what he might ideally earn.

The case of countries at different levels of development

When two countries are very unequal as to development, a country whose economy is agricultural alongside an industrial country, the principles just laid down about surpluses and deficiencies will still hold good, but differences are most likely to be found in the nature of those surpluses and deficiencies. In countries where people are only just at subsistence level it does not mean that, because they are over-populated, or seem so, they cannot do with any immigration or that emigration of any kind would necessarily benefit them. Take, for instance, the one extra person who might be capable of helping them really increase their food production: he will actually reduce the over-population because this notion of over-population is an entirely relative one.

So we can let this idea of a man's utility stand, in terms of those he finds himself amongst and their joint environment.

Now, still confining ourselves to the consideration of two coun-tries, let us see what situation may arise with migration.

Four possible situations

Migrations of people of one occupation, or, to put it more exactly, of one particular skill, as between country A and country B, may be classed in four categories, as follows:

Advantageous for A. Advantageous for B.
Advantageous for A. Disadvantageous for B.
Disadvantageous for A. Advantageous for B.
Disadvantageous for A. Disadvantageous for B.

In this context the words 'advantageous' and 'disadvantageous' must be taken in the sense defined above, by reference to the number and nature of occupations followed. Of course, if you are going to cling to the rather imprecise notion of over- or under-population as an absolute, then other considerations will naturally arise, even on the actual economic plane.

It does seem as though the fourth case, in which both countries suffer by the migration, ought, *a priori*, to be out of the question. However, it could happen that the interests and individual decisions involved might fit in with none of the collective interests.

The situation in industrial countries

In industrial countries, the lack of personnel falls into very different categories:

Highly qualified people. The lack of these is always being pointed out and is due to two main causes:

(a) Speed of technological progress. The training men get always lags behind inventions in the very forward - looking professions.

(b) Demands for higher and higher qualifications. Here again, it is not just a question of absolute value, the scarcity factor enters into it, too.

Time was when a man who could read and write was looked upon as very highly qualified. With that ability alone he could get all sorts of well-paid jobs. Now it is so common or garden as to have no longer any value of itself. To come nearer our own time, ability to drive a car used to be a real qualification forty years ago. Now this, too, has lost its scarcity value.

Thus, up to a certain point, qualifications are linked with scarcity value. So we are back at the same conclusion about the relative value of a man's occupation.

Menial, unpleasant, or difficult jobs. In industrial countries having a reasonable educational system, people no longer come forward to do certain jobs, either because they do not pay well enough, or be-cause they are not attractive (domestic work), or because they are too heavy (this is especially true of the building trade), or, in the last resort, because the person doing them has to get himself organi-zed, as is the case with rural craftsmen or, for that matter, craftsmen in towns.

Somewhere between these last two categories and pretty well at the opposite pole, we find occupations in which there is a labour short-age, say, when the demand for them has increased, as in teaching, or else when the pay and working conditions have not kept up with the cost of living (general practice or nursing).

Contrariwise, there is a perpetual surplus of labour in professions which have always enjoyed popularity, such as the arts, or in occupations that have a high standing socially, or are supposed to be light, so that lots of people want to get into them (the business world). Surpluses are also to be found in office jobs for people with-out many qualifications, but the situation here varies a good deal, from country to country and even more so, according to the educa-tional systems and schedules in each country.

A survey of the situation as it affects various countries

The most striking labour force is that of modern Switzerland, which falls principally within the second category of low-grade workers.

E

The number of foreign workers has risen to 750,000 (monthly average, which leaves out of account any seasonal peaks). This represents 26 per cent of the working population and more than a third of the whole salaried labour force.

These foreign workers mostly hold low-grade jobs, either in smelting, or building, or the hotel trade. On the whole the Swiss workers themselves, thanks to the general education and technical training which they get in their own country, are equipped to fill the higher sorts of employment. By reason of this, *they needed a second working population to complement their own.*

A similar phenomenon has come about in other industrialized countries, though on a lesser scale.

The United Kingdom has had to call on immigrants from Malta, from Ireland and from Jamaica, etc, France on Italians first, then Spaniards and Portuguese and finally on Algerians. The German economy needed Italians too, then Greeks and Turks. Sweden gave entry to Danes and Finns, and so on. As for the United States, from the beginning they have always made use of a sub-proletariat composed of blacks and Puerto Ricans.

The situation is entirely different in communist countries. Not only is their industrial evolution less advanced but, more important still, the considerations of marginalism and job distribution, which applied to the other countries mentioned, are not valid in their case. It is not only for economic reasons that international migration is considered undesirable in such countries. In spite of the obvious way in which they might complement each other's needs (surplus of peasants in Poland and shortage of them in Czechoslovakia, for example) the Economic Union of countries behind the Iron Curtain has only taken very tentative steps in the way of organizing migrations.

Yugoslavia, however, has been an exception here, by authorizing the departure of workers for capitalist countries and even by signing agreements on these lines.

MIGRATIONS OF HIGHLY SKILLED WORKERS AT THE PRESENT TIME

These days migration generally takes place from a poorer to a richer country and this is what we are now going to consider, leaving out of account our second category, quoted above, of labourers and workers in other unpleasant trades. In most cases their migration is advantageous to both countries concerned, at any rate in the short term view. The under-developed country gets rid of its surplus population, which will be sending home its savings, while the developed country is supplied with workers for the jobs none of the indigenous population wants to do any more. If you take a long term view you might, perhaps, form a less favourable opinion of all this, particularly if you look beyond the economic aspects of it all. Nevertheless, the very fact that they do complement each other's needs means there is a profitable exchange of services.

The same thing does not hold good for the other two categories of personnel which the developed countries are always after. To take the highly qualified immigrants first.

Engineers and scientists

Here very highly qualified people only are involved. Most emigration takes place in the direction of the United States. From 1956–7 to 1962–3, 34,572 highly qualified immigrants were admitted to the United States. Of these 25,727 were engineers, 8,422 were scientists and 423 held advanced degrees in the social sciences. Doctors are not included in these figures.

Of this total, 15,248 came from Europe. Expressed as a percentage of the scientific and technical graduate force in the countries of origin, this figure represents 8 per cent in Germany's case, 7 per cent Great Britain, 15 per cent Holland, 16 per cent Norway, 17 per cent Switzerland.

Mr Quintin Hogg told the House of Commons that, in aeronautics alone, 1,300 experts have already emigrated from Britain to the United States.

Last December, six American firms were in London, interviewing 700 top engineers and electronic engineers, with a view to signing them on.

The Argentine is affected equally seriously. It all goes to show that the phenomenon has become more extensive still in the last few years. In 1965, it was estimated that the United States requirements for engineers would reach 1,400,000 by 1970, which would leave them 500,000 short if they could not fill the gap as far as possible by immigration.

Selection is at work on two levels. In the first place, it applies to men who have, by taking a series of examinations, given proof of their outstanding quality in particular fields. Then, from amongst these picked men, there is a second kind of selection which is carried further and is, no doubt, a better guide, because it is applied to men who have already gained experience in their chosen field.

Economic consequences. It is very difficult to appreciate these fully or even to assess them at all, because a 'multiplier' factor enters into it that defies all kinds of measurement. What additional productivity is achieved in any country by means of the contribution made by one highly qualified man ? Decidedly, such a contribution must be a high one. In any event, one must beware of measuring the loss to his country of origin in terms of what it cost to train him. The very fact that such men have to undergo the kind of double selection mentioned above makes their value in terms of productivity very much more than the mere cost of their education because of the way in which the work they do can increase the national income with all sorts of indirect repercussions.

If we have to assess this in terms of quality, we may well imagine that, far from reaching any saturation point, the progress made is self-amplifying, one thing leading to another almost mechanically. Thus the weeding out of the very best men inevitably becomes almost automatic in certain professions : just as all professional men above a certain level within any country gravitate towards big cities, so it can become essential for the career of some gifted scientist that he take off, sooner or later, for some world capital.

Such a movement, which would give this metropolis a definite technical lead, would be followed up by a positive commercial balance, and by capital and technical investments made by the dominant country in the other countries, which would henceforward be unable to stave off their own decline.

This is still only hypothetical, but it deserves attention because, once a certain stage is reached, it will be impossible to arrest the movement.

In October 1966, for that matter, M. Robert Mayolin sounded the alarm at a Common Market meeting: 'If the Common Market is destined to remain the chief importer of discoveries and the chief exporter of brains, then the six countries who go to make it up will be condemning themselves to a kind of accumulative under-development which will soon make their decline inevitable.'

What lies behind emigration. The country to which people go can naturally afford to pay the immigrant a higher salary than he can get in his own country. There is this discrepancy not only because the host country is more technically advanced but also, and above all, because the firm or the whole economy are on a bigger scale. Moreover, it is not just an increase in earnings that the emigrant is after : indeed, this may be a secondary consideration. A man of great culture, particularly a man who is outstanding all round, wants work that really stretches him, a laboratory at his disposal, a whole business to control. This is where training and expansion again enter into the picture. In the same way, the ease with which things can get done, the legal and administrative set up, are all involved.

Doctors and paramedical personnel
Scientists apart, it is people in the above categories who are particularly attracted by highly developed countries. The need for doctors, nurses and the like is felt pretty generally throughout the world.

The Naraghi report. Realising the importance of this phenomenon, the United Nations Organization asked the Naraghi of Iran to prepare a report on it.

Completed some months ago, this report has not yet been made public and it would seem that the United Nations authority are hesitating about doing so because of the possible repercussions. We can give some of the figures here :

The United States is employing 20,000 foreign doctors, a great number of them from Latin America. Out of 13,000 Iranian medical students, 6,000 took up practice in Iran (1 to every 4,200 inhabitants) and 7,000 in the United States. American teaching hospitals are turning out 7,000 doctors a year, as against a requisite number of 14,000 for their hospitals alone.

Every year 150 nurses leave Chile for the US. According to another source, 78 per cent of the Iranian students visiting US, in all subjects, stay there permanently.

The American immigration law of 1965 encourages this intake of brain workers.

Nor are the US the only country to drain such people away from under-developed countries. In England there are 4,000 doctors and 9,000 nurses from abroad, chiefly India and Pakistan. Of recent years France has taken in more doctors and teachers from Togoland than it has sent there. It has been estimated by some people that Western Europe is making up to herself, in quantity if not in quality, all the technicians she loses to the US, by taking them from her old colonies.

Some observations about this, with suggested remedies

The value of a man. Is it true that an under-developed country supplying manpower to a highly developed one suffers a loss that is greater in effect than is the gain to the latter ?

In the case of doctors and nurses this is undoubtedly so, in terms of human life, because of the diminishing power they thus have to reduce their high death rate. We must, however, allow here for the fact that such a doctor may not be made the best use of in his country of origin.

When it comes to engineers and scientists, there the case is different. It may happen, especially when you are dealing with very exceptional men, that the higher productivity that is achieved in his new country through the contribution of such a man is something of greater importance than the loss in production or earning power incurred by the country he left behind. This is the same thing all over again, though in a different context, as the problem of town from country, but having none of the compensations that you get within a country. You can already see the beginnings, here, of some international kind of compensation.

There are two reasons why it is impossible to assess the economic value of any man :

Our society not allowing slavery, cannot set any money value on any of its members.

You cannot possibly analyze the indirect effects on productivity brought about by the efforts of one particularly clever man.

It is precisely because there is this vagueness that public opinion remains unawakened to the dangers of the situation. If some foreigner were to come and steal 1,000 tons of steel from another country and take it back to his own, everyone would be united in denouncing the theft, as an act of piracy. When it is a clever man who is stolen, the material loss is much greater yet no feelings at all are roused in the matter.

This is the price we have to pay, a disadvantage that we have to accept, for the priceless gift of liberty. In communist countries where men are not free to leave their homeland this phenomenon simply does not arise. In this way, Negro and Asiatic students, having trained in free countries, almost all go back to their country of origin, or at least do not stay in the place where they had their education.

There is another reason why the public mostly remain unmoved by all this. Market economy always gives the impression of a super-abundance so that people easily come to think there is an absolute surplus of goods. In human terms the phenomenon is even more marked because everyone can see the unemployed men whereas the jobs they might get are not visible to the eye, so that people get a vague belief that there just are too many men in all countries, which are thus over-populated as far as jobs are concerned. All sorts of ideas are based on this one supposition.

It is also to be found in the us, but over there the importance of picking the best has been generally accepted enough to stop people worrying when they see a whole lot of extra workers immigrating.

A general corporate, or professional Malthusianism can also be sensed, so that people seem indifferent, or even indulgent, to the problem. If someone is going, they say, then that leaves a job for someone else, whereas someone coming in is going to take a job from other people. This kind of microeconomic point of view is very common, and takes no account of the essential phenomena of growth and development. In France, for instance, it is responsible for the refusal of entry permits to highly qualified men on the grounds that they would simply be rivals for the men on the spot.

Here again, such ideas have much less currency in the us which, being so much bigger, thinks of competition as a driving force.

The strong and the weak. Generally speaking, any alliance between the weak and the strong, however well intentioned, is fraught with danger for the weak. There always comes a moment when self interest makes itself felt and strength is brought into play, however discreetly.

It has often been said that the economic and financial aid given by the highly developed countries to the Third World has been compensated for by the unfavourable development of trade terms. Most of the economic experts seem to lend credence to this but it has never yet been proven. On the contrary, the emigration of the experts, the creaming off of the best in favour of the more highly developed country is a vivid example of how delicate are the relationships between a strong and a weak country.

The utmost attention and sustained effort must be paid to preventing the brazen law of inequality from prevailing.

The action which might be taken against all this. Of course for those who look on all this favourably or who just do not care, there is no need to propound any remedial measures. However, we must guard ourselves against that frame of mind which is so often encountered and proves so tempting, whereby the danger is underestimated. It is very difficult indeed, just from first principles, to stand out against this attitude.

What must be done at the outset is research: the extent of the phenomenon must be noted, uncertain as it still is. Then it can be evaluated and all its repercussions, as far as possible, followed up.

Two counter measures come to mind, brakes and compensations, which might act interchangeably.

First, migration might be absolutely forbidden and a strict control set up, but this would necessitate a previous agreement between the different countries and would very likely not be honoured, especially not where it really mattered. It will seem hard to forbid a man to work at something which will really stretch his capacities to the utmost.

Secondly, that the under-developed countries should be reorganized so as to be able to offer better working conditions to their citizens; this would be acclaimed everywhere. Surely we must make some effort along these lines. Nevertheless, it would be unwise to think such plans would solve the problem.

Dr Naraghi makes the suggestion that international universities and research centres should be set up. This question ought to be gone into. One thing is certain, and that is that if some sort of regional agreements could be made, this ought to make emigration less attractive, either from Latin America or the Far East, from the Arab countries or Black Africa. The Common Market, as it has

functioned so far, is a model of how not to operate : a purely mer-
cenary approach leaves out of account a man's full value and pays
no heed to the positive co-operation which might be achieved,
especially where scientific research is concerned.

There is also talk of paying some indemnity to the country from
which the skilled man emigrates. This would be paid partly by the
state and partly by the firm employing him in his new country. In
principle, this is a fine idea but, all the same, there are serious
difficulties to it. Not only does it require the full approval of the
countries at the receiving end but also it would come up against the
problem of assessing a man's value in any particular case. There
would be a great temptation to base the whole calculation on mere
book-keeping, totting up the cost of his education, that is. Such a
method would call for the sort of compensation which would be a
mockery, although pretending to resolve the problem.

Other methods, again, might be put forward, all connected with
various kinds of international co-operation. But the vital thing to be
decided is what end capitalist society has in view for itself. If what
it wants is to arrive at a strongly centralized organization with one
country dominating all the others, then its job is already done.
Should some higher concept of life prevail, then our world must
take stock of what means it has for realizing its aims.

Comments

R. Illsley

When two distinguished scientists disagree as fundamentally as Drs
Beijer and Sauvy, it is simplest, in the first place, to seek the cause in
inadequate or contradictory data. We do indeed suffer from a lack of
good data and this lack applies to most aspects of international
migration – its extent (particularly among professionally qualified
people), the reasons for migration, the characteristics of migrants,
and the latent benefits and disadvantages to exporting and receiving
areas. This situation leaves plenty of scope for disagreement about
what, if anything, should be done to regulate the flow of migrants.

Two problems arise in assessing the extent of migration, the first
relating to the permanence of migration, the second to the volume of
compensatory movement. In many branches of professional work a
period abroad has become an accepted part of the educational process and the full advantage of such an experience may only be
reaped from an extended stay. At present it is difficult to calculate
the net or permanent loss. Secondly, we know that a movement from
country A to country B may be, at least partially, balanced by a movement from country C to A. The true loss to any country can therefore
only be calculated after allowing for compensatory movements.
Both deficiences are potentially rectifiable by further data collection. For this purpose, however, we need more than the usual
national census statistics on the age, marital status, occupation, etc.
of the population by place of birth, last residence, and nationality,
because these are the statistics which give rise to our present uncertainty. The appropriate model is not one of exchange between
two countries but one more comparable to that of world trade, of a
pattern of export, import and re-export involving many countries.
The 'brain drain' from Britain to N. America can only be evaluated
if we take cognizance of her net gain from Commonwealth immigrants, whilst the serious loss of trained manpower for Commonwealth countries must be set against the increased skills of their
nationals returning after several years of education and experience
in Western industrial societies and programmes of technical aid.

Full evaluation also requires more specificity in the occupational
roles of migrants. If we lose, for example, a large number of medical
doctors trained to operate our general health services they are a net
loss of this country and a net gain to importing countries, who
receive a qualified service worker trained at somebody else's expense.

If, however, we lose a medical scientist to a country more able to exploit his skills we may reap some return from advancements in medical science which ultimately are shared among the international scientific community. Scientific research workers form a significant part of Europe's 'brain drain' to N. America, while Europe's gain from the under-developed countries consists more of service workers who may now be essential, for example, to the manning of medical and nursing services. It is arguable that the result of this complex inter-migration is a marked gain to the richest countries, a partially compensated loss to the older industrial countries and a large net loss to under-developed societies. In the absence of really appropriate data this must remain a supposition.

There are two accepted methods of studying the motivation of migrants. The first is to ask the migrants themselves about their motives. We must be clear, however, that the responses give us only the migrants' self-perceptions and/or rationalisations. This is clearly relevant for it may be the image of a country, rather than the reality of it, which attracts or repels. Explanations flowing from such data tend to be individualistic or psychologistic, rather than sociological or structural. The individual feels pressures in his day-to-day work or living standards and his responses are likely to centre around these personal experiences, but at another level of explanation or action the problem may stem from disjunction between role expectations built up during training and role performances after training, from the structure of the profession, or a conflict between class and national interests. Such reasons are not likely to be explicitly stated by a respondent, particularly in answer to a simple questionnaire. A simple example comes from my own studies of young migrants in northern Scotland. Migration from the countryside to the city was significantly higher among persons whose family of origin had been broken or disturbed by the death or separation of parents. The reasons given for migration centred around training, jobs or housing and in one sense this was a reasonable explanation. An interesting category were those where the father had died and the family contained several daughters; the range of occupations for girls was limited in the countryside and the father's death led to a re-appraisal of the family's interests and a move into the city. You can seek the reasons for migration in family disturbance, in sex ratios, in occupational opportunities or in the distribution of industry, but the best explanation lies in a social process rather than the perceived and stated 'reason' of the respondent. Questions to professionally qualified migrants frequently attempt to assess the relative importance of personal income, promotion prospects, status, research facilities, etc. The responses undoubtedly have some validity but we know that these influences are frequently interrelated rather than neatly separated and specific, and that all of them may often be more use-fully described in terms of differences between exporting and import-ing countries in professional organization and hierarchies, professional socialization and social class identification. This leads to an alter-native, or rather a supplementary, method of studying motivation based on a thorough analysis of the situation of migrant and non-migrant populations at both ends of the migration stream. Part of such a study would contain a traditional demographic and social-statistical type of material. A great increase in understanding might accrue, however, if such studies were carried out on particular professional groups, where it would be possible at the same time to study professional organization, conflict between structure and ex-pectation, the relation of class to professional and national interests, and those other social-structural factors which might well be the most profitable points for administrative and political intervention. It is for this reason that I welcome Dr Last's study of the medical profession.

A further area of uncertainty relates to the characteristics of migrants. This of course is closely linked to their motivation. One can infer something of the characteristics of migrants from their motivation or, alternatively, something of their motivation from their characteristics. Disquiet arises at the thought that we are losing our brightest and best national products. Professor Sauvy rightly drew our attention to selective migration and its possible consequences, and particularly to migrant populations of 'high quality'. He sug-gested that selective migration might be one reason for the superior height and weight of North Americans. Plenty of evidence has now accumulated to show that out-migrants from an area are taller and heavier than sedents. The processes involved are complex and difficult to interpret. There are equally firm data showing that within a given society upper socio-economic groups are taller and heavier than lower socio-economic groups – indeed there is a continuous association between height and socio-economic status. In Western industrial societies migration, both internal and international, runs at a continuously high level in the professional, managerial and highly educated groups. My own studies suggest that long-distance migrants are taller than short-distance migrants; the reasons again are com-plex, put at the simplest economic level it seems reasonable to assume that one might move a 1,000 miles for an extra £1,000 p.a. but not for an extra 6d. an hour. The differences in stature between Europe and N. America are paralleled by similar differences in Britain itself. Present-day Scots, as a population, are shorter than the English, and the Northern English are shorter than those living in London and the

South-East. The general migratory movement in Britain is from North to South. Is the difference in mean stature therefore an indicator of genetic selection? Here we have to be cautious. Potential stature may be genetically determined but environment probably plays a very important role in deciding whether an individual reaches his genetically potential height. I would suggest that the superior height of migrants reflects their socio-economic composition and that the superior height of the Southern English and the North Americans reflects their superior living standards. In this connection it is noteworthy that second- and third-generation Americans are substantially taller than their immigrant forbears. One must also bear in mind the relativity of social-influenced characteristics. Migrants from Northern England are taller than sedents, but they are shorter than the resident population of the Southern areas to which they migrate. To the native born American, immigrants from Europe have frequently appeared as a stunted, unhealthy population even though they may have been superior physical types in their European background.

Similar problems arise when we turn to intellectual characteristics. Migrants in Western industrial societies tend to have higher intelligence test scores than sedents – although, of course, there may be certain migratory streams with opposite characteristics. Again this derives largely from their socio-economic composition, and furthermore they may not show any superiority over the population into which they migrate – this depends to some extent on the cultural characteristics of the areas between which they migrate. The position may appear very differently if, like Dr Last, we look at a narrow socio-economic stratum. In Dr Last's study it was not the best graduates who had the highest rate of migration, and both he and other participants made the point that those who had achieved the best examination results in their early careers were most likely to show a successful career pattern in our own society. Ultimately this comes back to the problem of motivation; some stay because they are successful and because the structure of the profession is favourable to them; others leave because they are unsuccessful, because their profession does not provide opportunities to meet their expectations. Some of our medical doctors have stayed in Britain because the National Health Service has provided them with the opportunities for good and egalitarian medical practice, while others have left for the US because that same medical practice did not yield financial rewards befitting a doctor.

The latent effects of migration are almost by definition more difficult to evaluate. One important effect stems from the fact that frequently we are dealing, not merely with the migration of individuals, but of families. Professional men, in general, marry highly educated women, so that when we lose a married scientist we lose not only the resources put into him but also into his wife, their joint work-capacity, and their ability to transmit the most sophisticated culture of our society to the next generation. Not all our losses however are pure losses. The loss of scientists to more advanced areas results partially from our attempt to give them a period of further training abroad and many return to pass on the benefit. Developing countries gain from our educational system and lose a proportion of their skilled manpower in the process. As Dr Beijer points out, there is one rather peculiar sense in which the loss itself brings compensations in that it draws attention to defects in our system, which, if acted upon, will lead to far-reaching improvements. It would be interesting to know how far the 'brain drain' from Britain has stimulated or hastened much-needed changes in our universities and in the structure of our professions. This may, however, be poor consolation to the developing countries which do not have the resources to fight back.

This conference itself is an example of the most powerful of the latent advantages of professional migration. The results of most scientific research are not confined to a single nation. Just as one generation climbs on the shoulders of another, so do we all gain in some measure from the scientific progress of more advanced societies and the loss of our native scientists returns to us as a benefit if their skills can be more successfully exploited elsewhere. We need to ask how far we are concerned with absolute or with relative gains. Is a technological advance beneficial in itself, wherever it originates, provided that ultimately it is diffused? Or is it only beneficial if, by occurring in our own country, it narrows the technological gap between ourselves and more advanced societies? We are concerned here with a question of fact, at present almost immeasurable, namely the extent to which advances are diffused to the ultimate benefit of less advanced economies. Professor Sauvy touches on a point very germane to Scotland when he discusses the relationship between the weak and the strong and suggests the possibility that an outflow of talent and strength may, when it reaches a certain point, be irreversible and cumulative. But the problem also raises questions of political values. Do we measure the results of the process in terms of absolute gains and losses in national wealth and living standards, or in changes in the relative wealth of the strong and the weak, in which case the latter might be regarded as a loser despite large absolute gains. The answer depends on how far we attach importance to national identities or believe in the desirability or possibility of international integration free from domination by a single power. Scientists and academics generally are reaching the point where many feel that their community, their friends, the people with whom they identify are not their nationals, or their neighbours, but their professional colleagues wherever they live, and it would seem retrogressive to restrict free flow between them. The chances are that it would also be uneconomic.

General Discussion

G. Beijer, W. Brand, W. Brass, C. Clark, M. Drake, H. J. Habakkuk,
G. F. Hammersley, T. H. Hollingsworth, R. Illsley,
J. M. Last, and J. N. Wolfe.

This was a rather involved discussion, and apart from a few straightforward methodological points is not easy to summarize succinctly.
The main effect of the various contributions was to put the problems
involved in sharper focus, and it became apparent during the discussion that greater precision was necessary if really useful statements
were to be made about the so-called 'brain drain'.

Last really started the methodological theme, taking up a point of
Illsley's to agree with him that the motives for migration were very
difficult to assess, and asking how one could obtain accurate answers
to questions about why people migrate. Illsley felt that we should
place less emphasis on people's statements, and more on their
actions. In other words as he put it: 'You can learn a great deal not
just from what people are and from what they *say*, but from what
they are and what they do.' Thus, rather than asking people how they
felt about migration he suggested techniques such as examining the
way they fitted into the career structure both of their country of origin and of the country to which they migrated. In this way one could
find out, for instance, whether they were people who had failed to
make the grade in their country of origin, and see whether by migration they became more successful – in terms of higher status, better
financial returns, and so on. Illsley suggested that facts like these
could be more easily interpreted than those obtained by asking people
to examine their own motives. Brass reminded the seminar that very
few studies really looked at all the people they should look at. Most
studies sampled either people who remained in a country, or those who
returned, or sometimes those who emigrated, but not all these
groups. He suggested that the right methodology would be to compare those who stayed with those who came back and those who
never emigrated at all; most studies are as he put it 'highly selective
in the type of people they look at.'

The difficulties of interpreting the present statistics were indirectly
highlighted by Drake, who pointed out that, according to the appendix of Beijer's paper, Norway appeared to lose more engineers as a
percentage of the output of science and engineering graduates than
any other country. He suggested that this was misleading; Norway
tended to send many students to study overseas who then appeared

in statistics of this kind. When Drake was at Oslo in 1956–7, one-third of the Norwegian university students were studying outside the country. The figures are, thus, to some extent an artefact of the Norwegian educational system. At that time a student would obtain the same loan no matter where in the world he chose to study.

Beijer returned to the question of the causes for emigration, mentioning that a study had been done by the Dutch government in 1956 to find out the motives people gave for emigrating. They had a sample of 1,000 people, 400 in Australia, 400 in Canada and 200 in Latin America. In a two year follow-up of these subjects it was found that 25 per cent of the reasons they had given for their original decision were in fact fictitious, thus throwing considerable doubt on this type of enquiry.

The general discussion started in a very unfocused way and, as will be seen, the inadequacy of this approach gradually became apparent. Last, in an opening comment, said that he was convinced sanctions were of no value and what we required were incentives to keep people in their countries. Wolfe took up this point and claimed that, to put the matter somewhat crudely, the situation was essentially one of supply and demand. He then suggested that 'one obvious thing one could do about it is to raise the incomes of the sort of people one wants to keep at home to a sufficient level. Now this may not be the most attractive solution, but I would think myself that it is almost certain to be one possible way of solving the problem. When people say they cannot *afford* to raise academic and professional salaries to such a level as to curb the "brain drain", what they are really saying is that they do not *choose* to raise academic and professional salaries to that level. And of course if you have got mobile people you cannot really expect to have a professional salary level which is all that different in different countries without getting a very considerable movement of people between countries.' He went on to point out that there are of course other ways of increasing the job satisfaction of scientists and other professionals. For instance, their rate of promotion, access to equipment and so on can be improved. Some of these measures may cost more money than raising salaries although others certainly cost less. A rather simple method of raising job satisfaction was to improve the opportunities for intellectual interchange and stimulus. Wolfe found it rather curious that until very recently countries outside America had not taken steps in this direction, and remarked that seminars of the kind being reported did increase job satisfaction and thus probably the intellectual stimulus and productivity of individual academics. Nevertheless he said, 'Ultimately it has got to be faced that people get the brains that they wish and the basic problem is that many of the countries which are experiencing "brain drain" are experiencing it because they do not have the will to take the steps to avert that kind of movement.' He admitted, however, that one of the great satisfactions of travelling between countries was a kind of intellectual excitement, and that no matter what one did to salaries and academic positions this excitement would remain. He went on: 'I would really suggest that in a fundamental sense, intellectual movement between countries is something which will occasionally get out of hand, and gets out of hand if the exporting countries either fail to match their supply situation to the demand situation domestically, as has happened occasionally in Britain since the war, or alternatively if they cease really to be very concerned about the number and quality of the professional and scientific personnel whom they keep at home. If these conditions can be checked, the outflow I think will be checked.' Last supported Wolfe's point by referring to the changes in the supply and demand relationship in British medicine. The changes in this relationship within the National Health Service in the first ten or so years after the war had a profound effect on the movement of general practitioners. In particular it affected their migration from the places where they lived in their youth to those in which they finally settled in England and Wales. Moving on to the migration out of Britain he said 'I feel sure that you are absolutely right that the fashion in migration from Britain by people in the medical profession has been set by rather violent swings in the supply and demand relationship both in the service and the academic sphere.'

Beijer also partly supported Wolfe, pointing out first of all how research into the situation in highly-developed countries had produced a table of the percentage of the national income spent on scientific research. The percentage in the United States was more than double the equivalent percentage in France, and France had the highest level in Europe! However some governments have indeed been active in sponsoring a return movement of scientists. Western Germany paid to scientists and engineers returning to Germany a lump sum, which was related to the income differential experienced, and also made some allowance in the tax situation. Finally Beijer commented that people who return to their country of origin often find it very difficult to re-adjust. This can be seen in the case of skilled personnel returning to Pakistan and India. They have expectations of the kind of life they had lived, for instance in America, and in this way they come to feel that they are foreigners in their own country. This, Beijer felt, certainly contributed to the 'brain drain' from some countries, and it could be argued that it was a mistake to give a European education to people from these countries, but that this must be a matter of policy.

F

As we shall see, discussion of the type of educational system a country should have re-appears later, but it is convenient to continue with the main theme – the supply and demand relationship, and the effects of migration.

Brand pointed out that there were often compensatory elements. He admitted that he knew of no studies of the phenomenon, but he would hypothesize that the movement of people also involves questions of trade. His point of view was that many people migrating have an interest in obtaining goods from their countries of origin and that this must be included in the balance of losses and gains. More importantly however he claimed that the crucial question was the kind of world which we wanted to live in. He personally did not grudge the 'brain drain' to the United States, regarding them as the policemen of the Western world, and he was therefore prepared to lose some personnel in order to maintain the United States in its present powerful position. Furthermore he believed that the future lay in a larger Atlantic community. And with special reference to Holland, he pointed out that it was a very small country, too densely populated in his opinion, and it should be pleased if a number of its people moved away. His points came together in some ways when he said 'I believe very strongly that Holland really must have access to stronger markets in order to exist, and for people to move helps in this way to spread Dutch culture, Dutch characteristics and the Dutch outlook on matters.' Behind a great deal of the discussion of the 'brain drain' there lay a matter of philosophy or ideology; a belief in the sort of world or country you really wanted.

It was at this point that the first shift of emphasis became apparent, although a precursor of this was a remark made by Last at the beginning of the discussion. He had pointed out that in a report recently published by the Pan American Health Organization the migration of scientists from positions in Latin America to the United States had been shown to be very serious under certain circumstances. The important point was that a developing country cannot afford to lose men who were leaders and teachers in their profession and, moreover, that once this migratory movement has started it is very difficult to stop. Beijer had later qualified this statement by pointing out that while he agreed in the case of Venezuela or Columbia, he felt that the point did not hold so well for the Argentine, Brazil and Chile. However the *theme* underlying Last's remarks was taken up again by Habakkuk. Habakkuk's statement is reported at some length, as it contained the roots of a good deal of the discussion. He started off by saying 'Dr Beijer reinforced by Dr Brand really persuaded me that, so far as Europe is concerned, the migration of brains is not a major problem in the sense that if it assumed proportions which were

thought to be excessive by some criteria or other, the actions necessary to redress the balance would be presumably within the ability of
European countries to undertake. But I think in the case of an under-
developed country the position is very different. Particularly an under-
developed country like India in which the university population
has the fortune or misfortune to speak the same language as the
richest country in the world, and is therefore peculiarly vulnerable to
the temptations of a fuller life and a larger income.' He expanded on
Last's points saying that the real damage was not the loss of individual brains. It was the breaking up of the teams of which many of
these men were the leaders. In a country which has a small stock of
first-class ability it is extremely difficult to replenish ability and to
recreate teams once they have broken up. Thus he felt it was the
migration of people in their thirties and possibly even in their forties
which was the most damaging form of migration, and it was not
easy to see how the supply and demand mechanism described by
Wolfe could work in the case of India. As he put it 'It is very difficult
to see how a country so poor could afford to pay even the brightest of
its stars income equivalent to that of an MIT professor when MIT was
in a bidding mood.' Furthermore he pointed out that in India and in
some other countries there is an important institutional factor that if
the remuneration of a scientist is set by the government there is
usually some relationship between that salary and the salaries in the
Civil Service. But there is no international market in civil servants.
If the Americans were to start bidding for the civil servants of other
countries this would no doubt bring an increase in academic and
professional salaries generally! Nor did he feel that the intellectual
satisfaction generated, for instance, by international seminars, as
suggested by Wolfe, was of any great value in the Indian case. While he
conceded that an increase in such seminars would doubtless increase
job satisfaction among British scientists he felt such an increase would
have the effect in general of raising job dissatisfaction among
Indians; after every visit to Europe they return more dissatisfied.
Habakkuk's final remarks show the clear distinction between developed and under-developed countries, and how they should be considered separately in discussion. 'I think that in the case of Europe
there are certain self-correcting mechanisms. The disparity in opportunities and salaries, after all, are not all that great, and migration
sets in train steps to persuade people to return. Furthermore the
disparity is not so great that those steps cannot be successful. But
the disparity between countries like India and America, to take two
extremes, is so great that the flow once started will tend, I think,
to accelerate, and for that I do not really see any obvious remedy
among those that have been suggested.'

Brand returned to the discussion to agree that despite what he had said about Europe he felt that for the developing countries the 'brain drain' really was a most serious problem. A possible suggestion that had occurred to him was whether there could not be a World or United Nations corps of really first-class people from the under-developed countries who would be prepared to go back to their countries of origin under certain conditions. His idea was that they might be put at the disposal of their countries and paid international salaries.

Wolfe however returned to the attack, claiming that the problems of the under-developed countries could be grossly exaggerated. He felt that it was possible to establish centres of great excellence even in countries like India, and in the field of economics this had been done in at least one Indian centre. The technique used was to promote a number of people into senior positions at a very youthful age, regard-less of the fact that this meant they became senior to older people. By these means their income levels, while still lower than those of the United States, had been sufficiently satisfactory in Indian terms to make it attractive for them to stay. In contrast he pointed out that effecting the return of nuclear scientists from America had only been made possible by the decision to build a very large machine in Europe. This had made it feasible to attract high-energy nuclear physicists from America and to build up a centre at an international level. Competitive pressure to build even larger machines was then created, and Wolfe estimated that the process had now gone so far that the total equipment costs per high-energy nuclear physicist in Europe might be as high as £150,000 per man by 1975. Furthermore the *annual* cost in equipment and so on to support these physicists would be something like £40,000 per year per man. As Wolfe said 'these are rather high figures and they indicate just how expensive it may be to attract and retain scientists by other means than by raising their salaries. I should have thought myself that this was likely to be repeated in many other lines, and in fact the cheapest way in which to keep your scientists is to pay them.'

Habakkuk responded to Wolfe's comment by claiming that the Indian department to which he referred bore out his own point. He claimed that its members were always on the verge of accepting an offer to go elsewhere, and indeed that two of its leading experts had just departed, one to MIT and one to Columbia. It must remain, he said, a rather fragile institution even though the Indians have made an attempt to pay younger men much larger salaries than those nor-mally expected in India. The salaries and intellectual facilities re-mained meagre compared with an American university, so that the future of such an experiment must remain very much in doubt.

Hollingsworth supported Habakkuk on this point and took up the example of the nuclear scientists. He suggested that not only is it rather doubtful whether the salary level of nuclear physicists could be raised to match those paid in the United States, but also that they would be unable to do anything unless provided with equipment. Thus, one would be landed with a double cost which was continually mounting. He too believed that the problem was one of supply and demand, but seemed to see it as one of the supply of educated people at very high levels versus the occupational opportunities. Here we can see returning the theme of the sort of education which should be made available. Hollingsworth queried whether in under-developed countries sufficient money was being spent on low level education as opposed to high level. He felt that the production of a large number of university graduates in India may well be a very foolish thing to do given the limited resources available. It might be an unpopular move to decide that, a few hundred people apart, no one was going to be a scholar of international repute but all were going to be literate. Nevertheless this might be the kind of measure that India needed. Certainly Hollingsworth felt it would prevent the 'brain drain' in rather a drastic manner, because one could afford to pay the small number of top men the international going rate. At the same time the majority of people, more highly educated than they are at present, would be able to find a useful place in the occupational structure. The Indian educational system seemed to be built on the British élite model which had been dogging European education for long enough, and to Hollingsworth this seemed a mistake. In saying 'after all it is nonsense to say that we need more scientists if we don't pay for them, and if we don't pay for them then presumably we don't need them,' he seemed to be in agreement with something Wolfe had said earlier. However his conclusion was not that we should pay more, but perhaps that we required rather different people. For instance he suggested that in this country we should perhaps be concentrating our efforts on producing more technicians for industry rather than more highly-educated scholars.

Drake took up this theme by looking at the problem in a related but slightly different way. 'There is no point in increasing pay unless the whole community, the whole society is educated into wanting to use people in the way they feel they are wanted in other parts of the world. This is essential, I think, to the problem, and the idea of paying seems to me not the answer at all.'

Clark suggested that the Japanese case supported Hollingsworth's suggestions. He admitted that there was probably an important linguistic element in the Japanese success in that they spoke European languages badly and their scientists and technicians had felt only a small temptation to emigrate. The combination of the linguistic factor and a rather strong sense of national obligation had provided a sort of barrier behind which they had been able to organize their education in a particular way. They spent the money firstly on universal schooling. Later they considered it reasonable to send the top specialists abroad for their education, while progressively developing their own high schools and universities. In this way they built up a very good educational system without losing many people. The practical conclusion Clark drew was that it might well be wiser for each developing country to develop its own universities, perhaps behind its own language barrier, rather than send any more men abroad than was really necessary.

Brass took up the same points when he spoke about medical training in the under-developed countries. He suggested that a good deal of this training had been directed towards the wrong type of person, that is, not people to do the general work of their own country but people suitable for doing the rather specialist work going on in the United States and the United Kingdom. A good deal of this training goes on in Europe, and he recalled talking about work in rural Africa to medical students, and two Nigerian students commenting that they had been fascinated to hear about rural Nigeria, because they had never been there and had no idea what work there would be like. In Africa and India a great deal of the work that should be done by doctors was in fact being done by people trained at a much lower level because very few doctors would do the kind of work that was required. 'They appear not to have been trained to or have accepted the view that working in fairly primitive areas can be an exciting and useful kind of work.' He emphasized what was clearly coming out of the discussion at this point, that people were talking about many different things at the same time. As he put it 'I can't myself raise very much interest in say, the luxury trade in doctors between the UK and US, or for that matter, the luxury trade in atomic scientists between India and Europe.'

Last elaborated on Brass's point by saying that in a Latin American country with very similar problems, Columbia, the question of training people at different levels to perform professional tasks raised acute questions of national pride. He had recently visited medical schools in Columbia, and in three of them any idea of training people to a standard slightly below that of North America or Europe was quite unacceptable. In one school, however, they were going ahead to train people in this way, and he felt that it might help some of the problems. Nevertheless as he put it 'this is a major difficulty in any developing country, that national pride intrudes into any realistic approach to this question of training people appropriately to meet the country's needs.' Brass mentioned that at a recent meeting in India of the World Society of Medical Education there was a very strong consensus of opinion that a lower level of training on a larger scale was highly desirable but, as Last commented, this had still to be accepted by the politicians.

Hammersley returned again to the variation between one 'brain drain' and another 'brain drain'. He pointed out that there were teachers of different kinds and at different levels, that doctors and engineers were one thing and astronomers another. Much opposition to the 'brain drain' was a result of an indiscriminate desire to keep people in one place which, for many professions, was surely not necessary. Indeed he suggested that in many fields it was simpler and cheaper to import ideas from elsewhere rather than develop them at home, and he cited the Japanese in support of this idea. He wondered for instance whether, rather than bothering about research into atomic energy, we in Britain should not simply have decided to buy everything from the United States. In this way we might be far better off in a large number of other scientific areas, instead of having concentrated our resources on a large number of physicists working in the nuclear field.

The overwhelming impression with which one was left at the end of this session was that there are indeed different kinds of 'brain drain' and it was a mistake to regard them as equivalent. And furthermore, the problems of Europe are quite different from those of Africa and India. A great deal more very detailed research is required before any real conclusions can be drawn.

Techniques and Methods of Study

W. BRASS

A generation method for projecting death rates

N. CARRIER

Calculation of family structure as a demographic
example of the organizational power of matrix
notation in mass arithmetical operations

with prepared comments by P. Cox

CHAIRMAN

E. Grebenik

W. BRASS

A Generation Method for Projecting Death Rates

The forecasting of population growth and its components, to serve as a basis for economic and social planning, is one of the main responsibilities of applied demography. Assessments of how well this function has been performed have almost always been depressing and have resulted in some classics of criticism, e.g. Dorn.[1] Views on how accurate forecasting might be with the use of the most 'modern' and effective techniques have varied over time and among demographers. At present we are moving from a period of widespread pessimism into one of modest and limited optimism.[2] Although the stimulus has come from real advances in the understanding of demographic processes the efficacy of these for improving actual projections has, in my view, still to be proved.

In any attempt to prophesy the future there are, of course, ominous imponderables. It may be that luck will continue to be a dominating influence on success. Nevertheless, consistently good guessing must be based on a critical analysis of trends in the past. An important element in such a study is the search for significant measurements, that is, aspects of the observations which reflect most clearly the patterns and potentialities of change. The development of such measurements of fertility, particularly over the reproductive life of generations of women rather than for cross-sections of the population in time periods, has been the most important advance for demographic forecasting. For various features of these studies see Glass and Grebenik,[3] Ryder,[4] and Freedman, Coombs and Bumpass.[5] There has, however, been surprisingly little attempt to investigate the nature of the trends and fluctuations of series of vital rates, or to examine projection procedures empirically by application to such observations. Some of the findings from the outburst of research into stochastic processes, particularly those on commercial and industrial forecasting, might have been applied usefully to population measurements. Exploratory work in this field has been done by Kpedekpo.[6]

The study of mortality projection has been particularly neglected. One major cause, no doubt, has been the fact that in developed populations, which possess more data and demographers, changes in fertility have a larger and more immediate effect on growth rates than changes in mortality. However, the trends of death rates by sex and age have an important influence on the population structure. Adequate forecasts are particularly necessary for man-power studies, particularly in those occupations, such as medicine, where supply is to a large extent controlled by planning decisions.

Standard methods of projecting age-specific death rates by fitting trend curves of various shapes to series of observations and extra-polating have not been particularly successful. Fluctuations in rates for an age group are substantial and erratic. Over any extensive period the apparent trend varies; except when projection is for only a brief interval ahead, slightly different shapes of curve and/or techniques of fitting can lead to greatly divergent estimates. In practice, it has been common for projections to be made from an inspection of past trends, based on no very clear principles, plus an assessment of the likely modifications in the future. It may be that such methods give better results than more systematic procedures, but this does not seem to have been tested by empirical examination. The subjective element is too large for an experimental verification.

More than thirty years ago Kermack, McKendrick and McKinlay [7] proposed and studied a method of mortality projection which was, in my view, soundly based on the principles required for an effective procedure. Their work is referred to in most of the textbooks on demographic techniques but on the whole is regarded as of historic interest only. There appears to have been little, if any, attempt to develop its application further. The present paper gives such an extension.

The method of Kermack, McKendrick and McKinlay (KMM for short) starts from specific death rates by sex and age for succes-sive generations, that is sub-populations of persons born in the same period. In practice it is usually convenient for the length of the periods to be five or ten years and that of the age groups for which the rates are calculated to be the same. Kermack et al. suggested that the ratio of the specific death rate of one generation to that of the previous one for the corresponding sex-age group could be taken as a constant. If the constants are estimated for a series of successive, incomplete generations, that is, those which have not ended their life span, the set of values can be used to project death rates into the future. Thus, at a given time, the comparison of death rates up to age 75 for generations born 80 and 75 years previously gives a value for the appropriate constant. Multiplication of the known mortality of the older generation in the age group 75–9 years by the constant supplies the estimate for the younger one. Similarly, comparisons between the generations born 70 and 75 years previously leads to estimates of the death rate in the younger group at 70–4 and 75–9 years from the known, and from the previously estimated measures respectively for the older generation. The process is continued to generations recently born. It follows, of course, that the mortality projections must relate to persons already born. Estimates thirty years in the future can only be for death rates above this age. For the important man-power applications the limitation is not serious. It is possible to devise consistent procedures for extending the estimates to lower ages but they will not be considered here.

The KMM method depends on two completely distinct ideas which will be considered separately. The first is that a simple relationship between different mortality patterns can be established. In the particular application it is between generation death rates but this is not an essential element. The advantage of such an approach for projection is that multiple trends are summarized by a small number of series of measurements. Efficient indices of this kind will average out part of the fortuitous fluctuation in individual age-specific rates; if the summary measures have a basis in the fundamental nature of the underlying processes, time changes are likely to be more systematic and apparent. There are also considerable practical advantages in the simplicity and consistency of the procedures.

The main criticisms of the KMM technique have implied that the relationship (or model) assumed was not wholly satisfactory. Kermack, McKendrick, and McKinlay themselves, admitted that it was not applicable at ages under five years. For generation projections from mortalities known to five years or above, the limitation is minor. More important is the weakness at the upper ages where death rates have decreased less, proportionately, than in the earlier years of life.[8] Over the past 10–15 years there has been much development of model life tables which describe 'average' patterns of mortality at different levels, as shown by the experience of many populations. An inspection of the best known of these systems, published by the United Nations,[9] shows that the ratio of the death rate in a high mortality population to that in a low at ages 5–14 years may be twenty times as great as the corresponding value at ages 70–9 years. An obvious possibility is to examine other relationships based on model life tables. Most of these systems have been developed in the form of standard tabulations of measures rather than mathematical relations. They would be difficult to apply to the present problem without heavy calculations. Some years ago I proposed a model system which is, in fact, a simple extension of the KMM relationship. It will be used here.

For convenience of exposition it is easier to express the KMM method in terms of the force of mortality μx, that is, the instantaneous death rate at the point of age x, rather than the rates for age groups. The relation can then be written as $\mu x^* = c\mu x$, where the asterisk distinguishes a different mortality pattern and c is a constant. Alternatively, solving the differential equation gives $\ln(lx^*) = c\ln(lx)$, where lx is the life table probability of surviving from birth to age x and ln stands for the natural logarithm.

There is no reason, *a priori*, why time changes in the probability of dying at any age should be in a constant ratio to the proportion still alive, as assumed in the K M M relation. They might as reasonably be in a constant ratio to the proportion who have died, giving the relationship $\ln(1 - lx^*) = c\ln(1 - lx)$. More generally, they may be affected by both. A simple model for incorporating this is $Yx^* = \alpha + \beta Yx$ where Yx stands for $\frac{1}{2}\ln\{(1 - lx)/lx\}$ and is called the logit of $(1 - lx)$ [note that logit $lx = -$logit $(1 - lx)$]. Logit functions are widely used in bio-assay studies of responses of animals to drugs. It is possible to interpret the above relation analogously, on the concept that death is a response to a 'dosage' of time on a particular scale. An equal improvement in resistance at all parts of the scale does not lead to the same proportionate fall in death rates at all ages, however, because of the varying percentages of the population in the dosage response intervals.

If β is fixed at the central value, one, the resulting relationship has a single, disposable constant (parameter) α. For a given Yx, as α varies, Yx^* describes a set of patterns of differing levels of mortality. For all of these, however, the differences from Yx in the specific death rates are greatest at the earliest ages and decrease steadily at later years, in contrast to the K M M relation and in accord with expe-rience. By varying the second parameter, β, the 'slope' of change in death rates with age can be altered and an additional flexibility in-troduced into the pattern. Various accounts of this model have been published elsewhere. [10, 11] It has been applied extensively in studies of the demography of under-developed areas, particularly in Africa.

Model relations can provide summary parameters, for either generation or time period observations, which can then be used for estimating trends. The second idea from which the K M M method stems is that the mortality of a generation, at later ages, is more closely related in some sense to that experienced in earlier years than it is to the general level of death rates at a particular time. This has been expressed as 'a generation carries its own mortality with it.' Evidence from the study of mortality from particular diseases [12] suggests convincingly that the death rate of an age group can sometimes be better interpreted from a knowledge of the earlier incidence for the generation. It is equally clear that some epidemics affect the rates, at a given time, of all or most of the age range. In none of these instances, however, is the effect simple. For example, a particularly high death rate from a disease at a given age may be followed by a relatively lowered incidence in the same generation at later years, because the number of high risk persons has been reduced. The attempt to examine the question directly by the analysis of observed rates is made difficult by these complications, and also by the interactions of generations and time. In most populations over the period for which adequate data can be obtained mortality has been falling. If the generation hypothesis is true a downward trend at early ages implies a reduction at later years and, therefore, times also; equally a general fall with period would occur at all ages. As a result the relative strengths of generation and period influences must be looked for in second order effects which are dominated by chance fluctuations.

In a sense, the best answer is that 'a generation carries its own mortality with it' to the extent that generation projection gives better results than time period methods. Some slight evidence will be given below that the model relationship used here may be a better representation for generation than for time period data, but little weight can be put on it. As a development of the K M M method the procedures are applied to generation data in the present paper. It seems likely that better results could be obtained by allowing for, or smoothing, both generation and time period effects, but a satisfactory method for doing this has not been developed.

The application of the logit relationship for the projection of generation mortality will be examined and illustrated on two series of life tables. These are for England and Wales (females) by five-year birth intervals of generations from 1841, and for Sweden (males) by ten-year intervals from 1775. The results for the sexes not shown are similar to those given, although there are some complications for England and Wales (males) due to war deaths, which will not be considered. The tables for England and Wales have been taken from Case, Coghill, Harley and Pearson,[13] but they were extended a further five years forward in time by the use of mortality data in the Registrar General's Annual and Quarterly Reports 1961-5. The Swedish generation mortality was calculated specially for this study from death rates in ten year age groups (five years at 0-4 and 75-9) over ten year periods. Only the simplest methods of calculation were applied and the results are, therefore, approximate. They are sufficiently accurate, however, for their purpose. Because generation mortality tables are constructed from rates for age groups in time periods there is always a slight indefiniteness about the dates of the births whose experience they represent. Thus, in the England and Wales tables the death rate of children aged 0-4 years in the period 1931-5 is the initial measurement for one generation. A few of those

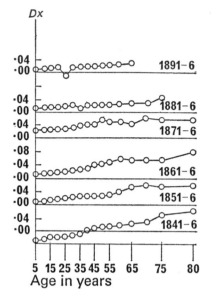

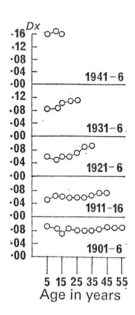

a) England and Wales, Females

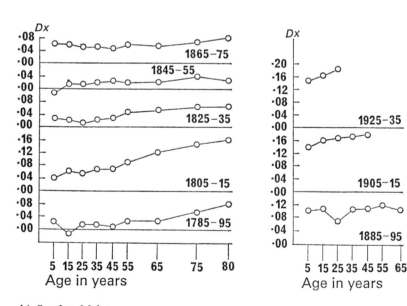

b) Sweden, Males

Figure 1. Logit Differences in Generation Mortality

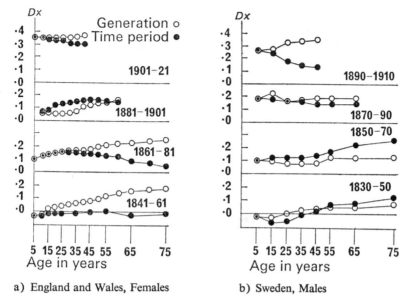

a) England and Wales, Females   b) Sweden, Males

Figure 2.   Logit Differences in Generation and Time Period Mortality

included have been born as early as the start of 1926 and others as late as the end of 1936. It is usual to specify such a generation table by the mid-year around which the bulk of the births were clustered, in this case 1931. The convention is adopted here.

The assumed model relation between successive generation mortality patterns can be written as $Dx = Yx^* - Yx = \alpha + (\beta - 1) Yx$, that is, Dx is the logit difference. For the single parameter model with β equal to one the relation reduces to $Dx = \alpha$. In application and presentation it is often convenient to work with the Dx rather than the Yx. For the two sets of life tables the Dx are plotted in figure 1. Only every second generation interval is shown for compactness of illustration. Since the model is linear in the logits the relations hold (although with different values of α and β) if the Dx are plotted against Yx values for any of the series of generations. To save changing the scale for every set of points, therefore, the Yx measures for the 1876 and 1875 generations have been used throughout for England and Wales, and Sweden respectively.

Since the Dxs are differences between larger quantities they are particularly sensitive to chance fluctuations and there are erratic points on the graphs. In the England and Wales data the effects of the 1914–18 war at ages within the range 15–40 years are particularly notable. As a broad description of the variation in the Dx with age,

G

a linear relation in the logits seems not unreasonable. In some of the graphs there is a tendency for an upward slope over the middle adult years to flatten out at the older ages, 65 and upwards, particularly for England and Wales between the 1851 and 1871 generations. Of course, a better representation could be obtained by the introduction of a third parameter into the model, but in most cases it would be very close to zero and satisfactory estimation would not be possible. It is clear that the single parameter model with β equal to one is not, in general, adequate, although some of the sets of points for more recent generations could be satisfactorily graduated by a constant.

Figure 2 gives comparisons of Dx values for generation and corresponding time period mortality patterns, that is, those based on the same death rate in the youngest age group. In order to exhibit effects more clearly the generation intervals have been made wider. As a result those divergences from linearity due to effects which are consistent over time are emphasized and the transient ones reduced. The departures from linearity are, on the whole, rather greater for the time period mortality patterns than for the generation values. It appears that mortality projection may be more accurate when based on generation observations but, as pointed out previously, the question is complex and the evidence slight.

The KMM method based on the proportional death rate relation has already been described. The procedure with the logit model is similar. The technique is particularly simple with only the one parameter. As Dx is then assumed to be constant its value at the oldest observed age common to the two successive incomplete generations is taken to hold at later ages. Since the lx measures and derived logits cumulate probabilities of dying to age x there is no need to use Dx values other than at the latest age for estimation. The full set of estimated differences and, therefore, logits can next be built up working from the most recent complete table (in the present paper 80 years is the highest age included). From the derived logits the lx of the generation life tables are obtained. Probabilities of dying and death rates in age groups can be calculated from the lx and rearranged as time period measures if required.

If z is the last age for which there are corresponding lz measures in two successive incomplete generation tables the logit relationship can be written $Yx^* - Yz^* = \beta(Yx - Yz)$. The substitution of an estimated β allows Yx^* measures for a younger generation to be derived from those already found for an older. The procedure, then, continues as in the one parameter case. Various ways might be adopted for the estimation of β. If the model relation was exact the most obvious would be from the equation $\beta = (Y_b^* - Y_a^*)/(Y_b - Y_a)$ with a and b chosen as the lowest and highest ages for which measures were known. In practice a would be 5 years and b the upper age reached by the younger incomplete generation. If less reliance is placed on the adequacy of the model over the whole range, a would be taken as not much lower than b on the argument that the trend near the upper limit will be a better forecast of what happens beyond it. In other words the pattern of change at 5 to 15 years might have little rele-vance to tendencies at 70 to 80. On the other hand, the shorter the interval between b and a the greater the effect of chance fluctuations. In the calculations here a was taken as fifteen years below b for England and Wales, and twenty years below for Sweden (for which the measures were only obtained at ten year intervals). For the younger generations where b was 15 years or below β was not esti-mated directly from the corresponding observations. Instead it was taken as the average of the last three βs which had been estimated as above. The indications from the data were that, with very short age intervals, the effect of chance fluctuation on the estimated β could be so great that it was safer to assume a continuance of the trends in previous generations. These rules are, of course, arbitrary but inspec-tion of the observations suggests that something of the kind is re-quired to give the most satisfactory results.

The problems of estimating β discussed in the preceding paragraph occur in a more general form when the whole procedure for deter-mining a trend for projection (or extrapolation) is considered. The one parameter model with $\beta = 1$ is, for many of the generations, not a good description of the mortality pattern relationship. On the other hand the estimation of the single parameter is 'robust', that is more stable, when subjected to erratic fluctuations in measures. The two parameter model is a better representation but the estimated β may be very inaccurate. The effects of an error in β are large when the projection is for many years ahead for a generation which is still young. There is evidence (from mortality patterns in countries with a wide range of death rates) that *on average* β will not vary greatly from unity over a long enough period. In such a situation the intro-duction of the extra parameter may not give more accurate extra-polation. Analogous problems occur in industrial and commercial forecasting from time series. Recent work[14,15] has shown that a successful approach is to compromise between the needs of stability and sensitivity by using appropriate weighted-averages of the con-trasting estimates. In the present context this means taking a level of β somewhere between the estimated value and one.

Projections have been made in four ways:
1. Method A: with the logit one parameter model.
2. Method B: with the logit two parameter model and β estimated from the observations as described.

3. Method C: with the logit two parameter model and β taken mid-way between unity and the value used in Method B.

4. KMM Method: with the proportional relationship; the constant ratios were calculated from mortalities at 5 years to the oldest age for the two generations compared.

No claim is made that these procedures are optimum among the systems considered. In C the equal weighting of unity and the estimated βs is the simplest approach. Preferable estimates of the proportionality constant for the KMM method might be devised. To determine the 'best' rules would require extensive calculations on long series of life tables for many populations.

The projected mortalities for England and Wales (females) based on the data up to 1926 and 1936 are shown in Tables 1 and 2 respectively. The former projections are for 20, 30 and 40 years ahead (that is, for the five-year periods preceding the beginning of 1946, 56, and 66) and the latter for 20 and 30 years. Similar results for Swedish males based on 1930 and for 20 and 30 years ahead (the periods 1940–9 and 1950–9 inclusive) are given in Table 3. The apparent anomaly that the Swedish estimates start at an age five years lower than the projection period occurs because the first age period of 0–4 is a five- and not a ten-year interval. In practice it would have been rather later than 1930 before the projection for the youngest generation was made. The projected mortalities have been expressed in the form of probabilities of dying in age groups in time periods, and the corresponding tables estimate survivors at the given ages from an initial 10,000 people. They are compared with the values observed, and the current rates in the period immediately preceding the base year are also shown for comparison.

A quantitative measure of the relative accuracy of the projections could only be made from some form of weighting of errors at different ages. Since the most appropriate weights would depend on the particular purpose it is doubtful if the outcome would have much meaning. Overall, however, the comparisons show that the modified two parameter method C has substantial merits. This is seen particularly clearly from the survivorship ratios. Since these are cumulated measures they reflect 'average' agreement over an age range rather than in the specific features of a restricted interval. For the uses of forecasts the former type of agreement is generally the more important. The characteristics of the KMM projections are as would be expected in the light of the criticisms made earlier. Results at younger ages are mainly good but the estimated probabilities of dying in the later years of life are too low, and survivorship too high. For Sweden the A single parameter estimates are satisfactory but for England and Wales they overstate mortality because of the systematic deviations of Dx from constancy. The performance of the b two parameter projection is more variable although there is a tendency for the rates at older ages to be underestimated. The erratic agreement of the estimates with the observations in particular age groups is inevitable because of the fluctuations and inconsistencies in the mortality changes. The strength of the modified two parameter method c is that it takes advantage of the signs of trends in the level and pattern of mortality but is not overwhelmed by them. The resulting projec-tions are in excellent agreement with the observations in some examples, and in no case are they highly divergent. There is little indication of systematic pattern in the differences. Further study is required to refine the techniques and establish the range of their applicability.

References

1 H.F.Dorn, 'Pitfalls in population forecasts and projections',
    Journal of the American Statistical Association, **45** (1950) 311.
2 I.B.Taeuber, 'Future population trends', Background paper for the
    United Nations World Population Conference (Belgrade 1965).
3 D.V.Glass and E.Grebenik, 'The Trend and Pattern of Fertility in
    Great Britain: A report on the Family Census of 1946', *Papers of
    the Royal Commission on Population*, Vol. **6**, (HMSO, London,
    1954).
4 N.B.Ryder, 'The process of demographic translation', *Demography*,
    1 (1964) 74.
5 R.C.Freedman, L.C.Coombs, and L.Bumpass, 'Stability and
    change in expectations about family size: a longitudinal study',
    Demography, **2** (1965) 250.
6 G.M.K.Kpedekpo, *Ph.D. thesis* (Aberdeen University 1966).
7 W.O.Kermack, A.G.McKendrick, and P.L.McKinlay, 'Death
    rates in Great Britain and Sweden', *Lancet* (1934) 698.
8 See, for example, the comments in United Kingdom, Royal
    Commission on Population, Papers **11**. *Reports and Selected
    Papers of the Statistics Committee* (HMSO, London, 1950) p. 71.
9 United Nations. *Age and Sex Patterns of Mortality: Model Life
    Tables for Underdeveloped Countries* (New York 1955).
10 W.Brass, 'Uses of census or survey data for the estimation of vital
    rates', United Nations Economic Commission for Africa Seminar
    in Vital Statistics (Addis Ababa 1964).
11 A.J.Coale (ed.), *The Demography of Tropical Africa*, (Princeton
    University Press, Princeton, in press.
12 For example. R.A.M.Case, 'Cohort analysis of cancer mortality in
    England and Wales, 1911–54, by site and sex', *British Journal of
    Preventive and Social Medicine*, **10** (1956) 172.

13　R. A. M. Case, C. Coghill, J. L. Harley, and J. T. Pearson, *Serial Abridged Life Tables: England and Wales* 1841–1960 (The Chester Beatty Research Institute, London, 1962).

14　R. G. Brown, *Statistical Forecasting for Inventory Control* (McGraw-Hill, New York, 1959).

15　G. A. Coutie, O. L. Davies, C. H. Hossell, D. W. G. P. Millar, and A. J. H. Morrell, 'Short-Term Forecasting', in: *ICI Mathematical and Statistical Techniques for Industry, Monograph No.* 2 (Oliver and Boyd, Edinburgh, 1964).

TABLE 1a　Comparison of projected with observed mortality, England and Wales, females: 1926 base, 20 years ahead

Age group in years	Current	Observed	KMM	Projections A	B	C
			Probabilities of dying in age group			
20–	0·0154	0·0103	0·0063	0·0083	0·0091	0·0087
25–	0·0169	0·0110	0·0087	0·0113	0·0127	0·0120
30–	0·0186	0·0116	0·0142	0·0136	0·0144	0·0140
35–	0·0226	0·0142	0·0177	0·0183	0·0188	0·0185
40–	0·0272	0·0183	0·0210	0·0237	0·0245	0·0231
45–	0·0365	0·0263	0·0291	0·0322	0·0269	0·0303
50–	0·0505	0·0375	0·0356	0·0432	0·0385	0·0409
55–	0·0733	0·0539	0·0495	0·0603	0·0496	0·0547
60–	0·1090	0·0825	0·0713	0·0896	0·0705	0·0798
65–	0·1665	0·1320	0·1133	0·1423	0·1110	0·1267
70–	0·2550	0·2103	0·1796	0·2287	0·1806	0·2041
75–9	0·3823	0·3251	0·2926	0·3607	0·3063	0·3334

Age in years	Survivors to given age from 10,000 at 20 years					
20	10,000	10,000	10,000	10,000	10,000	10,000
25	9,846	9,897	9,937	9,917	9,909	9,913
30	9,680	9,788	9,851	9,805	9,783	9,794
35	9,500	9,674	9,711	9,672	9,642	9,667
40	9,285	9,537	9,539	9,495	9,461	9,478
45	9,032	9,362	9,338	9,270	9,229	9,259
50	8,702	9,116	9,066	8,972	8,982	8,978
55	8,263	8,774	8,743	8,584	8,636	8,612
60	7,657	8,301	8,310	8,066	8,207	8,141
65	6,822	7,616	7,717	7,343	7,629	7,491
70	5,686	6,611	6,843	6,298	6,782	6,542
75	4,236	5,221	5,614	4,858	5,557	5,206
80	2,617	3,524	3,971	3,106	3,855	3,470

TABLE 1b   Comparison of projected with observed mortality, England and Wales, females: 1926 base, 30 years ahead

Age group in years	Current	Observed	KMM	Projections		
				A	B	C
			Probabilities of dying in age group			
30–	0·0186	0·0061	0·0068	0·0093	0·0101	0·0098
35–	0·0226	0·0083	0·0105	0·0148	0·0159	0·0154
40–	0·0272	0·0124	0·0182	0·0192	0·0216	0·0197
45–	0·0365	0·0193	0·0251	0·0267	0·0249	0·0266
50–	0·0505	0·0295	0·0310	0·0398	0·0345	0·0372
55–	0·0733	0·0449	0·0441	0·0587	0·0448	0·0512
60–	0·1090	0·0719	0·0645	0·0866	0·0668	0·0762
65–	0·1665	0·1183	0·0947	0·1338	0·0971	0·1144
70–	0·2550	0·1948	0·1467	0·2140	0·1493	0·1798
75–9	0·3823	0·3154	0·2430	0·3460	0·2507	0·2964

Age in years	Survivors to given age from 10,000 at 30 years					
30	10,000	10,000	10,000	10,000	10,000	10,000
35	9,814	9,939	9,932	9,907	9,899	9,902
40	9,592	9,857	9,828	9,760	9,742	9,750
45	9,331	9,735	9,649	9,572	9,532	9,558
50	8,990	9,547	9,407	9,317	9,294	9,304
55	8,536	9,265	9,115	8,946	8,974	8,959
60	7,910	8,849	8,713	8,421	8,572	8,500
65	7,048	8,213	8,151	7,692	8,000	7,852
70	5,874	7,241	7,379	6,663	7,223	6,954
75	4,376	5,830	6,297	5,237	6,145	5,704
80	2,704	3,991	4,766	3,425	4,604	4,014

TABLE 1c   Comparisons of projected and observed mortality, England and Wales, females: 1926 base, 40 years ahead

Age group in years	Current	Observed	KMM	Projections A	B	C
			Probabilities of dying in age group			
40–	0·0272	0·0108	0·0084	0·0133	0·0156	0·0139
45–	0·0365	0·0172	0·0148	0·0222	0·0214	0.0225
50–	0·0505	0·0261	0·0270	0·0327	0·0311	0·0321
55–	0·0733	0·0398	0·0383	0·0495	0·0424	0·0460
60–	0·1090	0·0647	0·0562	0·0805	0·0602	0·0699
65–	0·1665	0·1054	0·0851	0·1309	0·0875	0·1075
70–	0·2550	0·1768	0·1333	0·2090	0·1423	0·1735
75–9	0·3823	0·2837	0·2058	0·3339	0·2243	0·2761

Age in years	Survivors to given age from 10,000 at 40 years					
40	10,000	10,000	10,000	10,000	10,000	10,000
45	9,727	9,892	9,916	9,867	9,844	9,861
50	9,372	9,721	9,769	9,648	9,633	9,639
55	8,899	9,468	9,505	9,333	9,334	9,330
60	8,247	9,091	9,141	8,871	8,938	8,900
65	7,347	8,503	8,627	8,156	8,400	8,278
70	6,124	7,607	7,893	7,089	7,665	7,388
75	4,562	6,262	6,841	5,607	6,574	6,106
80	2,819	4,485	5,433	3,735	5,100	4,420

TABLE 2a   Comparison of projected with observed mortality, England and Wales, females: 1936 base, 20 years ahead

Age group in years	Current	Observed	KMM	Projections A	B	C
			Probabilities of dying in age group			
20 –	0·0137	0·0035	0·0075	0·0072	0·0045	0·0057
25 –	0·0148	0·0047	0·0093	0·0084	0·0054	0·0068
30 –	0·0159	0·0061	0·0101	0·0091	0·0063	0·0075
35 –	0·0193	0·0083	0·0124	0·0132	0·0089	0·0109
40 –	0·0237	0·0124	0·0179	0·0175	0·0114	0·0142
45 –	0·0328	0·0193	0·0252	0·0262	0·0149	0·0200
50 –	0·0458	0·0295	0·0355	0·0401	0·0212	0·0296
55 –	0·0659	0·0449	0·0493	0·0580	0·0326	0·0440
60 –	0·1004	0·0719	0·0751	0·0873	0·0590	0·0721
65 –	0·1552	0·1183	0·1125	0·1332	0·1067	0·1197
70 –	0·2456	0·1948	0·1779	0·2163	0·1915	0·2038
75 – 9	0·3709	0·3154	0·2900	0·3454	0·3180	0·3320

Age in years	Survivors to given age from 10,000 at 20 years					
20	10,000	10,000	10,000	10,000	10,000	10,000
25	9,863	9,965	9,925	9,928	9,955	9,943
30	9,717	9,918	9,833	9,845	9,901	9,875
35	9,562	9,858	9,733	9,755	9,839	9,801
40	9,377	9,776	9,613	9,626	9,751	9,694
45	9,155	9,655	9,441	9,458	9,640	9,557
50	8,855	9,469	9,203	9,210	9,496	9,366
55	8,449	9,189	8,876	8,841	9,295	9,088
60	7,892	8,776	8,438	8,328	8,992	8,689
65	7,100	8,146	7,805	7,601	8,462	8,062
70	5,998	7,182	6,927	6,588	7,559	7,097
75	4,525	5,782	5,694	5,163	6,111	5,651
80	2,891	3,958	4,043	3,380	4,168	3,775

TABLE 2b   Comparison of projected with observed mortality, England and Wales, females: 1936 base, 30 years ahead

Age group in years	Current	Observed	KMM	Projections A	B	C
			Probabilities of dying in age group			
30–	0·0159	0·0042	0·0078	0·0070	0·0037	0·0051
35–	0·0193	0·0067	0·0106	0·0093	0·0050	0·0068
40–	0·0237	0·0108	0·0129	0·0125	0·0060	0·0088
45–	0·0328	0·0172	0·0184	0·0219	0·0095	0·0144
50–	0·0458	0·0261	0·0311	0·0333	0·0152	0·0228
55–	0·0659	0·0398	0·0430	0·0492	0·0228	0·0340
60–	0·1004	0·0647	0·0658	0·0810	0·0374	0·0554
65–	0·1552	0·1054	0·0988	0·1293	0·0636	0·0919
70–	0·2456	0·1768	0·1594	0·2105	0·1316	0·1677
75–9	0·3709	0·2837	0·2523	0·3330	0·2613	0·2967

Age in years	Survivors to given age from 10,000 at 30 years					
30	10,000	10,000	10,000	10,000	10,000	10,000
35	9,840	9,958	9,922	9,930	9,963	9,949
40	9,650	9,891	9,817	9,838	9,913	9,881
45	9,422	9,783	9,690	9,715	9,854	9,794
50	9,113	9,615	9,512	9,502	9,760	9,653
55	8,695	9,364	9,216	9,185	9,612	9,433
60	8,122	8,992	8,820	8,734	9,393	9,112
65	7,307	8,410	8,239	8,026	9,041	8,608
70	6,173	7,524	7,425	6,988	8,466	7,817
75	4,657	6,193	6,241	5,517	7,352	6,506
80	2,975	4,436	4,666	3,680	5,431	4,576

TABLE 3a Comparison of projected with observed mortality, Sweden, males: 1930 base, 20 years ahead

Age group in years	Current	Observed	KMM	Projections A	B	C
			Probabilities of dying in age group			
15—	0·0394	0·0206	0·0181	0·0234	0·0212	0·0223
25—	0·0439	0·0225	0·0191	0·0268	0·0227	0·0249
35—	0·0522	0·0308	0·0309	0·0360	0·0323	0·0339
45—	0·0844	0·0650	0·0647	0·0673	0·0722	0·0698
55—	0·1677	0·1479	0·1449	0·1467	0·1495	0·1484
65—	0·3556	0·3354	0·3096	0·3312	0·2973	0·3143
75—9	0·3649	0·3560	0·3123	0·3525	0·3217	0·3318

Age in years		Survivors to given age from 10,000 at 15 years				
15	10,000	10,000	10,000	10,000	10,000	10,000
25	9,606	9,794	9,819	9,766	9,788	9,777
35	9,184	9,574	9,631	9,504	9,566	9,534
45	8,705	9,279	9,334	9,162	9,257	9,210
55	7,970	8,676	8,730	8,545	8,589	8,567
65	6,633	7,393	7,465	7,291	7,305	7,296
75	4,274	4,913	5,154	4,876	5,133	5,003
80	2,714	3,164	3,544	3,157	3,482	3,318

TABLE 3b Comparison of projected with observed mortality, Sweden, males: 1930 base, 30 years ahead

Age group in years	Current	Observed	KMM	Projections A	B	C
			Probabilities of dying in age group			
25—	0·0439	0·0135	0·0145	0·0209	0·0167	0·0187
35—	0·0522	0·0222	0·0189	0·0281	0·0236	0·0257
45—	0·0844	0·0532	0·0464	0·0543	0·0514	0·0530
55—	0·1677	0·1374	0·1214	0·1307	0·1348	0·1328
65—	0·3556	0·3258	0·2878	0·3142	0·3015	0·3081
75—9	0·3649	0·3401	0·2925	0·3442	0·2977	0·3205

Age in years		Survivors to given age from 10,000 at 25 years				
25	10,000	10,000	10,000	10,000	10,000	10,000
35	9,561	9,865	9,855	9,791	9,833	9,813
45	9,062	9,646	9,669	9,516	9,601	9,561
55	8,297	9,133	9,220	8,999	9,108	9,054
65	6,905	7,878	8,101	7,823	7,880	7,852
75	4,449	5,311	5,770	5,365	5,504	5,433
80	2,825	3,505	4,082	3,518	3,865	3,692

Calculation of Family Structure as a Demographic Example of the Organizational Power of Matrix Notation in Mass Arithmetical Operations

In recent years, there have been many examples of the applications of matrix algebra to demographic research (for instance many books and articles by Nathan Keyfitz), but in general it has been the elegance and power of matrix theory that has been the central point of the application. With such advanced applications available, the power of far simpler aspects of matrix notation may escape notice, although they are of great value, and should properly come into prominence with the availability of electronic computers to permit the making of substantial arithmetical calculations, providing that the operations can be organized adequately.

This note describes a specific example of a large calculation where the organizational power of matrix notation was required. Although the example is very specific, the kind of situation with which it is concerned is by no means limited to demography but could occur where any Markovian-type process was involved.

THE PROBLEM

The example considered relates to a specific generation of women in England and Wales, approximating to women born between mid 1922 and 1923 (but other generations could be treated similarly) and relates to the age structure of their children at the latest convenient date, actually when they were aged exactly 41, around 1964. The data on their fertility were derived from the actual data published by the Registrar General of England and Wales that related to this generation but some simplifying assumptions were made.[1]

No special interest attaches to the initial manipulation of these data and it will suffice to outline the results produced. These were true birth order rates, comparable to those introduced by Glass and Grebenik,[2] but relating to the generation whilst Glass and Grebenik made their calculations for marriage cohorts. This means that the rates produced here relate to the fertility behaviour of the generation in the 12 months period when the generation moved from their sixteenth to their seventeenth birthdays, from their seventeenth to their eighteenth birthdays, etc. Like Glass and Grebenik, the rates show, for each of these years, the probability that a woman who started the year with no children should end it having had just one child, and similar probabilities for women starting a year with 1, 2, 3 ... 11 children. The calculations were carried up to such large family sizes out of curiosity although much saving in the arithmetic involved, with but trivial loss of information, would result from truncation at a small family size, since so few women extend their family building to such large sizes. An innovation of marginal value was to extend the concept of true birth order rates of Glass and Grebenik by a second set of such rates relating to probabilities that the women of each family size each year increased their families by two, that is had twins.

The 'single' and 'twin' true birth order rates for this generation derived from these preliminary calculations are shown in Tables 1 and 2.

APPLICATION OF TRUE BIRTH ORDER RATES TO FAMILY AGE STRUCTURE

The application of these true birth order rates to the problem of studying a family's age structure may be seen by a simple example. Suppose that we are concerned with the age structure of the children of this generation of women when the women were aged exactly 41. Then a child born in the year between the woman's twenty-fourth birthday and twenty-fifth birthday, for instance, will be of age $41 - 25 = 16$ l.b.d. The age (when the woman is 41) of her other children will be determined if it is known in what year of her life they were born.

The assumptions made require that a woman either has one live born child in a year, has twins, or has no children at all. Thus the sum of these three probabilities must be unity and, as two are known (the probabilities that she has one or two children) this constraint fixed the third. Starting with no children on her sixteenth birthday (illegitimate fertility was ignored), a woman may follow one of three alternative paths to her seventeenth birthday, namely by having one child, two, or none. Thus the generation arrive at their sixteenth birthdays in a single stream, but split into 3 in their passage to their seventeenth birthdays. Again each of these 3 streams splits into 3 in their passage to their eighteenth birthdays, so that they arrive there in 9 streams and so on. There are therefore 3^{25} different paths by which they may proceed to their forty-first birthday, except that a maximum family size of 12 had been imposed. Even with this constraint, there are many millions of alternative paths.

It is not conceivable that, of the many problems that arise concerning family age structure, any would involve the printing out of all these possible paths, for the list would be unwieldy. It will be

presumed that either an abbreviated list or some summary information requiring only that these paths enter the calculation at an internal
stage is necessary. In the treatment following, both simplifications
will be introduced so that their mode of application is apparent.

EXPRESSION OF FAMILY BUILDING IN MATRIX FORM

The 'state' of the generation at exact age x may be represented by a
vector $V(x)$, in which the ith element $v(x,i)$ is the *proportion* of the
generation at exact age x who have by then borne $i-1$ children. If
$s(x,i)$ is the single true birth order rate of women aged x with $i-1$
children and $t(x,i)$ the corresponding twin true birth order rate, then
a proportion $s(x,i)$ of $v(x,i)$ will move to state $v(x+1,i+1)$; a
proportion $t(x,i)$ will move to state $v(x+1,i+2)$ and the remaining
proportion $[1-s(x,i)-t(x,i)]$ will move to $v(x+1,i)$. If the matrix
$T(x)$ is therefore defined to have elements $s(x,i)$ in the diagonal immediately below the principal diagonal, elements $t(x,i)$ in the diagonal
below this, $[1-s(x,i)-t(x,i)]$ on the principal diagonal, and zero
elements elsewhere, then:
$$T(x).V(x)=V(x+1)$$
From this it follows that:
$$T(x+1).V(x+1)=V(x+2)$$
and thus that:
$$2T(x).V(x)=V(x+2)$$
where,
$$2T(x).=T(x+1).T(x)$$
and if $nT(x)$ is similarly defined, that:
$$nT(x).V(x)=V(x+n)$$
If we were not concerned to know the ages of the families of this
generation in single years, but were content to know them in age
groups, simplification of the generation's transition into 'stages' by
compressing the transition matrices in this way would thus be simple.
For instance, if we were only concerned with whether their children
were aged 0–4, 5–9, 10–14, 15–19, or 20–4 (when the generation of
women was 41), the 25 single year transition matrices could be
compressed into 5 composite transition matrices $5T(16)$, $5T(21)$,
$5T(26)$, $5T(31)$ and $5T(36)$. Such composite matrices are shown in
Tables 3a to 3e.

It should be noted: firstly, that no assumption of *constant* fertility
is involved in this process–the estimates of actual (and thus different)
fertility from year to year have been used in the calculation; secondly,
whereas the data concerning the true birth order rates would need to
be calculated and left in a readily accessible form, for example by
punching out onto cards that could be reread easily, the amalgama-
tion of the single matrices into the composite (in this 5 year case)

form would in general be peculiar to the problem under examination. And in any event, the years of the generation's life that corresponded to particular ages of child would change from year to year, that is, twelve months after the compression mentioned above had been appropriate, a different compression would be required to identify children in these same age groups.

It may sometimes be helpful in grasping the import of a path through two or more of these composite matrices (or of a path through single year matrices), and in particular of identifying the elements that are the appropriate probabilities associated with the path, if the matrices and vectors are thought of as physically translated as shown in the figure.

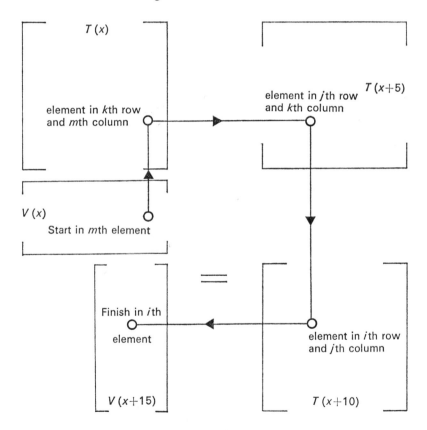

The 'typical' path shown is that of a woman having $m - 1$ children by her xth birthday, $k - 1$ by her $(x + 5)$th [that is having $k - m$ children between her xth and $(x + 5)$th birthdays], $j - 1$ by her

$(x + 10)$th and $i - 1$ by her $(x + 15)$th birthday, [that is having $i - j$ children between her $(x + 10)$th and $(x + 15)$th birthdays].

The product of the probabilities that are the matrix elements at the turns in the path is the probability of a woman who starts from the mth element of the starting vector following the path shown, and the product of this product and the proportion of women who start from the point shown, that is the mth element of the start vector, is the proportion of all women of the generation who follow this path. This is not the value of the ith element of the final vector, since this state may be reached in many other ways.

APPLICATIONS

In mathematical form, the probabilities and their product could readily be written down in symbolic form and, for any required summary, it would be necessary to write down symbolically what constraints had to be imposed for the passage of the women along the path shown to contribute to a particular part of the summary. In high level symbolic languages similar (or if anything simpler) expressions can be formed to produce the required summary.

An example of a summary prepared from the previous data is shown in Table 4. The specification of the summary is that it is required to know the distribution of this generation on their forty-first birthday by the joint ages of their youngest and eldest children in 5 year age groups. (Proportions in the cells will fail to sum to unity by the proportion who were childless.) The symbolic statement of the requirements to build up this table would be as follows: if $p(i,j)$ denotes the element in the ith row and jth column of the composite matrix for ages 36–41 and q,r,s,t, suitably suffixed the elements of the matrices for ages 31–6, 26–31, 21–6, and 16–21, it will be noted that we are only concerned with the elements in the first column of the matrix for ages 16–21, since we have required that women at age 16 have no children. Further the row of exit from the 16–21 matrix is the column of entry to the 21–6 matrix and similarly for later matrices. Thus a typical probability product is: $p(i,j).q(j,k).r(k,m).s(m,n).t(n,1)$.

No contribution to Table 4 (proportion of women with youngest and eldest children of various ages) can be made by women with no children. Thus we need only consider the possibility of i lying between 2 and 13. Nor can a woman have had more children by age 36 than by age 41. Thus j is restricted to the range 1 to i and similarly k to the range 1 to j, m to the range 1 to k and n to the range 1 to m.

Allowing i, j, k, m and n to take all values within these restraints in turn, the product of the probabilities shown is calculated for each combination. It is then necessary to determine to which cell of the

table the product should be added. If $i \neq j$, the youngest child is 0–4.
If this is not so, but $j \neq k$, the youngest child is 5–9.
If this is not so, but $k \neq m$, the youngest child is 10–14.
If this is not so, but $m \neq n$, the youngest child is 15–19.
Otherwise, the youngest child is 20–4.
A similar set of logical tests, starting at the other end, that is testing first whether n is not 1, and, if it is, whether m is not 1 etc., determines the age of the eldest child.

Applications of this type would arise, for instance, in the evaluation of family allowance schemes if payment depended in any way on both parity and age.

The essence of the concept is this: whereas there is no great difficulty in considering one path, and, in mathematics, making it typical by symbolic representation of its turning points, in high level computer languages a comparable set of statements implies not algebraic, but arithmetic relationships, and controls the arithmetic evaluation of the solution.

Notes and References

1   One simplification was to ignore illegitimate fertility (and it would by no means be easy to include it in a realistic manner). A second simplification was to leave out consideration of marriage. It would complicate the calculations, but by no means make them prohibitive, to introduce subdivision of the generation into those who married at different ages.

2   D. V. Glass and E. Grebenik, 'Trend and Pattern of Fertility in Great Britain', *Papers of The Royal Commission on Population* **6** Part I (1954) p. 170, section 13 et seq.

TABLE 1   True birth order rates – singletons

					Previous children							
AGE	0	1	2	3	4	5	6	7	8	9	10	11
16	0·00121	0·00000	0·00000	0·00000	0·00000	0·00000	0·00000	0·00000	0·00000	0·00000	0·00000	0·00000
17	0·00594	0·20692	0·00000	0·00000	0·00000	0·00000	0·00000	0·00000	0·00000	0·00000	0·00000	0·00000
18	0·01484	0·17475	0·18949	0·00000	0·00000	0·00000	0·00000	0·00000	0·00000	0·00000	0·00000	0·00000
19	0·02978	0·17547	0·12897	0·31206	0·00000	0·00000	0·00000	0·00000	0·00000	0·00000	0·00000	0·00000
20	0·04855	0·17382	0·17164	0·30491	0·39499	0·00000	0·00000	0·00000	0·00000	0·00000	0·00000	0·00000
21	0·07004	0·18720	0·19670	0·24255	0·25885	0·30725	0·00000	0·00000	0·00000	0·00000	0·00000	0·00000
22	0·07944	0·15817	0·15863	0·17567	0·23758	0·33096	0·00000	0·00000	0·00000	0·00000	0·00000	0·00000
23	0·11063	0·19004	0·17941	0·20212	0·35409	0·32524	0·37167	0·00000	0·00000	0·00000	0·00000	0·00000
24	0·14970	0·21520	0·18961	0·22197	0·28555	0·19520	0·63061	0·46093	0·00000	0·00000	0·00000	0·00000
25	0·12552	0·18536	0·16003	0·18358	0·23624	0·26971	0·41023	0·16034	0·00000	0·00000	0·00000	0·00000
26	0·11287	0·17759	0·14107	0·16464	0·22111	0·23375	0·35399	0·60388	0·60408	0·00000	0·00000	0·00000
27	0·09976	0·15956	0·12473	0·15223	0·18763	0·26227	0·29237	0·48806	0·22436	0·00000	0·00000	0·00000
28	0·09164	0·15207	0·11286	0·13870	0·19541	0·25801	0·31328	0·33304	0·41706	0·75765	0·00000	0·00000
29	0·08635	0·13812	0·09974	0·12413	0·18369	0·24499	0·36241	0·40805	0·58048	0·68545	0·75215	0·00000
30	0·07878	0·13187	0·09304	0·10965	0·15361	0·20503	0·27038	0·26381	0·39933	0·43396	0·42652	0·50065
31	0·06596	0·10903	0·07423	0·09301	0·13137	0·17016	0·24205	0·25242	0·27040	0·30644	0·35057	0·24485
32	0·05591	0·09837	0·06706	0·08481	0·12294	0·17558	0·21747	0·28254	0·30141	0·41008	0·49650	0·06526
33	0·04920	0·08616	0·05983	0·07472	0·10492	0·14883	0·21214	0·23978	0·23013	0·36880	0·48133	0·23827
34	0·04339	0·07455	0·05397	0·06869	0·10085	0·14669	0·19100	0·21760	0·25123	0·38356	0·45125	0·09124
35	0·03350	0·06234	0·04874	0·06350	0·08688	0·13172	0·17111	0·21431	0·22587	0·30778	0·34633	0·24623
36	0·02870	0·04908	0·03941	0·05254	0·07263	0·10872	0·14666	0·17618	0·20820	0·32340	0·42160	0·16217
37	0·02306	0·03969	0·03327	0·04542	0·06645	0·09417	0·13383	0·16591	0·20174	0·24559	0·25430	0·17101
38	0·01735	0·03063	0·02942	0·04088	0·06414	0·08550	0·11796	0·15610	0·17773	0·21291	0·23757	0·18435
39	0·01323	0·02243	0·02135	0·03204	0·04846	0·07338	0·10173	0·14005	0·14913	0·18857	0·22857	0·20270
40	0·01540	0·02356	0·02332	0·02856	0·05566	0·07684	0·09797	0·12744	0·16443	0·20023	0·18842	

TABLE 2 True birth order rates – twins

AGE	Previous children											
	0	1	2	3	4	5	6	7	8	9	10	11
16	0·00000	0·00000	0·00000	0·00000	0·00000	0·00000	0·00000	0·00000	0·00000	0·00000	0·00000	0·00000
17	0·00004	0·00138	0·00000	0·00000	0·00000	0·00000	0·00000	0·00000	0·00000	0·00000	0·00000	0·00000
18	0·00010	0·00121	0·00132	0·00000	0·00000	0·00000	0·00000	0·00000	0·00000	0·00000	0·00000	0·00000
19	0·00021	0·00125	0·00092	0·00222	0·00000	0·00000	0·00000	0·00000	0·00000	0·00000	0·00000	0·00000
20	0·00036	0·00131	0·00129	0·00229	0·00297	0·00000	0·00000	0·00000	0·00000	0·00000	0·00000	0·00000
21	0·00064	0·00172	0·00180	0·00222	0·00237	0·00282	0·00000	0·00000	0·00000	0·00000	0·00000	0·00000
22	0·00070	0·00138	0·00139	0·00154	0·00208	0·00290	0·00000	0·00000	0·00000	0·00000	0·00000	0·00000
23	0·00112	0·00193	0·00182	0·00205	0·00359	0·00330	0·00377	0·00000	0·00000	0·00000	0·00000	0·00000
24	0·00158	0·00227	0·00200	0·00234	0·00301	0·00206	0·00664	0·00486	0·00000	0·00000	0·00000	0·00000
25	0·00142	0·00209	0·00181	0·00207	0·00267	0·00305	0·00463	0·00181	0·00000	0·00000	0·00000	0·00000
26	0·00148	0·00233	0·00185	0·00216	0·00290	0·00307	0·00465	0·00793	0·00793	0·00000	0·00000	0·00000
27	0·00130	0·00208	0·00163	0·00199	0·00245	0·00343	0·00382	0·00638	0·00293	0·00000	0·00000	0·00000
28	0·00137	0·00227	0·00169	0·00207	0·00292	0·00385	0·00468	0·00497	0·00623	0·00000	0·00000	0·00000
29	0·00123	0·00197	0·00142	0·00177	0·00262	0·00349	0·00516	0·00581	0·00826	0·00976	0·01071	0·00000
30	0·00136	0·00228	0·00161	0·00189	0·00265	0·00354	0·00467	0·00455	0·00689	0·00749	0·00736	0·00000
31	0·00107	0·00177	0·00120	0·00151	0·00213	0·00276	0·00392	0·00409	0·00438	0·00496	0·00568	0·00000
32	0·00098	0·00173	0·00118	0·00149	0·00216	0·00309	0·00382	0·00496	0·00530	0·00721	0·00872	0·00000
33	0·00087	0·00152	0·00105	0·00132	0·00185	0·00262	0·00374	0·00423	0·00406	0·00650	0·00849	0·00000
34	0·00089	0·00153	0·00111	0·00141	0·00208	0·00302	0·00393	0·00448	0·00517	0·00789	0·00928	0·00000
35	0·00063	0·00117	0·00092	0·00119	0·00163	0·00248	0·00322	0·00403	0·00425	0·00579	0·00651	0·00000
36	0·00050	0·00086	0·00069	0·00092	0·00127	0·00190	0·00256	0·00307	0·00363	0·00564	0·00735	0·00000
37	0·00044	0·00075	0·00063	0·00086	0·00126	0·00179	0·00254	0·00315	0·00383	0·00466	0·00482	0·00000
38	0·00034	0·00059	0·00057	0·00079	0·00124	0·00166	0·00229	0·00302	0·00344	0·00413	0·00460	0·00000
39	0·00024	0·00041	0·00039	0·00058	0·00088	0·00133	0·00184	0·00254	0·00270	0·00342	0·00414	0·00000
40	0·00016	0·00028	0·00027	0·00042	0·00065	0·00101	0·00139	0·00177	0·00230	0·00297	0·00362	0·00000

TABLE 3a   Transition matrix for ages 16 – 21

0·90224	0·00000	0·00000	0·00000	0·00000	0·00000	0·00000	0·00000	0·00000	0·00000	0·00000	0·00000	0·00000	0·00000	0·00000	0·00000	0·00000	0·00000
0·08394	0·44304	0·00000	0·00000	0·00000	0·00000	0·00000	0·00000	0·00000	0·00000	0·00000	0·00000	0·00000	0·00000	0·00000	0·00000	0·00000	0·00000
0·01257	0·40810	0·58233	0·00000	0·00000	0·00000	0·00000	0·00000	0·00000	0·00000	0·00000	0·00000	0·00000	0·00000	0·00000	0·00000	0·00000	0·00000
0·00113	0·11364	0·28317	0·47507	0·00000	0·00000	0·00000	0·00000	0·00000	0·00000	0·00000	0·00000	0·00000	0·00000	0·00000	0·00000	0·00000	0·00000
0·00010	0·02959	0·10919	0·39696	0·60205	0·00000	0·00000	0·00000	0·00000	0·00000	0·00000	0·00000	0·00000	0·00000	0·00000	0·00000	0·00000	0·00000
0·00001	0·00559	0·02513	0·12705	0·39499	1·00000	0·00000	0·00000	0·00000	0·00000	0·00000	0·00000	0·00000	0·00000	0·00000	0·00000	0·00000	0·00000
0·00000	0·00004	0·00018	0·00093	0·00297	0·00000	1·00000	0·00000	0·00000	0·00000	0·00000	0·00000	0·00000	0·00000	0·00000	0·00000	0·00000	0·00000
0·00000	0·00000	0·00000	0·00000	0·00000	0·00000	0·00000	1·00000	0·00000	0·00000	0·00000	0·00000	0·00000	0·00000	0·00000	0·00000	0·00000	0·00000
0·00000	0·00000	0·00000	0·00000	0·00000	0·00000	0·00000	0·00000	1·00000	0·00000	0·00000	0·00000	0·00000	0·00000	0·00000	0·00000	0·00000	0·00000
0·00000	0·00000	0·00000	0·00000	0·00000	0·00000	0·00000	0·00000	0·00000	1·00000	0·00000	0·00000	0·00000	0·00000	0·00000	0·00000	0·00000	0·00000
0·00000	0·00000	0·00000	0·00000	0·00000	0·00000	0·00000	0·00000	0·00000	0·00000	1·00000	0·00000	0·00000	0·00000	0·00000	0·00000	0·00000	0·00000
0·00000	0·00000	0·00000	0·00000	0·00000	0·00000	0·00000	0·00000	0·00000	0·00000	0·00000	1·00000	0·00000	0·00000	0·00000	0·00000	0·00000	0·00000
0·00000	0·00000	0·00000	0·00000	0·00000	0·00000	0·00000	0·00000	0·00000	0·00000	0·00000	0·00000	1·00000	0·00000	0·00000	0·00000	0·00000	0·00000
0·00000	0·00000	0·00000	0·00000	0·00000	0·00000	0·00000	0·00000	0·00000	0·00000	0·00000	0·00000	0·00000	1·00000	0·00000	0·00000	0·00000	0·00000
0·00000	0·00000	0·00000	0·00000	0·00000	0·00000	0·00000	0·00000	0·00000	0·00000	0·00000	0·00000	0·00000	0·00000	1·00000	0·00000	0·00000	0·00000
0·00000	0·00000	0·00000	0·00000	0·00000	0·00000	0·00000	0·00000	0·00000	0·00000	0·00000	0·00000	0·00000	0·00000	0·00000	1·00000	0·00000	0·00000
0·00000	0·00000	0·00000	0·00000	0·00000	0·00000	0·00000	0·00000	0·00000	0·00000	0·00000	0·00000	0·00000	0·00000	0·00000	0·00000	1·00000	0·00000
0·00000	0·00000	0·00000	0·00000	0·00000	0·00000	0·00000	0·00000	0·00000	0·00000	0·00000	0·00000	0·00000	0·00000	0·00000	0·00000	0·00000	1·00000

TABLE 3b Transition matrix for ages 21–6

0·56264	0·30156	0·11319	0·02001	0·00238	0·00020	0·00001	0·00000	0·00000	0·00000	0·00000	0·00000	0·00000	0·00000	0·00000	0·00000	0·00000
0·00000	0·35023	0·42543	0·17338	0·04252	0·00761	0·00078	0·00004	0·00000	0·00000	0·00000	0·00000	0·00000	0·00000	0·00000	0·00000	0·00000
0·00000	0·00000	0·37350	0·37800	0·17521	0·05967	0·01194	0·00163	0·00006	0·00000	0·00000	0·00000	0·00000	0·00000	0·00000	0·00000	0·00000
0·00000	0·00000	0·00000	0·31238	0·33226	0·24120	0·08267	0·02854	0·00292	0·00003	0·00000	0·00000	0·00000	0·00000	0·00000	0·00000	0·00000
0·00000	0·00000	0·00000	0·00000	0·19537	0·38808	0·20848	0·16883	0·03884	0·00040	0·00000	0·00000	0·00000	0·00000	0·00000	0·00000	0·00000
0·00000	0·00000	0·00000	0·00000	0·00000	0·18016	0·20479	0·44567	0·16763	0·00175	0·00000	0·00000	0·00000	0·00000	0·00000	0·00000	0·00000
0·00000	0·00000	0·00000	0·00000	0·00000	0·00000	0·13257	0·58928	0·27527	0·00288	0·00000	0·00000	0·00000	0·00000	0·00000	0·00000	0·00000
0·00000	0·00000	0·00000	0·00000	0·00000	0·00000	0·00000	0·44759	0·54659	0·00582	0·00000	0·00000	0·00000	0·00000	0·00000	0·00000	0·00000
0·00000	0·00000	0·00000	0·00000	0·00000	0·00000	0·00000	0·00000	1·00000	0·00000	0·00000	0·00000	0·00000	0·00000	0·00000	0·00000	0·00000
0·00000	0·00000	0·00000	0·00000	0·00000	0·00000	0·00000	0·00000	0·00000	1·00000	0·00000	0·00000	0·00000	0·00000	0·00000	0·00000	0·00000
0·00000	0·00000	0·00000	0·00000	0·00000	0·00000	0·00000	0·00000	0·00000	0·00000	1·00000	0·00000	0·00000	0·00000	0·00000	0·00000	0·00000
0·00000	0·00000	0·00000	0·00000	0·00000	0·00000	0·00000	0·00000	0·00000	0·00000	0·00000	1·00000	0·00000	0·00000	0·00000	0·00000	0·00000
0·00000	0·00000	0·00000	0·00000	0·00000	0·00000	0·00000	0·00000	0·00000	0·00000	0·00000	0·00000	1·00000	0·00000	0·00000	0·00000	0·00000
0·00000	0·00000	0·00000	0·00000	0·00000	0·00000	0·00000	0·00000	0·00000	0·00000	0·00000	0·00000	0·00000	1·00000	0·00000	0·00000	0·00000
0·00000	0·00000	0·00000	0·00000	0·00000	0·00000	0·00000	0·00000	0·00000	0·00000	0·00000	0·00000	0·00000	0·00000	1·00000	0·00000	0·00000
0·00000	0·00000	0·00000	0·00000	0·00000	0·00000	0·00000	0·00000	0·00000	0·00000	0·00000	0·00000	0·00000	0·00000	0·00000	1·00000	0·00000
0·00000	0·00000	0·00000	0·00000	0·00000	0·00000	0·00000	0·00000	0·00000	0·00000	0·00000	0·00000	0·00000	0·00000	0·00000	0·00000	1·00000

TABLE 3c Transition matrix for ages 26–31

0·60604	0·27543	0·10249	0·01449	0·00142	0·00011	0·00001	0·00000	0·00000	0·00000	0·00000	0·00000	0·00000
0·00000	0·43289	0·42979	0·11477	0·01950	0·00273	0·00029	0·00002	0·00000	0·00000	0·00000	0·00000	0·00000
0·00000	0·00000	0·53953	0·33078	0·10076	0·02393	0·00437	0·00058	0·00004	0·00000	0·00000	0·00000	0·00000
0·00000	0·00000	0·00000	0·47024	0·33175	0·14231	0·04359	0·01061	0·00138	0·00012	0·00000	0·00000	0·00000
0·00000	0·00000	0·00000	0·00000	0·34591	0·34447	0·19379	0·08886	0·02208	0·00453	0·00034	0·00001	0·00000
0·00000	0·00000	0·00000	0·00000	0·00000	0·24603	0·31753	0·27160	0·11273	0·04276	0·00867	0·00064	0·00003
0·00000	0·00000	0·00000	0·00000	0·00000	0·00000	0·14115	0·29896	0·23921	0·19014	0·10166	0·02666	0·00221
0·00000	0·00000	0·00000	0·00000	0·00000	0·00000	0·00000	0·05571	0·15992	0·29117	0·29185	0·15215	0·04919
0·00000	0·00000	0·00000	0·00000	0·00000	0·00000	0·00000	0·00000	0·04222	0·13292	0·26476	0·34539	0·21471
0·00000	0·00000	0·00000	0·00000	0·00000	0·00000	0·00000	0·00000	0·00000	0·03933	0·22192	0·43604	0·30270
0·00000	0·00000	0·00000	0·00000	0·00000	0·00000	0·00000	0·00000	0·00000	0·00000	0·13425	0·47673	0·38902
0·00000	0·00000	0·00000	0·00000	0·00000	0·00000	0·00000	0·00000	0·00000	0·00000	0·00000	0·49935	0·50065
0·00000	0·00000	0·00000	0·00000	0·00000	0·00000	0·00000	0·00000	0·00000	0·00000	0·00000	0·00000	1·00000

TABLE 3d Transition matrix for ages 31–6

0·77156	0·00000	0·00000	0·00000	0·00000	0·00000	0·00000	0·00000	0·00000	0·00000	0·00000	0·00000	0·00000
0·18621	0·63165	0·00000	0·00000	0·00000	0·00000	0·00000	0·00000	0·00000	0·00000	0·00000	0·00000	0·00000
0·03850	0·31512	0·72651	0·00000	0·00000	0·00000	0·00000	0·00000	0·00000	0·00000	0·00000	0·00000	0·00000
0·00347	0·04759	0·22725	0·66486	0·00000	0·00000	0·00000	0·00000	0·00000	0·00000	0·00000	0·00000	0·00000
0·00024	0·00513	0·03999	0·25906	0·55369	0·00000	0·00000	0·00000	0·00000	0·00000	0·00000	0·00000	0·00000
0·00001	0·00046	0·00549	0·06169	0·30441	0·42436	0·00000	0·00000	0·00000	0·00000	0·00000	0·00000	0·00000
0·00000	0·00004	0·00069	0·01229	0·10811	0·34633	0·30604	0·00000	0·00000	0·00000	0·00000	0·00000	0·00000
0·00000	0·00000	0·00007	0·00187	0·02786	0·16457	0·36257	0·24352	0·00000	0·00000	0·00000	0·00000	0·00000
0·00000	0·00000	0·00000	0·00021	0·00529	0·05319	0·22796	0·37539	0·22043	0·00000	0·00000	0·00000	0·00000
0·00000	0·00000	0·00000	0·00001	0·00058	0·00996	0·07756	0·22518	0·27756	0·10471	0·00000	0·00000	0·00000
0·00000	0·00000	0·00000	0·00000	0·00005	0·00146	0·02168	0·10987	0·25498	0·23814	0·05673	0·00000	0·00000
0·00000	0·00000	0·00000	0·00000	0·00000	0·00012	0·00394	0·04059	0·19913	0·45961	0·52841	0·36832	0·00000
0·00000	0·00000	0·00000	0·00000	0·00000	0·00000	0·00025	0·00545	0·04790	0·19754	0·41486	0·63168	1·00000

TABLE 3e   Transition matrix for ages 36–41

0·91043	0·00000	0·00000	0·00000	0·00000	0·00000	0·00000	0·00000	0·00000	0·00000	0·00000	0·00000	0·00000
0·08257	0·84945	0·00000	0·00000	0·00000	0·00000	0·00000	0·00000	0·00000	0·00000	0·00000	0·00000	0·00000
0·00666	0·13925	0·86639	0·00000	0·00000	0·00000	0·00000	0·00000	0·00000	0·00000	0·00000	0·00000	0·00000
0·00033	0·01058	0·12083	0·81724	0·00000	0·00000	0·00000	0·00000	0·00000	0·00000	0·00000	0·00000	0·00000
0·00001	0·00069	0·01170	0·15856	0·73916	0·00000	0·00000	0·00000	0·00000	0·00000	0·00000	0·00000	0·00000
0·00000	0·00004	0·00099	0·02148	0·21406	0·64064	0·00000	0·00000	0·00000	0·00000	0·00000	0·00000	0·00000
0·00000	0·00000	0·00008	0·00247	0·04025	0·27339	0·53413	0·00000	0·00000	0·00000	0·00000	0·00000	0·00000
0·00000	0·00000	0·00001	0·00023	0·00581	0·07051	0·32363	0·44266	0·00000	0·00000	0·00000	0·00000	0·00000
0·00000	0·00000	0·00000	0·00002	0·00066	0·01341	0·11258	0·36354	0·37844	0·00000	0·00000	0·00000	0·00000
0·00000	0·00000	0·00000	0·00000	0·00006	0·00185	0·02515	0·14526	0·35993	0·26498	0·00000	0·00000	0·00000
0·00000	0·00000	0·00000	0·00000	0·00000	0·00018	0·00403	0·03988	0·18460	0·36409	0·19586	0·00000	0·00000
0·00000	0·00000	0·00000	0·00000	0·00000	0·00001	0·00045	0·00783	0·06454	0·26819	0·43488	0·36658	0·00000
0·00000	0·00000	0·00000	0·00000	0·00000	0·00000	0·00003	0·00084	0·01249	0·10274	0·36926	0·63342	1·00000

TABLE 4   Proportion of women aged 41 on 1 January 1964 with the following families

Age of eldest child	Age of youngest child				
	0−4	5−9	10−14	15−19	20−4
0− 4	0·02126	0·00000	0·00000	0·00000	0·00000
5− 9	0·01042	0·05986	0·00000	0·00000	0·00000
10−14	0·03035	0·05756	0·11208	0·00000	0·00000
15−19	0·07100	0·10091	0·11988	0·10281	0·00000
20− 4	0·02283	0·02447	0·02389	0·01805	0·00852

Comments

P. Cox

In certain English examinations a question used to be regularly set in the form: 'write an essay on lobsters *or* the Court of Louis the Fourteenth.' One year there was a misprint and the question appeared as: 'write an essay on lobsters *and* the Court of Louis the Fourteenth'; it was a novel situation for the examinee. I was once confronted with a similar problem, when asked by a certain university publication to write a joint review on two books, and there appeared to be little or no connection between the one and the other. I accepted the challenge and wrote some sort of a critique, but in doing so I was forced to go far down to basic principles.

The contributions we have heard today, both extremely interesting, are not without their connecting links. But they do cover rather different ground and I think it might help, in inaugurating discussion, if I were first to generalize a little about demographic techniques and methods, and then see where these two contributions fit in.

Discussions on demographic methods and techniques are rather uncommon. For instance, at the World Population Conference recently there were twenty-three sessions, and only four of these were concerned with techniques. It seems an excellent plan to discuss methods today, and I congratulate the organizers on selecting this topic. It could be argued that demographers are normally more interested in results than methods. Certainly, discussions on the *principles* of demographic method are very rare, and it may be of some help to go to basic essentials and think first about definitions. 'Demography' almost defies definition because it embraces such a wide field of study, but 'method' and 'technique' at least are clear enough, and there is a distinction between them. Method is concerned with the collection and tabulation of data, and with routine interpretation. Technique is described in the dictionary as 'artistic execution', and demographic models and theories are evidently in this class. Both the contributions we have had today are very much in the region of technique. It may be useful to establish a few basic principles relating to the choice of demographic techniques and then examine the two contributions in the light of these.

I think I would put my first choice as being that between an ideal approach and an empirical approach; in other words, whether you collect the data first and form your theory afterwards or whether you form your theory first and then study the data in the light of that.

Demography is full of outmoded theories; but past data also may no longer have any validity in current conditions, and so experience proves little as to which is the more reliable. The best idea, therefore, is to have the data and the theory side by side. Both the contributions today fit in very well with that notion, although I have some slight reservations on points of detail which I will come to later.

Secondly, a basic condition for good demographic technique is having a purpose and knowing what the purpose is. This condition should not be difficult to fulfil, but one sometimes meets work in which there is a lack of purpose: the title of a paper is not borne out by the contents and this can be the cause of confusion. However, there is no confusion on that score today. Both our speakers have managed to do what they wanted to do extremely well by economical and satisfactory processes.

The next need in demographic analysis is a philosophy: this is important where prediction work is concerned. Prediction can very frequently go wrong. What can one say after the event? Was it really one's fault that the prediction failed or was it just bad luck? Some demographers speak of one prediction as being better than another because it was the more 'intelligent', at the time it was made, though the other has proved more successful in the event. I can recollect an example of this, going back quite a long way, when one alternative projection seemed quite unrealistic to its author when it was made, but it has turned out very well – indeed, is the best of the bunch. One must not push this 'intelligent' approach too far, because the test of a method must to some extent be its outcome. Mr Brass has been careful to examine the outcome of his own method. This principle probably does not apply to Mr Carrier's contribution, because he is not concerned with forecasting. His talk has given us a technique for building up a rather complicated picture from certain given basic data. It could, however, be tested, if suitable data were available, and the results should be most interesting.

A number of principles relate to the need for a clear understanding of the nature of the data and particularly to that for fitting the method used to the quality of the data. It would be wrong of me to go into too much detail, because both contributions you have heard today score very well, in this regard, but here again I have one or two reservations in detail which I will come to later on.

The next principle is one of multiplicity of approach. Look at a problem in two different ways, if you can, rather than just one. This is illustrated, I think, in Mr Brass's contribution, where he has used several alternative approaches. This brings me to a further principle: the need (sometimes) for compromise. This is again illustrated in Mr Brass's figures. He had two methods, both of which he regarded as extreme. He went on to find something in between the two, and scored a greater success.

I find it rather difficult to say very much on Mr Carrier's method, because it is highly technical, and new to me today. It seems extremely interesting, and I like particularly the ingenious way in which he illustrated it on the blackboard, by means of geometric rotation. I would have liked to ask him to go on and show us two more steps, in which case he would have needed an extra dimension! I did wonder, when he said that the only way to proceed was by means of additions to the size of the family. In practice, a large family might emigrate and be replaced by immigrants coming in with a smaller family. Again, if those with a larger number of children were selectively withdrawn by death there might again be a reduction in family size. His method is, of course, appropriate in relation to the fertility of a particular person, or the number of children born to a particular married couple. The practical utility of the method depends upon one's purpose. If one were costing family allowances, the complications I have mentioned would perhaps be a nuisance, although probably only a minor one. The problem is somewhat similar to that, which often arises in actuarial work, of evaluating complicated contingencies for the future: for instance, the chance of a man marrying and then going on to have children, of his wife being widowed, getting a widow's pension, and then remarrying. The evaluation procedures are complicated, and approximations may well be justified, even when a computer is used.

I now turn to Mr Brass's paper, which I enjoyed very much. I agree with what he said, but in order to stimulate discussion will make one or two controversial observations. First, he says that pessimism in the matter of forecasting mortality has given way to mild optimism. I doubt this. But even if it is true, the prospects of success in mortality projection do not really seem to be any better than they were. He says also that mortality projection is a neglected study. It is, however, a standard procedure now for mortality to be projected in actuarial calculations, although perhaps the theory of projection has not been greatly advanced in the process.

As he says, Kermack, McKendrick and McKinlay are a trio with a poetic, and satisfyingly Scottish ring to their names. I was rather reminded of Finlay, Cameron and Macpherson – who were apparently active at about the same time. But another gentleman with a K in his name, who should perhaps be mentioned in this connection, is Derrick who evolved in 1926, for the first time, this idea of parallelism between the mortality curves for generations. The theory Derrick advanced was that circumstances at the time of your birth determined your strength of resistance all your life. At the time when he

enunciated this theory it was hardly possible to test it in a very satisfactory way; but, as the years have passed, we have seen that parallelism doesn't continue; that there is a sort of 'wearing off', and the
generation curves come closer together in old age. The reason for
this is perhaps that the events that happen during one's life – wars and
economic depressions, and the new medical discoveries – have some
sort of 'secular' effect which waters down the generation differences.
The incidence of secular effects is greatest in infancy, and indeed the
generation effect starts by being a secular effect. A complete theory
of mortality ought to provide for both secular and generation effects.
Although I would agree with Mr Brass that the generation effect is
very important, I am not altogether with him in everything he has said
about the relative importance of generation and secular effects.

There are other ways of interpreting death rates. For instance,
Beard has regarded mortality as a product of secular, generation,
and age factors, and studied fruitfully lung cancer death rates on this
basis. His analysis came out rather well because he was able to explain
the generation effect, the age effect, and the secular effect in terms of
cigarette smoking. It is interesting to note that when this method was
tested on the differences between male and female mortality (much
of which could be due to things like smoking) the secular component
became unimportant and a good fit was obtained from the generation
component alone. Mr Beard's method, like that of Mr Brass, is more
flexible than that of Kermack, McKendrick and McKinlay, or of
Derrick, in that it offers a number of ways of adapting the method to
the circumstances, although, of course, this has its dangers as well.

Mr Brass has logit on his side, but has he got logic? Judging by
the results he quotes, methods A and B are not really more successful
than that of Kermack, McKendrick and McKinlay. Brass's method C,
on the other hand, is very much more successful, but we have to
remember that this is a compromise; with the best will in the world,
one wonders if this might to some extent be the result of hindsight,
and on this account one cannot be completely sanguine about an
equal success for it in the future.

In practice, people do not, on the whole, use the generation method
of mortality in projections. A cursory glance at a recent OECD
publication, which gives the official projections from a number of
countries, creates the impression that the secular method has been
employed more often. It is much more convenient for computation,
it is more comprehensive, it takes in the young ages and is, in some
ways, perhaps more convincing. In order to test the relative worth of
the generation and secular methods I went back to the mortality
projections which were made for the Royal Commission on Population, twenty years ago, which were on two alternative bases. One was

a generation method adjusted for 'wearing off' – not in the way that Mr Brass has done but by a rather different formula; the other was a secular method. Some simple tests against the actual experience of the last twenty years suggest a drawn battle between them, and I would not say that one method had proved to be any better than the other. In order to test this matter further I had a word with my colleague, Mr Martin, who is concerned with making the official population projections each year, and he confirmed that his own personal investigations led him to believe that the secular method was more convenient and successful than the generation method.

One has to recognize that there are some things which are quite unforecastable. The mortality predictions made for the Royal Commission have proved to be badly wrong at the younger ages. The mortality rate has declined faster than expected, and much more speedily than it had ever done before. This was due to new medical discoveries. Somebody may have foreseen this happening, but if they did they kept quiet, because there was nothing publicly announced by doctors or anybody else at that time. Today we do not know whether there is suddenly going to be a great improvement in the mortality in the older ages. New discoveries may come along, completely transform the situation, and invalidate all forecasts made on the basis of past experience.

General Discussion

W. Brass, N. Carrier, E. Grebenik, and S. A. Sklaroff

Owing to the relatively short time available, discussion of the papers by Brass and Carrier was somewhat restricted. Given the technical nature of both papers, many comments took the form of a request for information rather than a contribution to discussion. A point which was emphasized was that the techniques described in the papers were capable of a very wide field of application, but both authors made it clear that they themselves had not yet exploited them to any great extent. Carrier laid great weight on the fact that his paper was concerned with a technique of analysis, that 'you can answer almost any question' relating to the data given. However the data he used as an input was by no means in a raw form, having undergone a good deal of manipulation before being applied to the model. The central purpose of his paper was to illustrate the *organizational power* of his approach.

In connection with this, Brass suggested that the development of the matrix approach described by Carrier was, fairly clearly, heavily dependent on the use of high speed computers and their ready availability. Carrier agreed entirely, illustrating the point by saying that in a typical run he uses up to two minutes of computing time on a machine doing fifty thousand divisions a second, so that the gain was not just marginal! He went on, however, to repeat that the main point was the organizational problem. As he put it 'for organizational purposes you could write this on paper if you had millions of staff, but you could never find the paper you'd written it on. That's the main point I'm trying to make.'

The problem of random error was raised by Sklaroff in connection with Carrier's paper. Many applications of the technique might be on populations considerably smaller than a national one, and the question of random error would then become much more important. Carrier, in reply, pointed out that while it was quite true that stochastic processes became important when dealing with small populations, the cost of stochastic work on computers was very great compared with 'deterministic' work of the kind he had been describing. He suggested that a possible way round the difficulty would be to try and assess the stochastic element within the deterministic model. This might be done by taking a population of 50,000 (say) and splitting it into 50 blocks of 1,000 each. The variability in the answers for the fifty blocks might be taken as an indication of the stochastic element.

In the case of Brass's paper it was once again a major theme that his analysis could be applied more widely. In particular, work could be done on the analysis of fertility data. As he put it in response to Cox's criticism of a previous remark: 'I said somewhere that the study of mortality projection has been particularly neglected. What I meant by that was that no-one has studied mortality in the way I think they should have studied it, and similarly I might have said that the study of fertility projection has been particularly neglected for the same reason.'

Carrier made the point that Brass had very modestly suggested that there were only two really good systems for producing model life tables, the United Nations system and that of Cole, Demeny and Hoover. He himself, however, used a third system exclusively . . . that of Brass, the logit system.

In his concluding remarks the chairman drew attention to the work that is being done, especially in the United States, on stochastic model building, the use of computers for simulation, and the appearance of what he called a *rapprochement* between medical researchers and demographers. Typical of this work are studies of conceptive delays, and the measurement of biological fecundity.

The general impression created by the discussion was a realisation that many new lines of analysis had opened up recently and were continuing to appear. The possibilities appear almost endless and the amount of work which has actually been done somewhat meagre.

I

Population Forecasts
and Planning

W. STEIGENGA

The contribution of demography
to physical or spatial planning

with prepared comments by
J.N.Wolfe, H.J.D.Cole, and
P.Johnson-Marshall

CHAIRMAN

T. Burns

W. STEIGENGA

The Contribution of Demography to Physical and Spatial Planning

Since some difference of opinion exists as to the definitions of demo-graphy and physical or spatial planning, a few basic definitions are required if one is to consider the relationship between the two disciplines. Moreover there is a difference of opinion with regard to the type of contribution demography can make to the field of planning. In my own country, for example, the contribution of demography to planning was initially highly valued compared with that of other social sciences. Within the Dutch universities the chair of what we call in the Netherlands 'planology' (science of spatial planning) is often combined with or closely related to training in demography. This is more or less the result of a long tradition: before the Second World War and the early post-war years the contribution of social scientists was mainly restricted to calculating population estimates and describing the social and economic situation of the region involved. In this context, the role of the social scientist within the field of planning was passive compared with the more active role of, for example, the town planning designer. In later years the role of the social scientist working in the field of planning was no longer restricted to a social survey of existing situations and the calculation of demographic projections; his attention was more and more concentrated on the formulation of future socio-spatial structures. When the present role of the social scientist connected with planning is analyzed, the following functions are revealed:
1. the diagnosis and evaluation of the present situation and observable trends;
2. the calculation of projections;
3. the setting up of programmes for the constituent elements of plans – for example, for the types, size and number of amenities;
4. the formulation of alternative socio-spatial models;
5. the formulation of programmes of action designed to realise the planning goals accepted by the responsible authorities.

In moving from a more passive to a more active role in planning, the original relationship between planning and demography was changed. It became less clear than before, and a slight tendency to underestimate the significance of demography could be observed.

Demography
Not only the position of the demographer within the field of planning
needs further exploration; we have also to clarify what is the real
field of demography and demographic research.

In the demographic literature – in handbooks as well as in the
proceedings of national and international congresses on population –
one is confronted with different views of the limits of the field of
demography. The contents of some important British and French
textbooks on demography differ significantly from many American
textbooks. These American texts deal not only with what may be
called demographic analysis, but also with population problems in a
broader sense. Many chapters in these textbooks are dedicated to
topics such as the distribution of population, migration, socio-
economic differences between areas or regions, and many others,
depending on the author's interest.

On the other hand in textbooks written by authors like Barclay,
Pressat, and Henry, to mention only three outstanding Western-
European demographers, attention is restricted to purely demographic topics such as fertility, mortality, age composition, and natural
growth. The emphasis is on the methods and techniques of analysis.

The proceedings of recent international congresses on demography – most of them announced as population congresses – deal, for
example, with topics like 'urban development and housing.' When
reading the reports dealing with topics such as these one wonders
where demography begins and where it ends.

In order to avoid a dogmatic methodological approach it may be
useful to distinguish between three concepts of the contribution
demography can make to the complicated field of spatial planning.

In the first place, in preparing all kinds of plans (regional plans,
town and country plans, national plans) extensive information concerning the population is required. These data are mainly connected
with the demographic structure and can generally be provided by
official statistics. The opening chapters in most planning reports
provide this information under the heading of 'demography'. The
term 'demography' is used here more in a popular sense. The knowledge provided under this heading is *de facto* a social survey of the
existing situation based mainly on census figures.

More important is the second concept of the relationship between
demography and spatial planning; in this case demography is closely
related to the analytical contribution of other social sciences such as,
for example, human geography, sociology, or economics, and is
incorporated in their concepts. The quality of the demographic part
of the analysis depends either on a knowledge of demographic
techniques and methods on the part of the social scientist or on his

ability to co-operate with a professional demographer. This can be considered as an application of demographic research techniques in the field of the social sciences. From the planning point of view this kind of contribution is very valuable. For example, demography can play a part in the discussion of topics such as the size and types of housing, migration, school population recreation and certain types of population estimates.

The third concept of the contribution of demography to planning can be based on Barclay's definition of demography as a science. Barclay – like Pressat and Henry – stresses the analytical aspects of demography. Barclay considers demography as a science dealing with the process of replacement, especially in its two main aspects: the population aggregate and changes that occur during some period of observation. The direct use of demography lies in the ability to calculate future development of size and structure, either based on pure demographic data, or in connection with social and economic data.

From a planning point of view only these last two concepts of the contribution of demography to planning are of importance.

Spatial planning

In order to indicate some main fields of demographic interest within the field of spatial planning a description or definition of the aim of spatial planning is required.

Physical planning, or planology, or spatial planning – according to the Israeli, Dror – deals with a 'political decision-making activity, which is directed to enable, to promote, or to exclude certain developments.' Within a given society the aim of spatial planning is to create a spatial structure so that the society can obtain optimum use of space; or to put it in the words of a French planner, Rouge, planning aims at such an organization of space that a better balance between space and society can be obtained. Spatial planning may take the simpler form of a programme of recommendations, as well as the more elaborate form of a socio-spatial model.

In other words this kind of planning deals with the spatial organization of human society, with, for example, the pattern of population distribution, the social morphology of human settlement, the social or demographic composition of a population in a limited territory, the set-up of a residential area, the concept of a new town, and so on.

Planning as a social discipline is based on a thorough diagnosis of the existing situation, the disclosure of trends of development and the evaluation of both situation and trends. With the aid of this diagnosis alternatives can be developed based on different values. It is clear that the social sciences – including demography – will have to provide the elements for this diagnosis.

Demography and the process of realisation

The question arises of how demographic analysis can be considered useful for spatial planning.

Planning can be divided into two very important parts: the formulation of the target (in the case of spatial planning – future spatial structures) and the formulation of the process by which the target is to be realized. This process of realization is determined by trends caused by autonomous processes and by conscious intervention, mainly by governments.

When we first look at the process of realisation it seems possible that certain physical or spatial planning goals can be attained by influencing demographic components. Theoretically it may be possible to influence social development in order to lower or perhaps to increase the expected size of a population, or perhaps to influence the expected age composition. In that case the demographic structure is no longer a fixed datum, but is considered as an influencible variable to be used for attaining certain targets of spatial planning.

In principal two means of intervening in the demographic datum are at our disposal. In the first place it is possible to manipulate one or more basic demographic components such as fertility or nuptiality. It is my impression that the political means of changing the trends of fertility and nuptiality significantly are very restricted, and only successful under extraordinary circumstances. Up till now no physical planning policy has attempted to alter fertility or nuptiality in order to make the realisation of planning goals possible.

In the second place one can try to stimulate or check migration, or to change the pattern of population distribution. This is a more realistic planning policy aimed at controlling population development in the planning region.

From a spatial planning point of view the concept of accepting the demographic trends as given data is more in accordance with reality as we know it than the illusion of being able to change those trends significantly.

Some general aspects of the contribution of demography
to the goals of spatial planning

Demography can play a greater part in the detailed formulation of spatial planning goals.

This contribution is most important in determining accurately the number and size of amenities required for the citizens for whom plans are developed and designed. Many of these amenities are mainly determined by the existing age composition, and the expansion of certain age groups. Particularly striking is the fact that in Western society the number of dwellings required can be expected to grow disproportionately to the total population growth; the demand for dwellings for the elderly will grow rapidly in our Western society, because of the fundamental changes in the age composition. Because of the growing importance of educational institutions a detailed knowledge of the composition of the younger age groups is required. Every age group has its own space requirements, and Lewis Mumford rightly spoke of *planning for the phases of life.*

Any phase of life requires its own social and medical care, from maternity facilities to funeral homes and cemeteries, from crèches to old age pensions, from sports fields to theatres and nightclubs, from school libraries to general and specialized libraries, from active forms of recreation to all sorts of more passive forms of recreation.

In most cases the social and economic data determining the provision of space-requiring amenities have to be based on the specific demographic components of the local population. Planners have to pay attention to the characteristic demographic differences between residential areas. In most large metropolitan areas, we are not only confronted with increasing social differences between several types of residential areas, but also with remarkable differences in age structure. In a new residential area or a new town, amenities have to be planned for a very young and vital population in the beginning. What will happen, however, after the original generation grows older and the young find employment and home elsewhere? The population gets older and some amenities such as certain types of schools and social institutions will no longer be in full use. We can expect a certain cyclical movement in the relative importance of the distinct age groups. This, however, has its impact on the efficiency of the planned and realised amenities. In planning we have to consider the implications of these cyclical changes in the age composition.

However, the position of the demographer in the context of spatial planning is not unchallenged in every respect. A remarkable difference can be noticed when studying the development of techniques and methods of executing regional population forecasts.

The regional population forecasts

Traditionally demography has always been involved in making calculations for regional population projections. Notwithstanding this traditional task we can observe a remarkable change in the methods used for calculating regional population estimates, and I should like to illustrate this development by means of some examples from the Netherlands.

Before 1940 the most important population projections (for example those being made for the large urban municipalities,

Amsterdam and Rotterdam) were based mainly on a detailed demographic analysis of data such as local birth rates, local mortality,
nuptiality, and specific fertility, as far as these data were available.
These local data were compared, of course, with analogous data for
the country as a whole. With regard to migration the estimates were
based either on historical trends or on unproven economic expectations. That the planning region and the other regions in the country
were inter-related was not taken into account. Generally speaking the
region was considered as an autonomous area, independent of
economic and demographic development in the rest of the country.

To some extent just before the Second World War, but mainly
after the end of the war, different types of regional population projections were developed. I should like to mention here three types of
regional forecasts not based on analysis of pure regional demographic
data.

The demographic data in these types of forecast are no longer of
primary importance, but they have additional significance.

The first type was developed by an agricultural sociologist, Hofstee,
when working on the population projection of a provincial capital
town in the north. This town was mainly characterized as a centre
providing a market function in a rural area, with some minor additional industrial and service functions. Hofstee based his projection
on a detailed analysis of the various local economic activities. The
estimates for the future were mainly deduced from past economic
development, and information provided by the industry itself. To
some extent the author referred to the relation of this town to its
immediate vicinity, in this case the total area of the three northern
rural provinces.

This is the same type of regional forecast that was recommended
by a Swedish demographer, Hyrenius, in one of the meetings of the
World Population Conference in Rome in 1954. It is justifiable to
state that this type of regional forecast can only be applied to regions
with a simple economic structure and with a fixed hierarchical relationship between the settlements. More important is the fact that, in
one aspect, this type of regional forecast does not fundamentally
differ from more traditional demographic types of regional projections. For in both cases the region involved is generally considered
as autonomous and independent from other regions.

Quite different is the second type of regional forecast to be mentioned. This type was developed by a planologist in co-operation with
an economist just before 1940 (Van Lohuizen and Delfgaauw).
They tried to estimate the distribution of the national population
increase in the future over the economic-geographical regions of the
country as a whole. Their assumption was that the distribution of the

national increase over the regions would follow the pattern of an earlier period. A region was no longer considered in isolation, but just in its relation to the other regions and the country as a whole. The authors did not calculate a regional demographic forecast, but used national population projections calculated, for example, by the Central Statistical Office. However, the formulation of the assumptions was based mainly on historical considerations; changes in the economic structure to be expected in the future were not taken into account.

Confronted with the very complicated economic, social and demographic structure of the New Waterway region, I had to decide what type of regional population projection could adequately be applied. I decided that neither a pure demographic nor a regional economic projection could be used here as a consequence of the national demographic development and of some fundamental changes in the economic structure of the Netherlands.

Notwithstanding that the basic concept of the geographical population projection just mentioned was acceptable, the underlying historical assumptions had to be rejected. For it was clear that it was improbable that a projection of the future distribution of national population increase could be based on the same mechanism as in earlier decades. Thus it was necessary to formulate a great number of economical and political assumptions that would influence and determine the distribution of the expected national population increase over the country as a whole. Assumptions postulated were, for example: the maintenance of full employment, a successful industrialization policy, no overcrowding and diminishing of the agricultural sector, free internal migration, and a disproportionate increase of employment in chemicals and metallurgy. Along those lines a third type of regional forecast was developed. This type was partly based on an analysis of macro-economic trends and partly on an analysis of changes in the location of industrial and service activities. Based on these assumptions a relation could be calculated between the national population growth and certain national economic trends on the one hand, and the regional development on the other.

From an administrative-political point of view the advantage of this kind of forecast was that any change in the assumptions or the trends could be traced in its consequences for regional development. More and more within national physical planning, one is attempting to base future expectations of population distribution on, for instance, forecasts of the economic structure of the national population.

Thus nowadays we notice that planologists are accepting more and more the national population forecast, mainly calculated by the experts of the Central Statistical Office, and are attempting to study the changes in the relation of their region to the nation as a whole, in order to calculate the occupational population to be expected.

Notwithstanding the change in methodology by which the relation between planning and demography seems to be weakened, the aid of demography is still required to solve important questions. In particular the demographer will be needed to provide information on, for example, the specific characteristics of the age structure of the regional population to be expected. I have mentioned already the significance of taking into account the distinct age groups with regard to the required amenities. The demographer will have to calculate specifically the differences between the age composition of the national and the regional population.

In other problems too, the active contribution of the demographer is inevitable; how great the difference will be between the expected population and the result of a projection calculated only on the basis of the natural increase, in other words the quantity of migration in the future is a problem for the demographer. He will have to check the reliability and probability of the regional population projection from a demographic point of view.

The role of the demographer has changed, but not ended. This can easily be shown by the contribution a demographer can make to the planning of one of the most important amenities to be considered in spatial planning – the house.

The demographic base of the demand for housing

The demographer's most important contribution to housing policy and town planning is in calculating the number and types of dwellings required. The total number of dwellings required per 1000 inhabitants depends on factors such as the average size of the family and the proportion of unattached people not belonging to a family. The types of dwelling depend not only upon income and status, but also on the number, the age and the social structure of people forming a household or a family. To set up a housing programme for a region, a town or a residential area, a thorough knowledge is required of the composition of the population with regard to small, moderate, large and very large families. Moreover a more detailed knowledge of the composition of the unattached is desired with a view to the planning and construction of small apartments. From a demographic point of view the housing needs can be considered to be determined by family structure and age composition.

The population living in dwellings can be divided into three main groups. In the first place we have to deal with men and women living with and belonging to a family, as childless couples, young married as well as older couples, complete families (parents and children still being at home) and incomplete families (widows, widowers, divor-cees and separated persons living with their children). This is the main group determining the quantitative number of dwellings required.

In the second place one can distinguish a group of men and women not living with or belonging to a family, but either living alone or living with other unattached persons forming a so-called 'pseudo-family'. This group is getting more and more important as a result of demographic as well as of social changes.

In the third place one can distinguish a group of men and women living with (in other words participating in the household) but not belonging to a family. Examples of this kind of person are servants or relatives not belonging to the nuclear family involved, or strangers living with a family, perhaps as paying guests.

Based on this differentiation we can analyze the interplay of demographic and social factors determining the need of dwellings. To a certain extent we may say that the number of families is mainly determined by purely demographic factors such as birth rate, nuptiality frequency, age composition, and mortality. But only to a certain extent, for all kinds of social factors – albeit in a minor way – also contribute to the housing needs of the families. Nuptiality as such is determined by specific social factors. For example, the situation in the Netherlands has been changed by a relative increase in the number of marriages, and marriage at an earlier age, which has been an important factor in the demand for housing after the Second World War. Knowledge of these socio-demographic factors is most impor-tant for reliable estimation of future housing demands.

The demand for housing of the unattached is determined by social as well as by demographic factors. As far as the older unattached are concerned, recent changes in the age composition of the population as a whole are responsible for their expanding housing needs. In addition to this demographic factor, however, some important social factors influence the total housing demand of the old-aged. In former times the surviving parent found his lodging till the end of his life within the household of his children. Due to changes in social rela-tions and the economic position of the old-aged generally, the ex-panding group of elderly people prefer to live on their own in a small apartment.

The situation in the younger age groups is somewhat different. The increasing demand for small apartments in this group is mainly determined by social change, especially in the relationship between parents and children, and by the relatively favourable economic position of the younger generation now as compared with a few decades ago. In the past they could only afford to rent a room in a house occupied by a related or a strange family; nowadays – and here we look at examples such as Sweden – they prefer to establish an independent household by renting a small apartment of their own.

Housing need projections (such as have been published, for instance, in the report on the planning of the British New Town Hook) can only be carried out by well-trained demographers or by other social scientists well qualified in demographic analysis. The schedule concerning the distribution of dwellings by type and size, and even by location in special residential areas, can only be based on fundamental demographic facts. These facts are the main basis for further sociological and socio-ecological interpretation. In particular one has to take into account the internal changes within the family, such as the expanding, the stationary and the contracting phase, and the number of times a family moves from one place to another.

Final remarks

The contribution of demography to spatial planning is most important but constantly changing, sometimes weakened, sometimes intensified as the other social and economic sciences develop, especially as the scientific base of spatial planning develops. The contribution of demography reaches its peak in close co-operation with other branches of social science. This, however, is under one condition: the social scientist who makes use of demographic techniques needs a good understanding of demographic problems and of the methods of dealing with them.

Comments

J. N. Wolfe

Professor Steigenga has presented an extremely stimulating contribution and sets out a whole host of ideas.

I will touch upon only three or four points. The first of them concerns Professor Steigenga's discussion of the role of the social sciences in the field of planning. I agree that this role has not yet been satisfactorily defined. It would appear that the attitude of the planners is that the inclusion of the points of view of the social sciences is to be achieved by some kind of intuitive juggling. Economic, social and political considerations are to be handled by the planners in some mysterious and inexplicable way which nevertheless produces an acceptable synthesis. I would have said that the next step forward in physical planning would be the elimination of this intuitive aspect and the presentation of the results of planning as a clear set of cost benefit alternatives. Let me put it this way! Most of the choices made by the planner can be put in terms of the selection of a minimum cost operation, on the one hand, and the operation which the planner would like to persuade the customers to buy, on the other. It is rather like selling a luxury car. There is a standard version and there is a version with automatic gear shift, and the problem of the salesman is to explain why the version with automatic gear shift should be bought. The problem for the physical planner is very nearly the same. It is in the reconciliation of costs and benefits on accepted criteria that the next step forward in physical planning lies.

Now for the second point I should like to comment on Professor Steigenga's clairvoyant remarks on flexibility in planning. I entirely agree with him that it is not desirable as a matter of practice to fix a particular date and to talk about a population growth to that date without any consideration of what the population growth might be beyond that date. It is rather as though one were to consider an investment in a piece of plant and equipment with the notion that after five years this piece of equipment would definitely be written off and would be scrapped. Attempts to use a five years write-off period, as we know from capital budgeting theory, are bound to be wrong. There is a standard technique for dealing with this problem which allows one to go further forward, and to consider not only the effects and implications of a particular time period but the effects and implications of the probable outcomes over the whole range of future time.

It must be recognized, however, that when one goes beyond thirty years in the future the uncertainties involved are rather great, so that one would not want to give undue weight to the possibilities one might assume for that period. An expansion of what Professor Steigenga said is that it is not only necessary to consider what will happen beyond thirty years but it is also necessary to give some weight to the fact that we do not know clearly what will hapen in thirty years – or for that matter in five years. That is to say that there is a definite margin of uncertainty in all our forecasts, and particularly our population forecasts. What we are dealing with here is a random variable, and there are certain definite methods of procedure for dealing with random variables. We should take into account both means and variances, although I would agree that one has rather limited information as to the degree of variance of these forecasts. It is a frequent error of the physical planner to consider that the fore-casts on which he bases himself are in fact certainties. They are not certainties, and there is a great deal of action taken which might not be taken, or which might be delayed and postponed, if the proper weight were given to the uncertainty of forecasts.

There is, however, a conflict. A good deal of the mechanism of planning consists of a kind of sleight-of-hand operation in which one pretends to believe that something which is really rather doubtful is in fact certain; and by one's apparent confidence, one influences the actions of others, and so brings about, or helps to bring about, a situation which one desires. A desire for scientific accuracy conflicts with the need to look certain so as to convince others.

When, thirdly, one takes an area and attempts to change its popu-lation structure, what one is usually doing in practice is to increase population and to allow the age distribution and the skill distribution of the population to alter in whatever way it will as the result of the economic forces which are brought into play. Certainly one must face the question of what steps must be taken to attract the population into the area, but this question has not received as much attention as it deserves.

In this country the practical problem put to the demographer has been rather different from that posed by Professor Steigenga. The problem has not been to consider what the current industrial trends are, and to what extent these are going to shift population structure; because we have often adopted a conscious policy of attempting to change the population and to fix on areas to which population is to be drawn, and we have means of inducing industry to move to particular areas by providing cheap factories and cheap houses for the workers in these factories. We do this on a rather generalized basis through grants to development areas, and on a more detailed

basis by means of new town corporations and special housing corporations as well as by advance factory arrangements. In my
experience the choice of population target is often an arbitrary one.

The question of viability becomes a very important one when you
consider a particular small region. The question is what steps must
be taken and what kind of cost must be undergone in order to
attract the kind of industry which is required in an area. We tend
to take the view that the fundamental magnet for population growth
is, as Professor Steigenga's colleagues in Holland have suggested, the
question of jobs and industry.

Let me just touch now on the larger national aspect. The Government of the UK has, through various committees, been considering
the question of the distribution of population between now and the
end of the century. We have made a projection which envisages a
growth of population of perhaps 20,000,000 by the end of the century.
We have had to consider this in the context of a strong tendency for
the movement of population into urban areas, and an equally strong
tendency for the movement of population out of settlements having
populations below some critical figure. We do not yet know what the
critical size of settlement is. Some would say 150,000, some 250,000.
Others would pick on different figures in different circumstances.
But it is clear that cities and towns of fairly small size are going to
suffer, possibly absolutely, in the coming period. Cities of very much
larger size are going to grow, and this is a demographic fact which
compels a rethinking of the whole structure of planning. What is
required is a rethinking in terms of the problems of the expansion
of urban centres. We are faced with a consideration of the extent to
which we will allow the bulk of, let us say, 20,000,000 extra people
to flood into the existing urban centres and the extent to which we will
provide alternative locations for these people. There has been some
attempt to handle the problem by means of satellite towns, but this is
increasingly seen to be a difficult and not altogether attractive procedure. The currently announced planning studies are for two cities of
a population of 1,000,000 on Severnside and on Humberside. Two
new cities of this sort are not altogether unrelated to the problem of
the prospective pressure of population on existing urban areas. We
have also, in Scotland, a proposal for the expansion of the Dundee
area to a population of 500,000. But to what extent do we propose to
allow the existing urban centres to absorb remaining growth? And to
what extent will we seek other new sites for it? This brings us very
much to the question Professor Steigenga spoke of first – flexibility.
If we embark upon many more very large projects of the kind just
described, we may be faced with a very serious dilemma. Supposing it
works out that the pill intervenes and we do not have 20,000,000

K

extra people by the year 2000 after all. The Government will have been committed to (and will feel committed to proceed for a considerable way towards) the construction of these new cities. This will create a rather difficult position for the older cities. Can we accept a situation in which the bulk of population growth is directed to new cities and the existing cities cease to grow, cease to get the economic stimulus and the stimulus for development which comes from growth. I do not think that we can, and this is one of the reasons why in fact we have to plan for substantial expansion of the existing conurbations. This imposes a complete change in the point of view of the planning of British conurbations. Until now planning of the existing conurbations has been based upon the assumption that they were not to grow very much, and therefore any redevelopment of them would be of a modest sort easily left to local direction. If we are going to have to allow a very substantial rate of expansion in the existing conurbations, this means that we have a much bigger planning problem, which is really a national problem and must be treated nationally. Detailed decisions have to be decided or at least agreed at a local level and I am very much in favour of local participation. But I think that the major lines of policy are too important to be left in the haphazard and not always competent hands of local authorities.

Comments

H. J. D. Cole

Well, Mr Chairman, I find myself in two sorts of difficulties. First of all, Professor Wolfe said many of the things I intended to say – fortunately in some cases there are some elements of disagreement which I think are worth bringing out. In doing so, I should make it clear that I am expressing merely personal opinions, and not any official view. The second difficulty, I am afraid, is the picture that has been presented compared with precisely what is going on in Whitehall, particularly what I am doing in the shape of a really quite staggering amount of research, planning, and depth thinking. At the moment I have not got any proper staff, I have only been there eight months, and I have not been primarily concerned with the population in the year 2000. So please understand that really we have not made – and are not likely to make in central Government – the progress in providing a really decent picture of where we should be going that Professor Wolfe has been talking about. I would also like to make one passing comment on what he said about local authorities towards the end. I quite agree that from the planning point of view there must be some increase in scale, but I do not like the implication that seems to go with it that the gentlemen in Whitehall know best, or even that the gentlemen in the University know better, than the City Regional Planner based in democratic institutions and employing suitable staff.

First, I would like to go back to one or two things which Professor Steigenga wrote in his paper, because I think we must start with a full appreciation of our own uncertainties when it comes to demographic projection. We have heard a lot about the uncertainty over the 20 million population in the Netherlands and the 20 million extra population in Britain. I think we over-emphasize, however, the problem of the uncertainty of the total population. For many planning purposes we are not concerned with the most uncertain element in it – the number of schoolchildren – and we do have a very much greater degree of certainty about the numbers of other groups we have to plan for, such as the aged. One of the things I very much want to press on demographers is that they should not just tell us this is all very uncertain, but tell us what pieces of it are certain and which are uncertain, because there are different ways in which you should approach problems according to the degrees of uncertainty attaching to a particular estimate. To give a simple example; there might be a case for going hell for leather for the movable school in view of the uncertainty of the fertility rates, but there would be much less of a case for going for the movable old people's home. This is only intended to illustrate the point about uncertainty; I haven't gone into the economics of movable schools. The other feature of uncertainty I would stress is really connected with migration. Speaking in Scotland one has to be very, very conscious of how much of the Scottish future is tied up with how many Scots are going to continue to go right out of Britain in the next thirty years, and, in respect of migration out of Britain as a whole, the fact is that we know really very little about the economic reasons for emigration. We also have a great deal of difficulty predicting what will happen to all the migration controls in places like the United States. But, when you come down to what I am more primarily concerned with – regional planning – knowing how to approach the uncertainties about net migration, becomes, in many ways, much the most difficult element. I think Professor Steigenga produced, in his paper, a very good analysis of three methods of approaching the problem, and I share his preference, for the method which he has chosen to use lays primary stress on the element of employment demand. There is, however, interplay between demand and supply, as in so many cases, and when you are considering the distribution of the population around the country there are places where a supply of land is running out, partly because of the expanding demand for housing space by the poorer part of the population. The supply of land is also one of the factors that is likely to become increasingly important in determining the willingness of entrepreneurs to go elsewhere to set up their new businesses. After all, one main reason for studying in Whitehall this problem of the long-term distribution of population is that we are coming to the end, in many more places than London, of the way in which the planning problem has been tackled since the war – if a public authority has undeveloped space within it, fill that up first and thereafter consider overspill schemes and all that follows. I think Professor Wolfe, to a certain extent, gave a misleading impression of how far we have got in planning when he talked about what are really Development Areas and suggested that the same amount of thought has also gone into other areas. Frankly we have stuck to two problems at the centre up till quite recently. Firstly the problem posed by the overflow of population, in London in particular, but also in many other parts of the country such as Birmingham, Manchester, Glasgow, and so on, and secondly the problem of the high levels of migration and unemployment in Development Areas, primarily due to the run down of certain basic industries. The idea that there is a sort of general pattern that we have been looking at and a good sound basis of thought on what is happening and would be likely to happen to, say, Yorkshire or Edinburgh, and so on is just unsound. There has not been the staff for the job, and quite frankly I do not think the necessary thinking work has been done in the universities either. I hope that one of the purposes of the regional planning machinery, and why England followed Scotland in setting up a certain degree of regional planning, is to get a rather more comprehensive look at the issues.

One further point on what Professor Wolfe said. He said that we should get down to it and, instead of the planner dealing *ad hoc* with the various pressures on him, we should try and do some figuring, and work out the costs of various alternatives – to say, you can have that, and, if you are prepared to pay a little more, you can have something else. I am not sure that this is a wholly realistic approach. We are now working on such a problem in considering the feasibility of a new city on Humberside. There are certain aspects for which that approach is dead right, but he does perhaps suggest that we planners have more control over what happens than we do. We need to do a lot more to try to understand where, and to what extent, we can and should try to modify the underlying trends. Before we can do that we have to identify these trends, and I think we should start, when con-sidering the distribution of population in the long term, with a very clear idea of what would happen to the country as a whole if we did nothing. Frankly this material is not fully available because the operative factors are too complex for the kind of analysis that has so far been used.

Comments

P. Johnson-Marshall

I wish to comment in terms of questions because I think at a symposium of this kind it is usually questions one poses rather than answers. I was extremely interested in Professor Steigenga's paper, since a physical planner comes up against the points he has made all the time.

A physical planner's job is to make space decisions, or at least to advise his clients on the character and nature of existing urban settlements, but space criteria must be based on an assessment of human needs. We are still very far from achieving a good relationship with the sociologists, and still far from being able, as physical planners, to formulate our needs clearly enough. Mutual understanding is still a long way from achievement because it is only by an assessment of human needs that we can make correct and adequate space decisions. The difficulty is to make them in terms of maximum convenience for all kinds of human activities: take, for instance, the problem of residential density. The planner in the past has known too little about the types of people for whom we are planning, quite apart from income groups, but many of the problems of family size and the changing family structures are too little known, even when you begin to have adequate statistical information about the family structure in any community. One sees, in the past, cases in Britain where well-known residential estates were planned on the basis of an analysis of family structure and the provision of social facilities that related the family structure, as it existed at a point in time, to a particular space relationship in terms of schools. A classical case occurred in London where a particular family structure was taken, and this was applied to a physical layout. However the physical layout was built for at least the sixty years of the loan period sanction operated by the authorities so that the school buildings remained, but the family structure changed drastically during the next ten years. Thus the school provision first over-supplied and then under-supplied. This is the kind of demographic problem which we need to know a great deal about and relates back into the whole problem of flexibility of designing, particularly in residential neighbourhoods. In regard to the question of the Netherlands and Britain, I am always astonished, looking at the demographic map, to see the extraordinary differences in population densities between different parts of Europe, and this is certainly not always related to difficult geographical or climatic conditions. In the Netherlands, in particular, certain kinds of very tight space planning have had to be adopted as there is so little room to manoeuvre. In a sense, physical planning has developed a great deal out of dire necessity and, as I see it, space limitation does at least force accurate statistics. The need for a good statistical basis for physical planning decisions has probably come out more clearly, as Professor Steigenga has stated. The need is manifest for adequate information on family structure in terms of work spaces, schools, dwellings, and the amount in each case of the proportions of different spaces, and also the determinants each time in which the planner has to make some kind of density decisions. These space-needs change all the time. The *per capita* space-needs for industry vary drastically in different kinds of industries, and even in particular industries they vary, in a few years, in terms of, for instance, male and female employment and the adoption of certain kinds of mechanization. One change, for instance, is the office structure which one might see in New York now, which is a peak in terms of the fantastic density of office buildings. With the onset of computerization and mechanized techniques the need for this vast congregation of workers will be diminishing drastically, and may therefore set up a whole new basis for planning and a new image of city development. The problem of natural increase is that, in the past, the planner has tended to think in rather over-simplified terms of a planned population in new settlements, and has not allowed sufficiently for a double operation that goes on when you introduce a new population. It is increasing naturally all the time, and there should be a continual, close collaboration between planners and demographers. The effect of natural increase has probably not yet been studied adequately for physical planning decisions on population. In the New Towns there was an immediate increase, with the new conditions making the population higher than had been the case with the same population when they lived in the inner areas of cities. This again is a question which we need to know more about.

We have in mind the experience in Britain in the nineteenth century when the population explosion took place with the higher standards of development and industrialization. Initially there was a rapid increase, and then came the levelling off which we saw in the twentieth century. This leads to a whole series of very difficult questions in regard to the now well-known British prediction of the extra 20 millions. I question this, although I respect the reasoning of the demographers and statisticians. I know they are basing a great deal on statistical trends, but we have some biological problems and controls as well. The 20 million predicted increase is a very hazardous prediction in my view, bearing in mind the previous population changes that have occurred in the past. All this makes it impossible to have over-rigid statements looking ahead twenty years or more, but what it does mean as to the intention of the somewhat maligned 1947 Town and Country Planning Act of Britain, was the need for close reviewing of physical plans which is demanded at five-year intervals, and this whole operation of prediction being checked and reviewed should be a constant process.

Discussion

W. Brand, W. Brass, T. Burns, C. Clark,
D. C. Eversley, E. Grebenik,
T. H. Hollingsworth, and J. N. Wolfe

This paper provoked a lively discussion which ranged widely over many topics. Broadly speaking, there was general agreement that demographers can reveal misconceptions about what happened to populations in the past and is happening to them in the present, and can bring these events into sharper focus. A number of examples were given by various speakers and will be mentioned below. However in so far as the demographer was being asked to make a contribution to *planning* and thus frequently to provide *predictions*, opinion varied as to his usefulness. A good starting point is to be found in the comments of Grebenik and the chairman, Professor Burns.

Burns suggested that communication between planners and social demographers appeared to occur largely by chance. Little machinery seems to exist to encourage communication, and there is a large discrepancy between the size and range of topics studied by demographers and the pleas for more usable information from the planners. The planners protest that they are working in the dark; the demographers are interested in casting light on real but different problems. Burns wondered whether some kind of political machinery would not be necessary to prevent the relationship between the demographer and the planner (and vice versa) occurring in what he described as 'quite such a happenstance manner.'

Grebenik's reply expresses the point of view of one group of demographers so clearly that it is best quoted in full: 'I do not think it is surprising that administrators are never satisfied with what academic demographers do because, quite frankly, what the academic demographers can do is in my view extremely limited. Eversley in his contribution to the discussion (see below) has shown that there are a certain number of misconceptions which demographers can explode. We can and do, as part of our professional knowledge, analyze certain aspects of the population structure and point these out to administrators and planners, but fundamentally all we do is to explore the past. The administrators want to know what is to happen in the future. This I am afraid we cannot do. We cannot tell them anything about the future. I would be very hesitant, for instance, in saying anything reasonable about the future level of births in this country even for such a short period as the next five or six years.

How many demographers, for instance, foresaw the baby boom of the 1956–65 period, how many of them prophesied that births after 1965 would go down? How many people saw the reversal in the differential fertility of social classes which has been shown by the 1966 census? Who would have forecast that at present it is the highly-educated people who have the largest families? I think myself that we really have very little to offer on forecasts. Planners always want us to prophesy. They need population forecasts. They need, as Mr Cole has pointed out, some estimate of errors. When we do this we are not really talking *qua* demographers, because I do not think that as demographers we have yet arrived at an understanding of the factors which influence population increase or decrease. We can analyze what has happened but, I think, we still know very little about the factors which lead people to reproduce or to migrate, and we ought to acknowledge this lack of information. I think one of the reasons why civil servants and planners attack us is the lack of humility amongst social scientists in the recent past. Social sciences have become respectable subjects, and social scientists have claimed that they can deliver goods which they cannot in fact deliver. As far as understanding the population situation, regional or local, is concerned I can only echo the probably *ben trovato* words of the Member of Parliament who, when talking about the Cyprus situation, ended his speech by saying that anyone who claims to understand the Cyprus situation is misinformed!'

While this statement of the difficulties would be accepted by most of the participants some of them clearly felt that the job of the demographer did include operating in this area of uncertainty in the best possible way. Brass expressed these ideas very clearly in his contribution. He drew on his experience of planning in the medical field, where he had been concerned with the problem of deciding what the future production of doctors in the United Kingdom should be like. He pointed out that some of the lessons he had learnt and problems he had solved in this area were very similar to those in the physical planning field. Basically he made three points relating to the time-scale of operations, risk assessment, and the sort of assumptions which should be used.

The time scale involved in planning of this kind is very long indeed, and Brass endorsed Professor Steigenga's point that it is no use picking on a particular year, be it 1980 or 1990, and looking at the needs of the expected population at that time. Buildings and institutions have a very long life and take a long time to create. If one is concerned with the provision of new medical schools, for instance, twenty years may elapse between the plan and their first producing graduates. Those graduates may then be in practice for forty years or more.

The very uncertainty of projections means, to quote Brass, that 'a demographer working in this planning field has very much to be concerned with the problems of minimizing risks. In other words he's always got to consider what would happen if certain things go wrong. And I think it's at this point that he is really forced into the general planning field . . . he becomes intimately concerned with alternatives and with the costs of alternatives.' Brass went on to take up the point made by Wolfe in his prepared comment that variability and chance errors were to be taken into account in estimates or projections. Brass stated that here, as in many other things, social scientists were becoming concerned with something which statisticians were beginning to leave behind. Demographers, he claimed, should concern themselves with problems of minimizing risk in decision problems, with minimizing maximum risk, and so on, taking advantage of the considerable body of formal theory already developed. Later in the discussion Wolfe took up this point again, suggesting that a minimax procedure was only one of the possible forms of statistical decision-making procedure which could be used. He himself would prefer what he regarded as analysis at a more sophisticated level in which one considered alternative decisions between various mixes of risk and possible gains. This would mean the use in a fuller sense of the utility function which the planner or society imposes on the situation. Undoubtedly, however, there was substantial agreement between Brass and Wolfe that this was, as Wolfe put it 'the kind of way in which a realistic social science would deal with the problem of uncertainty of projections.'

The final point which Brass made was a very pragmatic one. He advised that in all planning of this kind one should try and minimize the necessary assumptions. In particular he felt that the sort of procedure, which was often followed, of looking at all the different facets of a problem separately and adding the bits together to arrive at a solution was very faulty. As an example he took his problem of the supply of doctors, saying it was far better to look at the population of doctors as a whole rather than decide how many of each type of doctor there should be (general practitioners, surgeons, radiographers, and so on) and then adding them all up. As he put it 'this kind of what one might call aggregative planning seems to me to be what is done in many circumstances . . . and that this very often is the worst way of doing these studies – it ignores inter-relations and all sorts of possibilities of transfer, and in practice it often gets very bad results.'

Brand suggested that one of the blocks to communication between demographers and planners arose from a disinclination on the part of vested interests to have problems of certain kinds discussed. He had been concerned with the economics of public health, and asked to what extent attention was being paid in Britain to the 'production function of public health.' He had raised questions in the Netherlands about the density of doctors and specialists, because he felt that figures were meaningless unless something was known about the rationale of public health provision. He then found that these were subjects which were not discussed due to the pressure of vested interests. In his country he claimed the same could be said of education and housing.

Brass felt that in the United Kingdom there was considerable interest in economic approaches to public health at least, and that vested interests were less opposed to such studies now than they were a few years ago. He cited studies which were being done in Manchester as examples, although he admitted that they were still on a very limited scale and far from having any great impact on practice as yet.

The other main line of discussion, as indicated earlier, was concerned with what the demographer *could* provide for the planner. There was a general feeling that these possibilities were not fully realised by people outside the field of demography and indeed by many people within it. Eversley made this point forcefully in his contribution right at the start of the discussion. The demographer can, as he put it 'slaughter vulgar prejudice.' He took issue with Johnson-Marshall who, in his comment, had made reference to the increased fertility in the New Towns. Eversley claimed that this had been looked at very closely (he cited the example of Crawley) and, given the sex and age structure and the marriage patterns, it appeared that specific fertility in the New Towns was certainly not higher than it would have been for the same people in their original locations, and indeed may be somewhat lower. Furthermore the demographer can provide critical planning data on household size, occupancy rates, and so on. As an example Eversley gave the estimation of household size: 'This is from a physical point of view by far the most important planning question. To put it in a very crude form, if headship rates were to remain at the level they were in England at the time of the 1961 census we should want '*x*' number of separate dwellings by the year 2000. If they were to fall to the Swedish level we should want '*x*' plus about 55 per cent or something like that, which is a very large number of families indeed in the physical planning sense. So what a demographer does want to find out is: what are the determinants of a fall in household size; what are the indications that we are going to follow the Swedish example of creating a separate household for all unmarried young people, or for old single people, widows, and so on. We have got quite a lot of material towards this.'

Eversley went on to discuss preliminary work which suggests that the degree of fission of households into smaller units in this country varies greatly by socio-economic group and by region. He pointed out that the old belief that household size is inversely related to socio-economic group turns out not to be true, as some of the highest socio-economic groups form large households. Nor should we be too surprised at this as they are more likely to keep children at school longer than the minimum leaving age, tend to have families at least as large as any other European population, and are more likely to employ hired living-in help or *au pair* girls. This general area is one in which a good deal of work has been done by the demographer and it represents a small beginning to the process of providing information of use to the physical planner.

Eversley's second example was drawn from the problem of predicting the behaviour of the labour force. He pointed out that female activity rates, for instance, depend not only on socio-economic group, fertility, and age of children, but also on how far wives live from suitable types of work. It is the demographer's job to calculate the relation of the factors one to another, a job which Eversley claimed the demographer can do better than the economist, who measures only one side of the problem.

Hollingsworth suggested another example of the ways in which demography may help planning in making a plea for what he called geographical demography. This sort of work has been neglected, probably because of the difficulty of getting data, by comparison with historical demography which at present is expanding rapidly. Yet it *is* possible to produce valuable information relatively easily in the geographic field. Purely as illustrations Hollingsworth took two unpublished studies which had been very easy to do and very quickly carried out. One related mortality and fertility indices standardized for age and sex in four wards of Glasgow. He was extremely surprised to find differences between the highest and lowest ward of the order of three to one in one case and two to one in the other. As he pointed out this is something which never seems to be taken into account because no-one regards it as their job to analyze it. Yet, clearly, such differences will be of the greatest importance if the overspill population from Glasgow comes from one ward rather than another. Hollingsworth's other illustration was drawn from the field of migration. Using the elector lists at three elections, he found that around a number of cities (notably London, Birmingham and Manchester) there are rings of ever-increasing rates of growth, and comparing 1959 with 1964 the maximum rate was at a range of about 50 miles from the city centre. Repeating this between 1964 and 1966 he found that the rings now met between Birmingham and London, for instance, and the areas were so large that the centripetal tendency bore no real relationship to where the cities really were. Hollings-worth's concluding comment put his point of view well: 'Now I mention this as something which doesn't seem to be discussed or done at all by anybody, and this means that we ought to spend a lot more time really considering what the spatial distribution of popula-tion is, rather in the way they used to in the nineteenth century.'

The difficulty of drawing inferences from this kind of data was pointed out however by Clark, who asked the question, unanswerable in this context, of whether the families were large because of their place of residence, or lived where they did because they were large families! Also on a polemical note he pointed out at another time that, contrary to Johnson-Marshall's statement in his discussant's comments, office building in New York was only taking place on Wall Street and Park Avenue, where all the visitors see it. The rest of New York he said was 'an economic desert so far as office building was concerned, and in fact virtually the whole of New York is an area of declining population and declining land values.' His final sentence, combining as it does the demographer's function as an exploder of myths, his tendency to clash with vested interests, and his intention of providing information of interest to planners, forms a suitable close to this account: '. . . some recent work done in Manchester indicates a heavy decline in land values. Now these are facts that city politicians and real estate agents will not even discuss; they are so contrary to what has been believed for so long, that urban land value is always going up. There is a very wide and planless diffusion of population going on with a rise in land values from rather low levels in suburban areas. This probably represents a net loss to land owners which nobody should mind about, but if (in the old congested cities) there is going to be a heavy decline in land values, that will make an immense difference to city planning, although there will have to be also an explosive change in the nature of political thought.'

Current Approaches to World Population Problems

W. BRAND

Population Growth and Economic Development

with prepared comments by
L. Tabah and G. M. Carstairs

CHAIRMAN

C. Clark

W. BRAND

Population Growth and Economic Development

In 1960 the world population, according to United Nation estimates, was about 3,000 million. By 1965 it had grown to about 3,300 million. Thus in five years there was an increase of 300 million, or an average of 60 million per annum. This annual rate of growth of 2 per cent in the period 1960–5 is assumed to be the result of a difference between an overall birth rate of 36 and death rate of 16 per 1,000. A rate of growth of 2 per cent signifies a doubling every 25 years, and, if the present rate of growth were to continue, there would be 6,000 million people by 1995, 12,000 million by 2030, 24,000 million by 2065 and 48,000 million by the year 2100. With 48 milliard people on earth, a figure reached in 135 years, the density of the population on the land area of the earth (1.5×10^8 km^2 – including the ice-covered areas of Siberia, Greenland and Alaska, and deserts like the Sahara and Gobi) would reach 320 persons per km^2. Such a density, only slightly less than that at present prevailing in the Netherlands (360 persons per km^2), would require, in my opinion, a strong world government to direct the activities of states and individuals. Whether this is a subjective view is not important. If the growth rate of 2 per cent were to go on unabated for a little more than 500 years, the density on the land surface of the earth would reach 1 million persons per km^2. I assume that almost everybody will agree that by then the moment of 'pathological togetherness' has arrived and procreation must come to a standstill. From this extreme extrapolation it may be deduced that, in the not too distant future, world population will have to be stabilized in order to provide every individual with enough living space. As all human beings seem agreed that a low mortality, say a life expectancy of 75 years of age, is desirable, it follows that the birth rate will have to come down to a level of 1000/75 or 13·3 per 1,000 in due course.[1]

Whether it is possible to determine when the constraint of space on population growth will become manifest, seems problematic. At first sight, a firmer foundation appears to exist for studies aimed at the determination of the optimal carrying capacity of the earth, or an estimation of how many people can be assured a reasonable standard of living in the light of available resources (cultivable land, minerals and fuels) and the technical progress which can be anticipated. In this approach too, however, difficulties abound. Though at present only 10 per cent of the land area of the earth is cultivated, the experts seem agreed that another 6 per cent could be brought under the plough. There is also agreement that it will be more economical to increase yields on the area already under cultivation than to expand the cultivable area. However, though this conclusion is borne out by the experience of the rich nations, in the poor countries higher agricultural production is still mainly achieved by increasing the crop area.[2] Without conclusive evidence, technicians generally assume that the means and methods developed in the West for increasing yields per land unit could similarly be applied in the tropical regions. A few years ago, however, de Vries[3] estimated that, in Asia, about 2·6 times the population of 1950 could be supported by the year 2000 through a 30 per cent increase in cultivated area and the doubling of production per ha which could still be achieved. He foresaw that an improvement in the diet of the expected Asian population of 3,990 million (based on the 1957 UN estimate) was feasible only if sea water could be effectively converted into irrigation water during the intervening period. Most experts seem agreed that synthetic or hydroponic food production offers no solution because of the high cost involved. The possibilities of the sea, encompassing 70 per cent of the earth's surface and at present only providing 1·5 per cent of our food requirements, are generally considered favourable, but not of a sufficient magnitude to affect the overall food situation.[4] Uncertainties again exist as to the reserves or, rather, exploitable reserves, of minerals and fuels. It can be calculated that as 90 per cent of the world's production of mineral and energy resources are consumed, at present, by the 30 per cent of the world population living in the industrial countries, annual production would have to be increased threefold in order to bring the poor countries, in which 70 per cent of the world population live, up to our level of consumption. Thus it can be demonstrated that supplies of many traditional mineral and fuel resources will be exhausted rather quickly if and when the rich areas' present level of consumption prevails over the entire world.

As far as energy is concerned, the emergence of new resources – atomic fission or even fusion, and solar energy – may present a boundless perspective, but for most metals the picture seems rather dim. Most 'futurists' appear to agree that, in the not too distant future, world population increase will have to come to a halt lest a return to a rather primitive existence for human life be in the offing. One of the most optimistic projections, that of Clark[5], suggests that a total of 28 milliard persons could be sustained by the earth at a decent level, but this figure will be reached in something over a 100 years if the present growth rate of 2 per cent continues. The work of the 'futurists' suffers, moreover, from several deficiencies. Their calculations are largely of a technical nature and do not consider the capital required to utilize existing resources more effectively, or explore new possibilities. Nor do they take into account the institutional obstacles in transferring the existing technical and organizational knowledge from the rich to the poorer parts of the world. The principal weakness of their schemes seems to be that they view the world as a whole, or as a common reservoir of wealth and knowledge which every nation could tap according to its needs, whereas in reality the world is divided into at least 200 states, each of which has to solve its own problems despite the lip service paid to international solidarity.

Having dealt all too briefly with the space and resource limitations of the earth in relation to population growth, I now turn to other more mundane aspects. Malthus thought that natural resources were finite and human beings tended to reproduce themselves in an infinite manner. He and other classical economists were apparently of the opinion that a higher wage or a larger food supply would raise nuptiality and thereby the birth rate, and thus quickly relegate mankind to its former level of living by virtue of the law of diminishing returns as applied to the land factor. However, population growth in Europe did not occur as a result of increasing fertility, but rather due to a decrease in mortality – from 36 per 1000 in 1740 to 23 per 1000 in 1840 in England. With a further decline in mortality, birth rate also started to drop in the by then industrialized nations for reasons, and with means, largely not envisaged by the classicists. The birth rate declined from 35 – 40 in the 1880s to 15 – 20 per 1000 at the present time so that, with few exceptions, the rate of population growth remained in the range of 1–1·5 per cent per annum. To escape the law of diminishing returns in agriculture, the classical economists recommended the expansion of industry, as here increasing returns could be reaped from unchanging inputs of units of labour and capital by means of technical progress. Thus, as Mill[6] in particular expounded, by exporting manufactured goods it was possible to pay for imports of food and other raw materials from overseas, which domestically could only be produced at increasing or prohibitive cost. In a study for the United States, Bennett and Morse[7] have shown that for the period 1870 – 1957 raw materials from agriculture, forestry, fishing, and mining were almost constantly obtained with declining inputs of labour and capital. This was largely the result of technical improvements and an extension of knowledge, together with decreasing population growth and a higher income, which caused a diminishing demand for resource-intensive goods and services, or a shift from scarce to more abundant raw materials. Though no comparable studies for Europe exist, I assume that they would show a similar outcome, namely, that due to the cumulative effect of technology and knowledge the law of increasing returns still prevails for our economies, and that there is no reason to suppose that until, let us say, the year 2000, we shall not be able in our part of the world to meet the challenge of emerging scarcities of certain natural resources through the expedient of technological innovation. As a result of the post-war agricultural revolution in the industrial countries, the development of synthetic substitutes, the more economical use of raw materials and their retrievability from scrap and waste, the dependency of the rich countries on overseas supplies of food and other raw materials has relatively diminished. Shifts in the industrial structure towards predominance of the services sector have contributed further here. Moreover, the developed countries can meet their needs for primary commodities through an increasing exchange among themselves. Between 1950 and 1964 the share of the poor countries in world exports declined from 32 to 20 per cent, and I would suppose that this share will decrease to 10 per cent by, let us say, 1980 if present tendencies continue. In the export of primary commodities, the developing countries accounted for 40 per cent in 1955 and for only 36 per cent in 1961. In foodstuffs their share came down from 42 to 34 per cent, in other agricultural raw materials and ores their share declined from 40 to 32 per cent, and only in fuels did their share rise from 57 to 63 per cent. The prospects may not be bright even for fuels if the North Sea plateau is thoroughly explored and motor cars driven by electricity emerge, as appears likely in our cities in view of the threat of air pollution caused by oil- and gas-driven vehicles. The decreasing importance of the developing regions in world trade is caused, apart from structural changes in the industrial nations, by the higher rate of population growth in the former, with increasing domestic consumption tending to restrict their export capacity.

Recent United Nations data [8] reveal that the increasing gap in living standards between rich and poor regions can be attributed largely to the higher population increase in the latter. In the period 1960–65 the gross national product of all less-developed countries taken together increased by an annual rate of 4 per cent.

As the annual rate of population growth was about 2·5 per cent, national product *per capita* only increased by 1·5 per cent during the period mentioned. In the rich areas gross domestic product rose by 4·4 per cent per annum, and as their population growth was only 1·2 per cent, *per capita* product grew at the rate of 3·2 per cent during the period 1960–65. I am not implying that the rate of population increase depressed the growth rate of the economy in the poor regions. In my opinion both phenomena are largely ruled by different factors, but I think that the high rate of population growth in the poor countries hinders their economic development and their chance of catching up with the richer nations. The high growth rate of the population (resulting from birth rates varying from 40 – 55 per 1000 and death rates of 10–30 per 1000) carries in its wake a high dependency ratio, that is, an unfavourable relationship between the numbers of children and potentially active workers. In the developing countries 40–5 per cent of the population falls into the age-group 0–14 while in the rich countries this group comprises only 25–30 per cent of the total population. Thus the share of potentially active workers (15–64 years of age) is 50–5 per cent of the total population in the developing countries compared with 60–5 per cent in the industrial countries. Around 1960 the number of economically active male workers as a percentage of the total male population was about 50 in the poor countries and 60 in the rich countries. The high proportion of children requires additional expenditure on education, but even in countries where the educational system was greatly expanded in the post-war period, the absolute number of illiterates or of children who could not attend schools, has increased. Furthermore accelerating population growth requires additional resources for housing. If the housing needs of the poor countries are projected in relation to expected population growth and rate of urbanization, astronomical investments seem required, quite apart from the desirability of replacing the slum dwellings in the urban areas by decent housing.[9] It may also be pointed out that education and housing are rather slowly maturing investments and substantial investments in these sectors will tend to dampen the overall growth rate.

Many economists, myself included, find the concept of the capital-coefficient (the ratio between physical and human investment, and income) also useful to demonstrate the impact of population growth. If the capital-coefficient is 4, then with a population growth rate of 2·5 per cent, 10 per cent of income has to be invested to provide the additional population with the same income as the existing population. As the savings ratio is naturally low at a meagre income level, substantial demographic investments are required when population increase is high, and little remains for economic investments or an improvement in income per head. A study by Paukert[10] confirms that in the fifties increases in income, which took place in a number of developing countries, have largely served to compensate for population increase, and little has remained to raise consumption per head, for investments, and as public revenue for collective needs. On the other hand, in the rich countries covered in this study, the increase in income which occurred has gone mainly to raise consumption per head and investments, while population growth has only absorbed a small part of the additional income.

With the aid of the capital-coefficient, it is also easy to indicate how much external capital inflow is required to achieve a certain target rate of growth. If annual population growth is 2·5 per cent, an increase of *per capita* income of 3·5 per cent seems desirable in order to diminish the gap in income levels between rich and poor nations. Then, with a capital-output ratio of 4, an investment quota of 24 per cent is necessary. If the supply of domestic savings is only 12 per cent, then 12 per cent or half the requirements for investible funds would have to be provided from abroad. In the recent past, the net aid flow from the rich to the under-developed world was equivalent to about 25–30 per cent of the latter's investment. It does not appear likely that the transfer of capital from the rich to the poor regions will rise as postulated, and thus a scaling down of the target of 3·5 per cent increase in *per capita* income and an effort to decrease the growth rate of the population in the under-developed regions seem necessary.

A similar conclusion can be arrived at by another approach. Assume again a population growth rate of 2·5 per cent and an increase in *per capita* income of 3·5 per cent for the developing countries. As at the typical income level of $100-200 *per capita* for the poor regions the income elasticity of demand for food is about 0·6, then, under the above assumptions, the food supply will have to grow at an annual rate of 4·6 per cent. Such a rate seems unattainable; *vide* the recent performance in the field of food production of the poor continents.[11] Food production in Africa, Asia and Latin America taken together has increased over the past thirty years at a rate of a little more than 2 per cent per annum. Most of the increase has been offset by population growth and thus food production per person has increased at less than one third of 1 per cent per annum in those areas. Thus this extrapolation also points in the same direction. Both the rate of increase in income *per capita* and that of population will have to be curtailed in order to set feasible targets.

In the above is implied that a high rate of population growth or a large number of children will macro- and micro-economically depress the savings ratio. There seems no factual support for Clark's argument[12] that a larger number of children will encourage the will of the head of the family to save in order, for example, to provide for the better education of his offspring. A glance at Dutch budget studies reveals that, at various levels of income, personal savings are higher in smaller than in bigger families. Neither is there any proof that population growth *per se* will raise the investment ratio and stimulate economic growth as Clark[12] and Hirschman[13] have surmised. For a number of industrial countries in the period between 1860 (or 1900, depending upon the availability of data) and 1954, no correlation can be seen between the rate of population increase and the rate of growth of national product.[14] The growth rate of the population varied from 1·4 per cent for the Netherlands to 0·8–1·0 per cent for England, Germany, Sweden, Italy, Switzerland, Denmark and Norway, and was thus of a different order than that now prevailing in the poor regions. For the Netherlands, it seems evident that though the rise in national product has been of the same magnitude as in other industrial countries, it has come down the ladder as far as product per head is concerned because of its higher rate of population growth. The facts do not support the opinion that an accelerating population growth will depress the wage level and thus induce entrepreneurs to seek outside markets. In the Netherlands, during the early post-war years, the Government consciously kept the wage level down through subsidies to promote exports, so that the economy could pay for the necessary imports (such imports amount to about 50 per cent of the Dutch national product) for our rapidly-growing population, but one cannot generalize on the basis of one isolated experience. In the developing countries, though the wage level may be low, this force is absent, because industrialization has an inward-looking bias or an emphasis on import replacements, and generally occurs behind high tariff walls so that their manufactured goods cannot compete effectively, price- or quality-wise, with the products of the industrial countries. It may be supposed that, with an equal growth in national product, a higher rate of population increase will relatively raise the demand for simple consumer goods and curtail the market for products requiring more processing. Thus, though industrial production in the developing countries may have progressed satisfactorily in the post-war period,[15] it could well be that, as a result of their higher rate of population increase, their investment pattern has been unfavourably affected–namely, that relatively fewer new techniques have been introduced than in the rich countries with their lower rate of population growth. In addition, in all probability there has been relatively more capital-widening than capital-deepening in the poor as compared with the rich areas, thus enhancing the technological gap and, consequently, the difference in labour-productivity between the two parts of the world. My review of the literature[16] brings me to the conclusion that the direction and rapidity of industrialization, or the diversification of the economy in general, depends foremost on income growth and thus that a certain growth rate of the population may be useful but not necessary. In my opinion the position of the Netherlands would be better if, in the recent past, our population growth had been of the same order as that in the surrounding countries, but this view is as yet hard to prove. In most poor countries, as I have said, the rate of population growth must be deemed excessive, in view of their limited savings capacity, and has been largely responsible for their falling behind the richer countries.

The last point which I want to bring up is the evidence that in the poor regions unemployment is increasing in the wake of the accelerated population increase. Here also no direct connection is implied, as institutional factors appear to some extent to explain that, for example, in India, labour is not more intensively used in agriculture to obtain larger outputs.[17] Population pressure in the countryside thus leads to an excessive outflow of people to the towns and to urban unemployment, as the modern sector, due again partly to meta-economic factors, absorbs relatively little labour.[18] In the light of the latter fact, Myrdal[19] has assumed that in many developing countries it will be necessary to adapt technology in agriculture to the fact that, for a generation or so, it will be able to provide additional employment at about the rate of increase of the rural population. Whether this is a feasible proposition I am not able to judge, though I may mention that in a paper by de Vries[20] it has been shown, probably on the basis of his experience in Java, that agriculture in already densely-populated countries could only create supplementary employment at a maximum rate per annum of about 1·5 per cent. The exhortations of the director-general of FAO, B.R.Sen, stating that food supplies will have to increase fivefold by the year 2000 (by 4·8 per cent annually or twice the rate now achieved) in order to provide a sufficient diet for the world population expected by then, make it safe to assume that labour-intensity in agriculture will have to be greatly increased in the developing countries over the coming decades if they are to be successful in the race between population growth and food supplies. Furthermore it would appear that, at the same time, in industrialization an intermediate technology (E.F. Schumacher) should as far as possible be applied in order that, for humanitarian reasons, an optimal amount of the potentially active population becomes involved in the process of modernization. This path also seems strewn with obstacles, among which may be mentioned the resistance to the introduction of methods of production which have been discarded in the industrial countries or which will maintain their technical backwardness vis-a-vis the rich countries.

On the basis of a recent United Nations projection it can be foreseen that between 1965 and the year 2000 world population will increase from 3,300 to 6,000 million. Under its assumptions the population of the rich countries will rise from 900 to 1,300 million, whereas in the poor nations the increase will be from 2,400 to 4,700 million. If this projected differential growth rate of the population – 40 per cent for the rich and 95 per cent for the poor countries – comes true it is likely, in my opinion, that the gap in living standards between the two groups of nations will widen.

A much larger flow of aid than is now being offered will be required, in the form of capital and technical assistance, to ensure that the gap between the poor and rich parts of the world does not become greater than it already is. A curbing of the natality rate also seems necessary if the developing countries are to succeed in improving the living standards of their inhabitants. Any percentage reduction in population growth will probably lead to a proportional increase in income per head in most developing countries.

References

1 On this paragraph and the next, see *World Population Conference*, 1965, I: Summary Report, UN (1966) especially pp. 259–71. Meeting B 10: Population and Natural resources.

2 Cf. US Department of Agriculture, *Changes in Agriculture in 26 Developing Nations* (Washington D.C., November 1965).

3 E.de Vries, *Population and Food Supply* (Dutch ENSIE, Amsterdam, 1959) Volume XI.

4 Cf. G.Borgstrom. *The Hungry Planet* (New York 1965).

5 C.Clark, 'World Population', *Nature* (May 1958) and 'The Earth can feed its People', *World Justice*, 1 (1959–60). A critical review of Clark's assumptions is contained in my book: *Population Explosion* (Dutch, 1961) pp. 58–62.

6 J.Stuart Mill *Principles of Economics*, 4th ed., (1898), Chapter III.

7 H.J.Barnett and Ch.Morse *Scarcity and Growth: the Economics of Natural Resource Availability*, (The Johns Hopkins Press for Resources of the Future Inc., Baltimore, 1964).

8 E.g. Economic Progress during initial years of development decade; major economic indicators for developing countries, *World Economic Trend*, UN, Document E/4059 (29 June 1965).

9 See R.C.Cook and K.Gulhati, Housing and Population Growth in Africa, Asia and Latin America in (Ed. S.Mudd) *The Population Crisis and the Use of World Resources* (W.Junk, the Hague, 1964) pp. 219–30 and J.Ettinger, *Towards a Habitable World* (Elsevier, Amsterdam 1960).

10 F.Paukert, The Distribution of Gains from Economic Development, *International Labour Review*, (May 1965).

11 Cf. FAO, *The State of Food and Agriculture* (Rome 1966).

12 C.Clark, 'Demographic Problems on a World Scale', *World Justice*, 6 (1964–5). June 1965

13 A.O.Hirschman, *The Strategy of Economic Development* (Yale University Press, New Haven) pp. 176–82.

14 S.Kuznets, Quantitative Aspects of the Economic Growth of Nations, *Economic Development and Cultural Change, Part I,* (Chicago 1956) and *idem,* Six Lectures on Economic Growth (The Free Press, Glencoe, 1959) Table I, p. 20.

15 See report mentioned under 8.

16 Cf. H.B.Chenery, 'Patterns of Industrial Growth', *The American Economic Review* (September 1960) and United Nations, *A Study of Industrial Growth* (1963).

17 See M.Paglin, 'Surplus Agricultural Labor and Development: Facts and Theories', *The American Economic Review* (September 1965).

18 W.A.Lewis, 'Unemployment in Developing Countries', *The World Today* (January 1967). See also data given by: W.Baer and J.E.A.Hervé, 'Employment and Industrialization in Developing Countries', *The Quarterly Journal of Economics* (February 1966) 88–107 and B.I.Cohen and N.H.Leff, 'Employment and Industrialization: Comment', *The Quarterly Journal of Economics* (February 1967) 162–64.

19 G.Myrdal, in the *1965 McDougall Memorial Lecture* given at the opening of the Thirteenth FAO General Conference, November 1965.

20 E.de Vries, Demographic and Economic Aspects (mimeographed) (August 1964).

Comments

L. Tabah

I thank you, Mr Chairman, for allowing me to speak in French. This will help me to avoid the sort of semantic misunderstandings to which M. Brand was just referring, and I am very grateful to you on that account.

I have a few comments to make about M. Brand's talk, which I found extremely interesting. I shall divide these comments, if you don't mind, into two parts: on the one hand, the purely demographic questions, which are absolutely vital, and on the other, his use of global growth models in dealing with population problems.

To take demographic evolution first, there is here a point which seems to me to be of the utmost importance, namely that the developing countries, which are now the focus of most of the problems connected with the future evolution of world demography and are all the time adding to our perplexities about it, have recently acquired a very strong growth potential. To make this clear I should like to make use of a little model and to take as an example one of the Latin American countries, say Mexico.

Let us suppose that, from now on, this country should continue indefinitely to have the same mortality rate as it does now but that, on the contrary, fertility should, artificially of course, undergo a modification which would make it diminish so sharply that eventually the population became stationary. In other words, that there should be an intrinsic rate of no growth at all. What would then happen? Well, first of all, of course, fluctuations would be seen in the annual birth rate and in the death rate and in the man-power age groups; and then, gradually, the population would stand still. It has been calculated that the relation between the population figure, once the standstill is achieved, and the one obtaining at the moment, is 1·70. That means that the age structure of the population in Mexico is so young that, even supposing it were subjected to a standstill as of now, even supposing all the women there used some really effective contraceptive method and that they wanted to limit themselves to the same number of children as European women have, even then the population would increase by about 70 per cent. This growth is, in the last resort, attributable to the potential strength pent up in the age structure and this, in turn, is explained by the fertility rate of past years. It seems to me that these figures are interesting because they allow us to make a distinction, in the present day population growth of the under-developed countries, between what is caused by temporary factors and what has been built in, in the past. Broadly speaking, you might say, if you like, that one-third of present day growth is accounted for by the rate built up over the years and two-thirds by the demographic conditions in the world today. Similar calculations have been made for about thirty different countries, some developed, some under-developed, and at different points in their history, and it must be admitted that no industrial country has, at any time in its history, reached such a high figure. France, at the present time, has a growth potential in these terms, of 1·2 and we have once fallen to an even lower figure, less than one per cent, just before the last World War. This means that, at that time, our age structure was so old that had our population been in a static condition, it would still have decreased. The fact that it did not do so is simply due to the decreasing mortality rate, on the one hand, and, on the other, to immigration. To take two more examples, the USSR and the US, both these countries have a relatively high growth potential, about 1·35 or 1·40; not much to choose between them.

The interest of such calculations seems to me to be that they prove one thing before we go any further: that, whatever success contraceptive planning may have these days in the Third World, it will be a long time before annual growth rates will fall below 1·5, not before the end of the century, simply because of the rate they have multiplied at in the past. That is why it seems to me both false and dangerous to lend any credence to the growing belief that contraception is the panacea which will produce a quick solution to the problem of under-development. We shall have to make considerable efforts outside the demographic sphere, and in the last resort it is economics which should have the first priority, as M. Brand has so rightly said just now. So much for my first point.

There are a few other points on the same demographic plane which all had a part in M. Brand's paper, and which cannot be avoided any longer today when population problems are under discussion. There is no doubt in the minds of all those who are following the population problems of the Third World closely that the present time is a decisive moment in world demography, in the sense that lower fertility rates are being obtained, on the Japanese model, by entirely artificial means. 'Induced' reductions in fertility (and, of course, I am putting this 'induced' in inverted commas) are being brought about by a new political approach to demography. This is what makes me say that for many countries the maximum population peak is in process of being left behind. There is, as we have seen, a very high growth potential, but we must not, on the other hand, take too black a view of the situation. My impression is that certain countries are undergoing an entire reversal of behaviour in this respect. This is what seems to me to be so very important. We are entering upon a new phase in the demographic revolution, whose main characteristic is a lowering in the fertility rate induced by artificial means. This decrease is, therefore, entirely different in character from what took place in Europe during the nineteenth century. The countries which have begun to reduce their fertility rate, and very quickly, are Formosa, Taiwan, Korea, Hong Kong, and Singapore. Of course, you will say, these countries are places in which very special conditions prevail, places that have even been called 'American fortresses', by which term I intend no sort of adverse political criticism – but a number of other experiments are being carried out now in some very big countries such as India and Pakistan. In view of the vast size of these countries you cannot, of course, expect quick results to affect the birth rate but, here again, it seems to me of fundamental importance that it should be a change in attitude of the people concerned, as well as their governments, towards demographic problems, and this leads one to think that there will be a real reversal in tendencies.

All such activity rouses great hopes in those of us who used to be classed as pessimists. At the same time, they do, I believe, lay us open to certain dangers or risks, and one would be wrong to try to cover these up. One thing we might do is to over-estimate what we can hope to achieve in this sphere, and this is what I would like to call your attention to: the hopes and illusions that may be involved in political theories about population.

In the first place, it must be recognized that the conditions underlying the cutting down of births in Europe are not to be found in any of the under-developed countries today. History, as they say, never covers the same ground twice.

Western Europe, as I do not need to point out to you, although it was the cradle of Malthusianism, has always been divided into two camps over the matter. On the one side we have the Anglo-Saxon, Scandinavian, Protestant zone and, on the other, the Mediterranean and Catholic one. Obviously, one is tempted to see a connection between the Malthusian doctrine and Protestant ethics, as Max Weber did in those well-known words of his about the origins of modern capitalism, which he shows as being closely tied up with Malthusianism. And you can, in fact, see a sort of straight spiritual line of descent from Calvin to Pastor Malthus, and to his followers today, which thus demonstrates how the link between Calvin's reformed church and the puritanical climate of the industrial revolution took on the shape it did because of historical pressures, and how the moral attitudes of the evangelical movement were always making people re-examine the social relationships to which those attitudes were supposed to be applicable. At first such conduct was based on restraint, self discipline, self control, but gradually the whole thing was rationalized and a calculating approach adopted, which was the forerunner of present-day neo-Malthusianism. You will be familiar with the resolution passed at the Lambeth Conference of 1930 on this subject, an altogether revolutionary one. Its whole way of thinking is founded on the Puritan tradition, in that it evinces certain specific characteristics: first of all, a *moral* one (the Anglo-Saxon people have always thought contraception preferable to abortion) next, a *middle class* one (there is an obvious contradiction in terms between having large families and accumulating a lot of money) a *feminist* one, after the famous trial of Annie Besant in 1877, and I would add a fourth, a very important aspect, in Anglo-Saxon countries anyway, which is the *medical* one. (For these people, the psycho-sociological equilibrium of the married couple cannot properly be based on practices which seem to them to be against nature, such as *coitus interruptus*, and which may, in the long run, bring about psychological troubles. All this, of course, is what Freud and a lot of other psychiatrists were trying hard to prove.)

All this holds together splendidly for the Anglo-Saxon section of Europe, but it is harder to swallow when applied to the Mediterranean, Catholic section, the more so because, as everyone knows, the lower fertility rate began in France.

I shall not dwell again on what causes lowered fertility, because you all know about it, but, all the same, there is a certain rationalism or individualism to be observed in it, over and over again. One thing is certain, and that is that one cannot expect the people in the under-developed countries, whose way of life is still so close to nature, who have got nothing, and who can look for no change in their social conditions, to deny their sexuality as people do in Europe, with very poor contraceptive methods at their disposal, even though they are not, as we are, subjected to over-stimulation of sexual appetite.

It is for this reason that research in the West has been based on the knowledge that contraceptive methods would have to be developed for people with very little will to control themselves. Of all the new methods produced I would single out the intra-uterine type of contraceptive. This has the great advantage of being, as it were, inoffensive to any cultural attitude, because it can be inserted in anyone, whatever her system of values and without any radical change in social thinking such as had to take place in Europe.

It is noteworthy that Western intervention in this field all hangs together very well and follows, as M. Brand also pointed out in his paper, what you might call the main lines of historical development amongst the under-developed countries. M. Brand states that the population of the world will double every 35 years, and this gives rise to some staggering figures: 6 million millions in 1995, 12 in 2030, 24 in 2064, and so on. It is plainly ridiculous to contemplate such figures and, unless we could raise the mortality rate, which we would not wish to do even if we could, what we shall obviously have to do is reduce the fertility rate to something nearer the mortality rate. Almost certainly future events will fulfil our expectations on this head. It is simply a question of time. Whether people like it or not, the odds in favour of contraception are already written into the future of the Third World.

What factors are there facilitating this movement and what ob-stacles stand in its way? First of all, the entire political set-up favours contraception. One soon realises, if one has any contacts at all with the under-developed countries, that the people there do not want to be 'manipulated' any longer. Their leaders want to direct the policies involved in such a private matter for themselves. Decisions which the various governments were chary of making when decolonization first took place, as though they had some complex about interference, are now being unanimously adopted. A real change of attitude is taking place. Proof of this lies in the fact that, at the last General Assembly of the United Nations in December 1967, one resolution received a unanimous vote, even from countries in which Catholic opinion is strongest, such as Latin America, and from certain socialist countries which were, until recently, so hostile to the whole idea. This vote recommended to the Economic and Social Council that it should give help 'whenever asked' to research into the tech-niques of population control. The task thus put upon the Council threatens soon to become one of its major technical assistance pro-jects for the Third World.

In the sphere of dogma, too, we are seeing a great reduction in the opprobrium which for so long put a brake on the movement, and now opposition is giving way all the time. To be more specific, it would seem that religious leaders are tending to take a neutral attitude. What seems to emerge as the central point of discussion con-cerns merely the methods of birth control to be employed, often with no other argument than the efficacity one. There you have a very sharp change in attitude which may be explained by an evolution in thinking about what is natural and normal in sex life, and this has been brought about by modern science, particularly psychology and psycho-analysis.

The third thing which has worked in favour of contraception is the fact that it seems to have been given a favourable reception by practically the entire Third World. Surveys have shown that when-ever the question is put to them openly, the idea of limiting the number of births finds a response in a need they have all felt. The very fact that the possibility of making some voluntary limitation on fertility is being debated is itself a strong stimulus to change in behaviour patterns. Proofs of this are legion. The large number of surveys carried out in these countries prove that the new methods are as readily accepted in rural districts as in towns. Questionnaires have been circulated in fourteen under-developed countries, amongst them the query 'Would you like to have no more children?' The results of this questionnaire were analyzed by M. Berelson and a comparison made. Here are some of his findings: replies in the affirmative varied from 42 per cent to 93 per cent in women who had had 3 children, and from 69 per cent to 95 per cent in those who had already had 4. These figures are scarcely any lower than those given in the US where they run from 62 per cent to 81 per cent. There is thus no doubt that contraception satisfies a need which is now felt pretty well everywhere. In point of fact, as comparison between all the surveys made in the eight Latin American countries shows, women usually have very little prejudice against birth control, even when they are Catholic. This interest in general birth control methods is soon apparent. You can see it from the surveys carried out in the eight Latin American capitals where the percentage of Catholic women who confessed to having used some form of con-traception varied from 49 to 93 per cent after the third child. How-ever, the methods they have used so far are not usually very effica-cious, and they do not use them very well either. The most common are the vaginal douche, periodic abstinence and *coitus interruptus*.

The further advantages of modern methods, on technical grounds, are obvious and I do not need to dwell on them because you are all familiar with them: they are reversible processes, which do not spoil the sexual relationship, to use which involves one decision only, and which are almost completely effective. There is no comparison be-tween their effectiveness and that of the methods used hitherto by people in Europe.

Yet another point here seems to me of paramount importance: it is that the method is one entirely confined to women. It would seem that people want to leave women in control of reproduction and free them from the consequences of male irresponsibility. There, to my mind, is one of the most powerful weapons that women could find in achieving their independence both in marriage and in society.

So much for the credit side, but that certainly does not mean that the problem is entirely solved. There are a great many difficulties which we should be wrong to underestimate. Indeed, if we do not recognize them for what they are we shall be in danger of compro-mising the advance that is being made. To make it seems logical, necessary, and simple enough to everybody. All we need to know is how far it is really feasible and what results could be achieved by it.

On the physiological plane, to begin with, enquiries in various countries show that the intra-uterine contraceptive may often be expelled, or that it may have to be removed for medical reasons, or that it produces side effects in quite a number of cases. As an example of this we have the research work carried out by R.E. Hall in the United States, which showed that in that country, where conditions are relatively favourable from the hygiene point of view, the percentage of side effects was as high as 36·9 per cent. The final figure for retention of this intra-uterine device is 60 per cent after 3 years. So you see that this is far from being a perfect method. One point which seems to me important is that there is a low success rate amongst young women with few children, whereas on the contrary there is marked success amongst women who have had 3 or 4. Statistics have since confirmed this.

Of course, the side effects I have spoken of so far are simply the immediate ones. We still know nothing about what might be their long-term ones. In fact, the fears people have felt so far about the new contraceptive methods are concerned far more with the long-term than with the immediate effects. Honesty compels one to distinguish, on this head, between what is certain and what is hypothesis. We all know how difficult it is to establish a fact: we have to set about it slowly, accepting nothing that is not fully proven and that always takes time. It behoves us to recognize how much pure speculation there is in what we are doing. Being short of time, we have often rushed our bridges, we have gone straight on to field experiments without submitting to the thorough laboratory study which strict experimental method would normally demand.

On the sociological plane, too, a certain number of dangers have come to the surface, dangers which might be envisaged if the new methods caused social irregularities, but, of course, here we are in the field of pure conjecture. One thing is certain, and that is that the whole notion of responsibility vanishes with the new contraceptive methods. But this threat is still in the realms of hypothesis and it is seen rather as a possible consequence than as something which might cause a setback to the work in progress.

The hardest obstacle to overcome in all this concerns the organization of it, how to see them all fitted, even. Many writers on this subject foresee that the point where a bottle neck in the spread of this intra-uterine contraceptive method might occur would be in the organization of some new programme. Such a programme must itself depend on a medico-social set-up that is very inadequate, so far, to cope with the health problem and might even prove harmful

M

to it in so far as health might be undermined by the new methods. In fact, the difficulties are many. You have not only to fit the new birth control appliances but, also, and more important still, to carry out clinical examinations so as to spot all the cases where their use is inadvisable and so stop it; also to give the women examinations regularly enough to discover cases of rejection in the early stages, and to keep up observation on the appearance and the development of side effects. All this demands the sort of medical and para-medical personnel which is usually entirely lacking, the more so because, in many countries, the patients demand women doctors (although this fact has not been established, yet, by any sort of sociological survey). It would hardly be surprising if, in countries where too many rings had been fitted, a lot of women began demanding to have them removed, there being not enough doctors to control it all properly.

All the same, it does seem to me a tenable argument that even if, for technical reasons, we had to abandon intra-uterine birth control methods tomorrow, and use something else instead (the laboratories are working on this now), the campaigns being conducted at present will at least have had the merit of setting in motion a kind of collective evolution in attitude, which it really seems likely will never be reversed. It has often been said that one of the main grounds for resistance to change is the fear of being out of step. These campaigns are just what is making possible a modification of group habits, instead of merely influencing individuals, because they bring out into the open, by means of discussion, a problem which individuals when left alone confront with personal prejudice, vacillation and the whim of the moment. In the last resort, it is this transformation in public opinion which counts above all.

To deal, finally, with the purely demographic part of M. Brand's paper, it seems to me that one really can say that tendencies are in process of changing. But it is no good having any illusions about the speed at which the movement may develop simply because it has built up a certain momentum so far.

That is the first point. The second one concerns those global growth models to which M. Brand so often referred. He said, in his paper, that the capital-coefficient is a useful instrument. I agree with him there. Right enough, such calculations are based on entirely abstract hypotheses and people are quite rightly warning us all the time against the idea that all the problems of the under-developed countries can be solved in terms of pounds, shillings, and pence. We are all agreed that mere financial bookkeeping will not suffice. All the same, to go to the other extreme, as so often happens nowadays, does seem to me equally mistaken. Even if it is not lack of capital alone which hampers development, you still cannot deny the importance of capital. Often, when people take this line they are trying to find a way of avoiding the problem of external aid which was mentioned at the end of the paper. To evaluate global supplies is a necessary operation, if only because it will give us any idea of what is being done in relation to what ought to have been done. No analysis of this is possible without some extensive breaking down of the data.

At the same time, to my mind, to evaluate the needs of the under-developed countries solely in terms of capital is only partially to cover the problem. We ought to try to go further than that and attempt, for example, to introduce a variable population figure into the growth models thought up so far by Harrod-Domar, Ichimura, Chenary, Ranis and Fei, Bruno and Goldberger, and others. We do have models of possible future populations for all countries: for instance, the United Nations have had some made. We could very well write further calculations into these, calculations such as all those who set up growth models will be familiar with. Thus we might hope to achieve something we have been cheated of so far: the integration of population variations into economic models.

Such calculations are of mixed interest. It may lie in the evaluation of the external aid a certain country with a certain demographic growth would need in order to achieve a certain *per capita* consumption, or even to attain a stage of development where it would be self supporting, that is to say, not need external aid.

When you are making this kind of calculation, you become aware that for many of the under-developed countries, in which the rate of savings rarely goes beyond 70 per cent of the net income, the annual population growth rate is 3 per cent, and the national interest rate on investments is 40 per cent (which means a capital-coefficient of 2·5, to put it at an optimistic level) and that these factors do not possibly allow of the *per capita* consumptions growing at 2 per cent per annum so long as investments represent at least 12 per cent of the national income. For the economy to be able to reach a state of internally-determined expansion, the first thing necessary is that the investment rate should be of this order. Few developing countries can, in actual fact, afford as of now to withdraw from their already inadequate *per capita* consumption such a high proportion of the national revenue for investment.

Equally interesting would be to find out what conditions would make it possible (after 'take-off') to maintain growth without relying on external aid, so that these countries might master their own problems. In other words, what variables can be relied on for this objective to be achieved? It will soon be seen, if you make such calculations, that needs are initially much higher than the capital which is actually being put at the disposal of the undeveloped countries.

But other conditions are indispensable too: there has to be a marked reduction in demographic growth, the inhabitants must greatly increase their personal savings, capital must be made to produce more, there must be some adjustment of the share of investments amongst the various sectors (more for a fixed social capital than for private consumption). It seems to me that it would be possible to pursue our calculations further than we have done so far in order to find out what, for each country, would be the necessary conditions for overall expansion, both demographic and economic. Doubtless the result would show that this would not be too difficult an achievement for some countries – Mexico, for instance – but much more so for others, such as Bolivia or Peru. We shall have to make an effort to regionalize our calculations. Then it will be seen that there is no such thing as under-development but simply under-developed countries, each of them needing different treatment.

Comments

G. M. Carstairs

I propose to speak about Dr Brand's paper which I read with great interest and profit. First of all I would like to say what a pleasure it is to speak of the paper of a distinguished colleague from Leiden. As he must know, Scotland has had many centuries of indebtedness to Dutch universities, not least to Leiden. It was three pioneers from Leiden who founded our medical school here in Edinburgh more than two centuries ago.

Dr Brand reminded us, in clear and forceful argument, of two of the most disturbing sociological problems in the world today. One is the inescapable demographic consequences of the trends of mortality already well established in this century. He reminds us that the population structure is such that population increase is going to go on at a rate which economic change cannot fully contend with; and it is a chill reminder that the disproportion between the well-off countries and the poor countries is likely to be exaggerated in the next decade. He talked particularly about the economic implication of the demographic trends to which he drew our attention. Dr Tabah, on the other hand, has talked about the possibility of changing these demographic trends, and has stressed the other side of the situation at which Dr Brand merely hinted – the possibility that fertility control is not only theoretically but practically obtainable. I thought that one of the most interesting points which Dr Tabah made was that a completely new factor enters the situation when women *know* that fertility can be controlled, that it has become not a theoretical but a practical possibility. This is comparable with the introduction of medical advances which control killing diseases. Once it is known that a killing disease need no longer kill one's children the situation is transformed, and mothers are no longer going to be content to tolerate the death of young children. I think Dr Tabah is quite right, that we are entering an era when mothers are going to cease to tolerate the inevitability of reproduction beyond the limits which they consider desirable.

I propose to speak particularly of another element of the theme at which Dr Brand merely hinted. What is going to be the consequence for human experience and for human behaviour if these trends of increase continue (as he suggested they are very likely to continue) and what is going to be the implication for human experience if the discrepancy between the rich and the poor continues to widen?

I was asked to address myself to this point recently and, after studying
the literature, I had to admit that there is very little clear information
from observations of human behaviour because, in general changes of
this order in the size of human populations take so long, and so many
variables enter into the scene, that it is hard to relate changes in
behaviour to any one particular factor such as that of population
size. It is much simpler with animal studies and there have been
some interesting studies of animal populations which have been
allowed to increase to intolerable levels of intensity. Rats, for
example: John Calhoun at the National Institute of Health in
Bethesda has published studies of the behaviour of rat colonies which
have been allowed to increase beyond the limits of normal rat expectation, where he found that in a very few generations, when the population became oppressively crowded, there was a striking breakdown
in rat behaviour, a breakdown which interfered with even such fundamental things as eating and drinking, with patterns of sexual behaviour, sexual dominance, and even sexual receptivity on the part
of the females. But to my mind perhaps the most striking of all the
interruptions of normal behaviour that he demonstrated was in
mothering. Here you might think is an instinctive behaviour pattern
that would be hard to alter, but in a few generations of rats exposed
to the oppressive stimulation of too many social conflicts, maternal
behaviour deteriorates. For example, when a rat's nest is disturbed
the mother rat will pick up the young and carry them gently one at
a time to a place of safety till they are all assembled there, and this
simple behaviour pattern became disorganized, in the overcrowded
rat communities, to such a degree that in two successive experiments
86 per cent and 96 per cent of all the litters in a crowded pen died
before reaching maturity. Some male rats developed into – I was
going to use a figurative term, and say psychopaths; they were certainly deviants in terms of rat society, they broke the rules, even the
crudest rules, of rat behaviour. These rats would attack and attempt
to have intercourse with females whenever they could, furtively
pouncing whenever they were out of the gaze of the more dominant
males in the community. They were hanging about the fringe of
society, grabbing and stealing. They even exhibited cannibalistic
behaviour. At the opposite extreme certain other rats assumed a
tyrannical control of larger and larger harems which they defended
against the weaker males. There are certain similarities between these
observations and others by Paul Leyhausen, an Austrian ethologist,
on cats. He started by watching cats in domestic back yards and
cities, and found that there were regularities to be observed in the
daily life patterns of domestic cats. Later, he observed pets in
confined and overcrowded surroundings and he described vividly

how the normal routine of cat life became severely disturbed. Perhaps the most striking phenomenon he observed there was the
emergence of tyrants, who dominated and bullied all the weaker cats;
and at the opposite extreme some weak cats became social outcasts
who were constantly the victims of attack. He ended his description
by contrasting the atmosphere in a normal colony of cats with room
to range, and this overcrowded pen in which there was an almost
continual hissing and growling, and never did the cats seem able to
relax and take their ease. It is, of course, a very long way from these
lower orders to any guess-work about human behaviour, but the gap
is a little less if one thinks of primates such as chimpanzees. Here,
curiously enough, the observation on the pathological situation long
anteceded the observation on the natural situation. When one thinks
of accounts of chimpanzee behaviour one turns at once to Sir Solly
Zuckerman's book of 1932 on the sexual life of primates (which was
said to have been advertised in London as the 'sex life of bishops').
Sir Solly Zuckerman observed chimpanzees and described their
behaviour very carefully, objectively – and quite wrongly – because
what he described was the behaviour of chimpanzees confined in
zoos, in a totally unnatural situation, with many more chimpanzees
to the area in which they have to live than is ever the case in the
wild. It is only within the last decade that observations have begun
to come in from observations of chimpanzees and other primates in
the wild state. There are two striking contrasts. One is that they are
not perpetually preoccupied with sexual mounting as Solly Zuckerman's apes were, but they have a mating season, as shown by the
greater frequency of births at certain parts of the year; and the other
is that they exhibit much less fighting in the natural state. This is a
particular instance of a very general observation of animals in the
wild which the ethologists have amply documented – the limiting of
aggressive behaviour by the concept of territory. There are many
species whose behaviour changes when they transgress the limits of
their home territory. Within that territory if an intruder comes they
will fight and win. When they go beyond their own territory they will
fight and lose against the same opponent, because it seems that to
fight on one's home ground is as important for an animal as it is for a
football team, and conveys some of the same advantages. This pro-
tective device is lost, of course, in conditions of overcrowding or
spatial limitation, so that fights will occur and the usual natural
expedient of retreat and exit from the situation is denied to the animal.
This reminds one of another observation by Dr Barnett, the zoologist,
in Glasgow University who notes that when rats in confined spaces
engage in combats the victor emerges, not only having made his
point and secured his ascendancy in the status hierarchy of the little

society, but he seems even to gain physically, and the vanquished seems to lose something physically. One can infer some metabolic process associated with the experience of defeat. Barnett points out that frequently you find dead rats that have experienced several defeats, but on post-mortem there is no obvious mutilation or severe loss of blood. Their death is probably something to do with the adrenal system, the response of the body to threat and danger, to fear and anger.

All these, however, are animal observations. What relation have they, if any, to human experience? One has to be speculative, but I think there are some analogies one can draw with human societies which are compelled to live with an excess of interaction, with individual interaction, and with an apparent inability to escape from the field. Dr Brand has reminded us that in the developing countries the rate of increase is twice as great in the cities, as in the country as a whole. One has only to think of the *barrios* on the fringe of great South American cities to be reminded of the squalid conditions under which these slum dwellers are living. You might say that although squalid and overcrowded, compelling an excessive amount of interaction, these conditions still offer a possibility of escape from the scene; and yet we know that the conditions of extreme poverty are such that there is an imprisonment imposed by poverty. It seems to the people in that situation that there is no alternative, no way out of the situation. One is reminded of those exhausted rats which have been defeated morally in repeated encounters and which succumb to their wounds even without physical injury. One is reminded too of the irritability of animals in captivity.

There is also some little evidence from human observation, particularly from two distinguished ethologists, Lorenz and Leyhausen, both of whom had the opportunity of watching human males in overcrowded conditions and captivity because they both spent several years in prisoner of war camps during the Second World War. They have commented on the change which comes over human behaviour under these conditions. One thing they both remark on is an excess of irritability. Lorenz, with typical gusto, said that the pimple on a man's nose, the accent with which he spoke, a trivial mannerism, could become unbearably aggravating, and the only solution which he found was to walk away from his fellow inmates and stand at the barbed wire looking out into the empty country until the irritation wore off. Other evidence has been advanced from conditions of even greater abnormality, by survivors of concentration camps; and they too, reported rather sadly that many of what we regard as the finer human attributes tended to be lost after months and years of contending with such extreme conditions. It was a very rare individual indeed, who could retain his sense of values and of conduct. On the whole, people became increasingly selfish, sometimes appallingly egocentric in their struggle for survival. A very meagre compensation, pointed out by a Dr Cohen, was that in those conditions psychosomatic disorders tended to disappear. (When he followed up some of his fellow survivors in civilian life he found many had developed peptic ulcers again in peacetime!) I mention these implications simply to underline the hints which Dr Brand gave us about the consequences for human experience of these population trends. One wonders what pitch of alarm the world as a whole must reach before social and political decisions are taken of the radical kind which Dr Brand pointed out would be necessary if the gap between poverty and riches is to be diminished.

General Discussion

W. Brand, W. Brass, G. M. Carstairs,
C. Clark, and A. Sauvy

The discussion consisted largely of two extensive contributions
(Sauvy and Clark) and a brief reply by Brand, together with a few
points arising from Carstair's prepared comments. Because of the
rather debate-like nature of the discussion it is presented in a similar
form here.

Sauvy started his comments by pointing out that the capital-
coefficient had been shown to be a somewhat misleading measure
when used as in Brand's paper. In particular he pointed out that a
single capital-coefficient cannot be applied both to population and
economic growth. In fact the use of this approach by the United
Nations in 1951 had led to considerable errors.

He then turned to the question of intervention to limit population
growth, and agreed with Brand and Tabah that it would not provide
an immediate solution although undoubtedly we should conduct
research into methods of population control. Whatever happened
there would be a considerable rise in population over at least one
generation. He pointed out that in some countries avoiding a rise in
population would require a fall in the birth rate so sharp as to be
absolutely absurd.

However, in Hong Kong, Singapore, Formosa, and Malaysia we
had observed over the last 12 to 15 years a quite extraordinary
phenomenon. Virtually alone of all the countries of the world, the
birth rate in these four countries has fallen. And immediately teams
of demographers, sociologists, doctors and so on went to these
countries to study this phenomenon. The statistics for these countries
are good and it is remarkable to find how the low birth rate has been
accompanied by a very low infant mortality. The infant mortality in
Singapore, for instance, is lower than that in Portugal or indeed in
parts of France. Sauvy suggested that this correlation between the
fall in the birth rate and a fall in infant mortality was highly significant,
especially as the fall in the birth rate commenced before any extensive
attempts at population control by, for instance, sterilization had
taken place.

These findings were consistent with studies which had been done
earlier by the Institut National d'Etudes Démographiques on
eighteenth century France. These discovered that the fall in population appeared to take place when some consideration for the child

as a person had come to enter people's consciousness. Sauvy suggested that with the fall in infant mortality children had ceased to be in a sense unimportant, and with the increasing consideration for their welfare had come a decline in the overall birth rate. He suggested that this was at least a possible line of enquiry and might prove an effective attack on the population problem; the active cultivation of the love of the child might paradoxically lead to a fall in the birth rate. At any rate this was a hypothesis worthy of further research which might prove an effective and humane technique of population control.

Clark took up many of Brand's points, commencing by saying that far from there being a danger of a world shortage of agricultural products or metals his sympathies were with the sellers of these goods. He claimed that technical displacement is going on at such a pace that there is little danger of such a world shortage. Indeed he found it somewhat curious that people were urgently demanding more world agricultural production on the one hand and on the other complaining that the exporters of agricultural products were obtaining steadily deteriorating terms of trade. However, at present the improvements in agricultural technology are taking place mainly in advanced countries. Clark pointed out that over the last few years he had constantly revised downwards his estimate of the amount of land required to keep someone fed. By American standards (which were probably over-generous) we now require about 2,000 sq. metres per person, and if our eating habits were those of the Japanese we could manage with a very much smaller amount of land.

Clark went on to discuss the work of de Vries, mentioning first how de Vries had arrived at what was now a generally accepted conclusion: that in a subsistence agricultural society, population and agricultural production must increase at approximately the same rate. It is only in a commercial society that there is any possibility of a discrepancy upwards or downwards in the rates of growth. Secondly de Vries categorized all the Asian countries by a composite agricultural measure, converting all agricultural production to kilograms of rice economic equivalent – not calorific equivalent but economic equiva- lent. In this way he was able to measure the stages of economic growth of subsistence countries, and Clark had found this technique ex- tremely fruitful. He was also very interested in de Vries' estimate that Asia could increase her rice production enormously in the next 40 years. Whereas de Vries was looking forward to the desalination of ocean water, Clark was rather more doubtful. The minimum cost at present for desalination of ocean water is 8 cents per cubic metre, whereas irrigation farmers are reluctant to pay more than about $1\frac{1}{2}$ or at most $2\frac{1}{2}$ cents. It follows that either food prices would have to be very much higher, or some entirely new process for desalination

is required – which seems thermodynamically impossible. Desalination would seem to be a prospect only for the very distant future.
Finally with regard to de Vries, Clark took up his point that, in a
country where agriculture still occupied half or more of the labour
force, the absolute number of people engaged in agriculture will
continue increasing for the next decade or two. Their absolute number will increase while their relative number declines, and de Vries
claims that we must make plans accordingly. Clark put the idea the
other way round, asking what is the maximum rate at which the non-
agricultural labour force can go up. He suggests that there is considerable evidence that it is possibly as high as 4% per year. At any
rate it lies between 3 and 4 per cent.

Clark then took up Brand's point that an argument for reducing
population growth in under-developed countries was that, although
the poorer countries have a rate of growth of natural product comparable with that of Europe, their rate of growth per head is less. For
Clark this conceals an erroneous assumption that if some population
growth stops, economic growth will go on at the same rate as before.
Clark is doubtful of this assumption, and suggests that there is a
good deal of historical evidence, although of a negative kind, to
indicate that periods of population growth, in due course and with
some time lag, stimulate economic growth. Several French economic
historians have complained that the lack of population growth in
the nineteenth century led to France's late start in industrialization.
Furthermore Clark pointed out that he had some allies among
economic theorists in claiming that economic growth is stimulated
by population growth in industrial countries. In addition to the work
of Hirschmann mentioned in Brand's paper he pointed also to the
work of Everett Hagen.

This led Clark on to consider capital requirements, and here he
agreed entirely with Sauvy. As Sauvy indicated, it is a great mistake
to treat the *marginal* capital output requirement as equal to the
average capital output requirement. In other words Clark claimed
that in many places you can look after increased population with a
much lower capital requirement than you need to start with. Every
process of development has some very large indivisibilities such as
constructing a transport system, an educational system, and so on.
These overheads have to be met whether by a dense or by a sparse
population. Where the population is sparse, as in Africa, it has been
shown that a population density of about 20–30 per square kilometre
is required before development can start at all, that is, before one
can even afford to build a road or clear away the tsetse fly. He
agreed that aiming at $3\frac{1}{2}$ per cent per head growth of real income in
the developing countries is understandable because this is what

Europe has been enjoying. Nevertheless he hoped that sensible eco-nomists would aim for the 1½ per cent rate which India has in fact obtained since 1950, despite many mistakes and contrary to the predictions of many scholars.

Clark went on to consider the income elasticity of demand for food which Brand had placed at about 0·6 for low income levels of $100 to $200 *per capita*. He agreed that this was so in many cases, but work being done in Oxford indicates an extraordinary variability and also a strong demonstration effect on the demand for food. Thus there are the two extremes, on the one hand the Siamese who have a rather low population density but, as a visiting agriculturalist put it, are compulsive eaters and on the other hand the Japanese who, even when fairly well off, still think it is a social duty to live on raw fish and rice. Clark claimed that this abstemiousness on their part played a very important part in accelerating the accumulation of capital and industrial development of Japan.

Finally he came to the question of population growth and savings. He had been doing some work comparing the rate of net savings as a proportion of net national product for a large number of countries over different periods. This study showed that population growth came out as a clearly positive factor; the higher the population growth – other variables being given – the higher the rate of savings. He himself regarded this as a purely empirical fact but claimed that it was supported theoretically by some economists, referring here to the Modigliani/Brumberg theorem which was developed entirely theoretically as a pattern of saving to be expected from a rational population equalizing its welfare on known expectations of earning and retirement. The theorem would support these empirical results. Furthermore the reserve bank of India published in March 1965 the rate of savings in India. In the first years of Indian independent development in the early 1950s the rate of net savings was 5 per cent of net national product. In recent years in spite of all that has gone wrong in India the rate has risen to 9 per cent. This represents a very rapid increase in savings which Clark claimed would not have oc-curred without the Indian population growth. Furthermore, whereas the 5 per cent rate would have allowed very little economic growth, the 9 per cent rate was more hopeful.

Brass took up Carstairs comments and pointed out that human beings become adjusted to conditions in a way which rats and other animals do not. Thus he asked whether problems of overcrowding and their possible mental effects were not a question of the distant rather than the relatively near future, of very much worse conditions than we have at present. He himself believed that the present econo-mic problems of population growth were of overriding importance rather than those Carstairs indicated. In reply Carstairs agreed that human beings were remarkably adaptable but that it took considerable time. The rapidly growing cities of Africa between the 1920s and the 1960s show similar patterns to those of Chicago between the 1860s and 1920s. There are certain similarities in the destruction of social ties and social constraints and in the formation of ethnic subgroups. Furthermore there is considerable similarity in the development of disorganized anti-social behaviour in these two situations, which he claimed have in common that the population, especially the least privileged members, are exposed to a radically different and less supportive social environment.

Brand in his final remarks felt that Tabah's comments were largely supplementary to, rather than critical of, his paper. Despite Tabah's comments on fertility control, he pointed pessimistically to the emphasis on fertility as a sign of manliness in Latin America and in Africa, where there is also a belief in the close association of fertility of women and fertility of the soil. He agreed with the criticisms made of his use of the capital-coefficient, which he regarded purely as a starting point for discussion, and looked forward to studies using it more precisely to improve the sort of exercise he had carried out. He took issue with Clark over the idea that a large amount of investment is initially required to create an infra-structure and that this created a relatively large capital output ratio. In his opinion this represented the worst possible advice for under-developed countries, who are already investing far too much in infra-structure. He instanced the building of roads where there is no traffic, and the practice of pumping money indiscriminately into education. He believed fervently in education as a factor in economic development, but in selective education rather than that found today in Latin America, Asia, and Africa which to him was opposed to development, as it led people away from their basic problem which was agriculture. While agreeing with Clark that the acreage required to produce our food is declining, he pointed out that even in the West the increase in production has only been about 3·1 per cent in recent decades, thus never approaching the 4·8 per cent or at the minimum 4 per cent which is required in the developing countries, especially in view of the very poor level of subsistence they have at present, particularly in terms of proteins and minerals. He turned to the fact that India intends to increase its food production to 120 million tons by 1971 from about 75 million at the present time. While he thought this was feasible by the extension of irrigation, the use of different varieties of wheat and rice and the extensive use of fertilizer, he was still doubtful whether it could be achieved in practice because he doubted whether there was the incentive to produce sufficient food. Illustrative of this point was the fact that while the critical thing was to raise fertilizer production from 400,000 tons to about 4 million tons there were still endless arguments in India whether this should be public or private production. To Brand this was nonsense from an economic point of view. He claimed that ideology should not enter the discussion; all that should matter was the production of fertilizer. All in all he doubted whether sufficient unity could be achieved among the Indian people to produce the food required, although he hoped that he would be proved wrong and Clark would be proved right.

Historical Demography

D.E.C.EVERSLEY
The validity of family and group statistics
as indicators of secular population trends

M.DRAKE
Age at marriage in the pre-industrial West

B.H.SLICHER VAN BATH
Contrasting demographic development
in some parts of the Netherlands
during the depression period of the
seventeenth and eighteenth centuries

with prepared comments by H.J.Habakkuk

CHAIRMAN
E. A. Wrigley

N

D.E.C.EVERSLEY

The Validity of Family and Group Statistics as Indicators of Secular Population Trends

The study of past populations, a branch of history or of demography little more than a decade old, presents unusual features of interest for the methodology of both disciplines. The approach to this type of research seems to have come simultaneously from both sides. Demographers found that certain aspects of their own contemporary in-vestigations would benefit from a comparative backward projection of data in a few advanced countries in which records had been kept for five or ten generations, and which had undergone, for instance, the process of 'demographic transition' which now so largely figures in contemporary sociological thinking.[1] Since usable vital statistics are often lacking in those countries which are of the greatest current interest, and since, in any case, these areas demonstrate stages of economic development in some ways analogous to those obtaining in some western countries hundreds of years ago, the tracing of changes over a long period of time is an integral part of the attempt to test current hypotheses.

For the historian, on the other hand, the approach to the demo-graphy of the past has come from acute dissatisfaction with certain types of explanation of causal relationships in economic and social history. He is no longer content to describe a mere sequence of events: he must know what were the causes and consequences of inportant structural changes. This applies especially to the periods of early industrialization; of the adjustment, in the nineteenth cen-tury, of marital fertility to reduced mortality, and other crucial epochs of secular change. Population change is no longer, as was once thought, merely a parameter: it is seen to be an essential part of the central mechanisms of evolution. The most recent history of non-European countries both serves to assist the historian to ask the right kind of analytical questions about the most distant past, and affords a standard of comparison for the modern demographer.[2]

Historical demography, then, may be defined as a branch of social science. Its techniques are in part borrowed from its parent disciplines – economic history, sociology, statistics – in part evolving in a more specialized way. 'Family Reconstitution', for instance, which was in the first place an attempt to 'recreate the populations of the past,' is by now subject to a set of rules which, though in origin perhaps statistical and sociological, apply only to this one field.

This paper does not seek to justify or explain every aspect of the work that is being done, but will concentrate on one particular problem which is being encountered in work now in progress. This is the question of sub-groups. The definition of the term is conceived in terms of either topographical or social selection – the latter including religious and occupational stratification, and that created by the rules governing marriage and inheritance in *bourgeois* and noble families. The term 'sub-group' is used in contradistinction to the idea of a 'national' population. We must stress here that it does *not* include the study of single parishes or groups of parishes which are being investigated either as a methodological exercise or as part of a national sample.[3] We can characterize this type of selection by saying that demographic investigations of particular localities are always prefaced by a warning that the findings have no significance except for this area, or when seen in conjunction with other elements of the wider sample.

To continue with the definition then, a topographical sub-group is one which has been chosen because it exhibits some special characteristic, which distinguishes it over a period of time from other elements of the wider population of which it forms part. Usually this involves relative lack of mobility between the locality in question and its neighbours; typically, therefore, it will possess certain island characteristics, whether the area is surrounded by water or by other obstacles such as mountains.[4] In each case the study depends on relatively infrequent inter-marriage between the 'islanders' and their nearest neighbours; the existence of a local (usually autarchic) economy; as well as some ethnic characteristic which provides the parallel with the social sub-groups yet to be described. To select only a few such studies, undertaken for various purposes and including research into demographic characteristics to a greater or lesser extent: Saville's chapter on the South Hams area of Devonshire,[5] Smith's work on the Cocos or Keeling Islanders,[6] and Stycos' investigations in Puerto Rico.[7] These are, respectively, sub-groups of the population of England, of Malaysia, and of the West Indies. (Leaving out the question for the moment whether the degree of 'representativeness' is the same in each case.) Again, the studies of Taiwan[8] are those of an island population of Chinese race, though in this case we are dealing with a much larger sub-group.

The social sub-group is rather different. Three variants may be distinguished: the compact self-segregated or enforced isolate (the North American Hutterite settlements, the Mormons,[9] the Mennonites,[10] the Jews in Europe[11]); the *élite* groups (which can again be sub-divided into local or national, the *bourgeoisie* of Geneva[12] being an example of the former and the British peerage an example of the latter[13]); the dispersed self-selected sub-group, of which the Quakers in England and Ireland may serve as one example, and Asians in Africa as another, and the castes in those societies which maintain them as a primary system of social division.[14]

These different types of investigation are common to historical and modern demographers, to sociologists and anthropologists, to geneticists and political scientists. They are all motivated by the desire to isolate a society which is in some way clearly different from other societies, and which can serve as a basis for systematic comparison. The 'purer' the case, the scarcer the records, and the greater the resort to archaeological evidence or oral tradition.[15] Historical demography therefore faces peculiar problems, because practically nothing except written information about births, marriages, and deaths will yield usable material. The majority of the studies mentioned here, therefore, are Western European if they go back more than 200 years, or at any rate relate to emigrant groups emanating from Europe.

The degree to which these various types of sub-group share the characteristics of their host community clearly varies greatly, and is not constant over time even for one group. Isolation may be relatively complete (as in the Cocos Islands) or of the mildest form (the Quakers in the last hundred years). The observed patterns of differentiation are not always susceptible to exact measurement. The survival of a common spoken or written language as the medium of daily communication is one indicator, but its efficacy depends on the extent to which the language of the host community is also known. (Jews spoke Yiddish in Central Europe but also knew modern German, or Polish; Sephardic Jews used Spanish or Portuguese as well as Dutch or English, and later on only the language of their host states.) The Serbs in Brandenburg preserved their Slav language, but were under German administration and spoke German to an increasing extent as a second language.[16] The Dutch Mennonites carried their language with them, but again increasingly adopted that of their environment as they moved from country to country.

Where religion is the decisive factor identifying the sub-group, the degree of isolation will depend on the strictness of the attempts to enforce endogamous rules. In some cases marriage out of the sect meant instant expulsion or even exile (this was generally true of persecuted minorities until the nineteenth century, but survived only sporadically after this). The biological significance of endogamy will depend, of course, on the size of the group involved. It has one sort of significance amongst the 1,000 or fewer Cocos Islanders, and quite another amongst the 2½ million resident Puerto Ricans. If restriction of marriage partners leads to later marriages, or the inability of a high proportion of young people to marry at all, the social consequences of separateness are clearly greater than if the laxity of rules or a high degree of communication between dispersed settlements of the sect or social group leads to more exogamous unions.

Where the identification of the sub-group depends on a social distinction alone, the degree of separateness achieved is also not a uniform factor. Thus, the British aristocracy in Hollingsworth's work is on the one hand clearly defined by a descriptive convention, be-cause both peers and their children are designated in the records as such. Peers, however, could and did marry outside their own class,[17] whereas in France the *ducs et pairs*[18] were much more likely to marry within their own ranks. When this social endogamy was localized, as in Geneva,[19] the chance of marriage is once again drastically reduced, and leads ultimately either to dilution through a change in the rules (and therefore virtually the dissolution of the local aristocracy) or to extinction by emigration or death.[20]

One might therefore conclude that the social or topographical sub-group is rather a bad subject for demographic studies. Its advantages are obvious: manageable size for the limited sort of project which is usually within the means of the research worker in this field, concentrated localized records (as on an 'island' or in the records of the *bourgeoisie*), or centralized or printed records (as with the Quakers and the peerage). Yet these advantages also show the defects. If the group is truly endogamous over a long period of time (say six generations, to make demographic comparisons pos-sible) and small, it is at least highly likely that it will show biological characteristics which make comparison with other populations invalid. None of the studies quoted are in fact of this kind. The Cocos Islanders recruited newcomers from Malaysia, and there was some cross-breeding of races. The Puerto Ricans are an international mixture of varying degrees of combination of Spanish, Negro, Indian, and American parentage. The Quakers received a large number of converts until about 1700, and then lost many, and recruited a good many more. Throughout the eighteenth and nine-teenth centuries their registers continue to record the burials of non-members as well as those who were still members but should not have been by strict rules. An analysis of surnames of brides and bridegrooms, and the compilation of a general index for well over 10,000 marriages studied by Vann and the present writer, suggests a high rate of turnover, Quakers marrying non-Friends were dis-owned or left voluntarily; on the other hand, many others married non-Quakers who were 'convinced' before marriage. The amount of inbreeding was relatively small.[24] The North American Hutterites also recruited from outside by marriage, but were stricter than the Quakers in their internal government.[21]

This kind of criticism, however, is too much influenced by a desire for biological purity derived from the study of animal strains. From the point of view of demographic history, the population under study is adequately defined and limited as belonging to the sub-group – that is living in the island locality, or acknowledged as adhering to the sect, or as being of a noble or *bourgeois* family – at the time the observation was made. This means that demographic studies of such groups will have to ignore, to some extent, the kind of genetic element which might be capable of investigation in a group of the purity of strain associated with laboratory-bred flies. Genetic inter-pretations are not excluded, since at any one time the great majority of peers, for instance, or of Cocos Islanders, or of Quakers (at least until recently) are descended from several generations of ancestors in at least one line which belonged to the sub-group.[22] Unfortun-ately, few studies seem as yet to have been made of anything except the proportion of marriages at one time which took place between partners both of whom were at this point inside the group – which is not at all the same thing as saying that they had between them two, four, let alone eight or sixteen ancestors who were all part of that group.[23] Nevertheless, where records are good, as they often are with the peerage, and especially where they include portraits,[24] it is often possible to trace strongly marked characteristics along with other demographic information. But the accent has to be on the 'strongly marked' – like the Hapsburg lip or the Romanoff haemo-philia. Unfortunately less marked characteristics which might have a bearing on vital statistics are much harder to trace. For instance fecundity (as opposed to effective fertility) is really not capable of being statistically interpreted. The reason for this is that the number of conceptions does not bear a constant relationship to live births over time, and that even neo-natal deaths are often omitted from the record. (We infer this from the relative absence of burials in some of the genealogies of children only a few days old, whereas, judging from modern statistics, there ought to be a great many of these in the days of very high infant mortality, which is recorded much more regularly.)

Moreover, investigations into fecundity presuppose knowledge of birth control practice. As Dr Wrigley has shown, it was practised in England early in the eighteenth century,[25] it was known in France, and it was almost certainly the rule in 'polite' circles in most parts of Europe. On present evidence, we believe that it was not widely

practised amongst Quakers until the middle of the nineteenth century, and not amongst the Hutterites to the present day. But corre-
spondingly, amongst the Quakers, true cases of sterility or very low
fertility (that is, where we are quite certain that the parents had no
more children than were recorded) are relatively infrequent, so that
it is unlikely that we shall be able to prove the genetic significance of
these occurrences. (Especially as the best attested cases, where 's.p.'
appears in the records, preclude, in their nature, a further trans-
mission of this characteristic.)

As far as genetic influences on the expectation of life are concerned, these are even more nebulous for groups of the kind we have
described. Apart from the fact that the cause of death is seldom
reported consistently,[26] let alone accurately in the modern medical
sense, the early records contain proportionately too many instances
of decease from violent causes (especially amongst the male aristocracy) and from the killer epidemics which swept through large
populations with little discrimination.

In other words, we are not really disadvantaged by the fact that
our sub-groups are not truly closed populations. However, their
relative isolation, to which reference was made above, which enables
us to identify their members at any point of time, still has many
advantages. For one thing, the possibility of relating demographic
experience to other variables is greatly increased. For an 'island'
community, facts of climate, endemic diseases, nutritional factors
and general environmental conditions may be relatively constant
over a period of time. The occurrence of crises (of subsistence, of
health, of political upheaval, or natural catastrophes) may be clearly
marked in the history of the community and precisely related to life
experience. For the social sub-group, the same applies if it is
localized. This factor will disappear if the group is dispersed, but
social and economic characteristics will remain. To name only a few:
for the peerage in England it may be assumed that all those recorded
were relatively affluent, so that malnutrition or lack of shelter would
play little role in their life expectation. Quakers did not become
ardent teetotallers until the nineteenth century, and we find distillers
and tobacconists in their ranks in the eighteenth. Nevertheless, their
testimony against excessive indulgence was strong from the earliest
days, and it is likely that they drank little alcohol beyond the ale
which was then the common drink in the absence of clean water.
They did not frequent inns except as travellers, and smoked very
little, and they did not serve in the Army or Navy (with very few
exceptions) or fight duels. The Hutterites led the life of agriculturalists
or artisans, as did the Mennonites.

It is often objected, when one speaks of the demographic study of a sub-group, that 'it is not like the rest of the population'. This is a truism. In the demographic sense, the average family does not exist. Recent studies have shown, for instance, that if one divides the current population of Britain into 28 local groupings (regions, conurbations, some sub-regions) and into the Registrar General's 17 socio-economic groups, one finds that the percentage of households with three or more children varies from 3 per cent to 15 per cent according to class and region. This reflects a multitude of variations in age at marriage, terminal education age, housing conditions, fertility, and mortality. It is therefore not meaningful to say that, for instance, the Westmorland Quakers of the late eighteenth century are not like the whole of the English population. No subgroup could meet this criterion, however chosen, except a sample of the whole drawn in a scientific manner. What is much more likely is that this particular group would in many ways resemble other people in Westmorland, and more particularly a similar social stratum (in this case, farmers, artisans, and professional men, but not labourers or aristocrats).[27]

The important methodological point, then, is not to try to find sub-groups which are in any way 'representative' of an average population, but to locate as many different groups as possible about whom anything at all can be said with more certainty than about the population as a whole; to try to say specifically what were the social, economic or biological characteristics of the sample, and then to show how both descriptive data and the demographic variables differ from any larger aggregates we may have.

If one takes a synoptic view of the studies already completed, one is immediately struck by the absence of the really poor. The spectrum runs from the respectable tradesman to the royal families. This is only what we would expect, and the question is whether this defect will preclude any future attempt to give a wider interpretation to the findings of successive studies. Peller,[28] in describing the European ruling families, compared their perinatal mortality in successive centuries with that observed in the General Hospital in Vienna between 1915 and 1923. The point of this demonstration is to underline that even between 1500 and 1699 the ruling families suffered fewer perinatal losses than the ordinary population in the twentieth century. Now, although the Vienna hospital had three 'divisions' (for patients of various degrees of affluence), the greater part of the mothers must have come from poor families – the middle classes still had their confinements at home in those days. Moreover, the period is one of war and post-war deprivation and even starvation. It is therefore surprising to note the absence of any really basic differences between the nobility of the earlier period and the poor

Viennese of the twentieth century, and if one takes twins (rather
fewer cases) the difference is even smaller. Peller also compares his
nobility with the tables for white Americans, and there again the
two populations are not so far apart,[29] the European nobles' children
in 1800-49 having about the same chance of surviving to fifteen
years as the white Americans in 1900-2.

In general, as Hollingsworth's work in the British peerage suggests,
mortality amongst the select groups moves in the same direction as
that of the population as a whole (where we know this), and this is
what we would expect. It would be dangerous to extrapolate back-
wards by inferring life expectations for the population as a whole by
assuming that these are always worse than those of the select groups,
in a constant proportion. What is likely, however, is that the fluctuations in mortality which are observable in sub-groups are also
reflected in the surrounding population.

Fertility is a slightly different matter. Although, as Henry, Hollingsworth, Peller, and others have shown, all the *élite* groups
experienced a decline in marital fertility rather earlier than the rest
of the population (though to only a small extent in the case of the
European nobility[30]) it would again be dangerous to conclude that
movements of fertility in earlier centuries showed fluctuations which
stand in any fixed relationship to the movements experienced by the
population as a whole.

French studies of local parishes, as well as the Geneva *bourgeoisie*
and the peerage, have already been presented in various studies in
synoptic form, and sometimes material from other researches conducted according to the method of Henry and Fleury is also shown
in a comparative manner.[31] This is no doubt legitimate, especially
where we are dealing with single parishes which are comparable if
only because the nature of the evidence is the same (the registers of
the Catholic church). If one includes social sub-groups, this is
sometimes unobjectionable[32] but if one describes fertility or mortality
it is possible that differences in the nature of the material make a
simple consolidation of tables a hazardous business.

Probably the best way of dealing with this situation is to present
statistical material in this comparative form only where the bases of
the comparison can be related to the differences between the populations under review, but otherwise can be said to be similar in reliability, completeness, and statistical methods used in calculating the
data. This requires a good deal of discipline on the part of the
researcher. There is a great temptation to use one's own methods,
especially in dealing with new types of data. Yet the existence of the
French (Henry/Fleury) method now makes it imperative to stan-
dardize presentation to a large extent. In other words, the categories

of modern demography need to be applied to historical materials. To give some examples: 'the age at marriage in the early eighteenth century' could mean: 'the average age of all males known to have married according to the usages of the Society of Friends 1700–49', or: 'the average age at first marriage of all French Canadian men and women who were born between 1701 and 1750', or: 'the age of marriage of all women who died ever-married in Sweden after 1750'. As a general rule, comparisons between populations, as opposed to those based on different periods in the same population, become hazardous where there is some obvious selectivity in the date. This has been pointed out by Hopkins with regard to the Roman tomb-stone inscriptions.[33] It applies to the 'Allegations of Marriage' cited by Chambers, which were for a long time the only useful information on English ages at marriage (because they were drawn from that small section of the population which used marriage licences).[34]

Perfection may, of course, be driven too far. For instance it has been objected that the Quaker material is not comparable with Anglican data because we have, in the case of the Society of Friends, birth records rather than baptisms. This means that certain children who died very young tend to be recorded in Quaker registers where they may have been omitted in Anglican records because they did not reach the baptismal font. But this sort of objection is not really valid. It means, as with all historical material, that individual pecu-liarities must be allowed for before the material is presented in its final form. It is a case of allowing, when evaluating Anglican registers, for a greater degree of under-registration of births, and correcting infant mortality rates so as to take into account the fact that babies were often many weeks or even months old before they were bap-tized, so that not all deaths within a year of baptism are strictly speaking infant deaths. These inconsistencies are, as it were, internal to each set of records, and they extend into the modern statistical period.[35] The peculiar Quaker nomenclature in the calendar, which forbade the use of the heathen names of months and makes it difficult in retrospect to identify whether 20th of the 1st month 1740 really means 1740 or 1741 (which we assume it must have done before the calendar reform of 1752), does not invalidate exploitation, but means careful editing of the raw material, even for comparisons between earlier and later Quaker registers.

The best way of looking at the place of the sub-group in historical demography is to assume that it is part of a continuous spectrum of possibilities at each epoch of the world population history. Today, we use model life tables to indicate the sort of population which may be represented by any more or less complete set of vital statistics.[36] That is to say, if, for any given group of people, we have only the age structure of one census date or some current birth and death statistics, we can calculate into what general model of life experience these partial data will fit. These life tables range from those applicable to an advanced 'Western society' with low birth and death rates right through the age structure, represented by something which looks much like an age square with a small pyramidal roof on top, to the broad-based and quickly tapering pyramid of a primitive population with high birth and death rates. The shape of the figure is determined by death rates, the width of each band, given the death rate, by the fertility of the population. In the past (and indeed at present) sub-groups within any given population can show as large a variety of life experience as any disparate set of nations today. For France, it is now possible to set side by side, in the eighteenth century, the *ducs et pairs*, the neighbouring Geneva *bourgeoisie*, and the parishes of Normandy. Amongst the first, the mean age of first marriage of males was 23·6 in 1700–49,[37] for Geneva it was 31·9 ± 1·5,[38] at Crulai it was 28·0.[39] Similar comparisons can be made for England (the Peerage, the Quakers, Colyton). With the help of a computer it will no doubt soon be possible, for any of these sub-groups, to construct a quasi-census at any given point, and indeed we already have a variety of early English census-type lists[40] to help us in this reconstruction at a fixed point of time. But even without this, the fragmentary rates which emerge from the study of sub-groups (infant mortality, expectation of life of cohorts) will enable us to fit these data into a framework of modern standards of comparison.[41]

With this procedure, the question of 'representativeness' takes on a different significance. Instead of hypothesizing about averages, we make surmises about the composition of the total population. Thus, we need no longer wonder whether the experience of life of a male earl was 10, 15 or 20 years greater than that of a 'husbandman' or an 'average Englishman'. Instead, we could ask what proportion of families with various given sets of vital statistics would be required to make up a total population which experienced certain assumed rates of increase (or decrease). There is now much more unanimity than there was a few years ago about the size of the population of England in the days of Gregory King, and we have the early nineteenth century censuses, including the age structures of 1821 and 1841. Much work has been devoted[42] to the attempt to reconstruct the birth and death rates that would have produced the survivors of 1821 and 1841, thus reaching back half way across the gap of ignorance between King and the censuses. The more sub-groups which provide data over a large part of the pre-census and pre-registration period that we investigate, both topographically and socially, the more feasible it becomes to make statements relating to the whole. A total given growth rate is made up in effect of the sectional rates of natural increase and decrease. A 'ducal' pattern of marriage at 28, an expectation of life of 45 years at birth, and an average marital fertility of 4·7 children might apply to 0·01 of the population. A 'Quaker' combination of marriage at 26, life expectation of 40, and 6·3 children might apply to 20 per cent, and so on.[43] This is likely to be, in the early stages of the exercise, rather a hazardous game, since each completed partial investigation will tend to produce yet another basic pattern. One has to treat this research as a succession of approximations.

Yet this is a more valid approach than the attempt to establish 'representative national rates'. Since ultimately the observed changes will have to be tied to changes in economic activity, social structure, and environmental experience, it is only right to link the data to groups which have identifiable combinations of experience. Even in recorded times, the varieties of local and sectional rates was so great that the well-known national series are quite misleading. Infant mortality in 1850 varied from over 300 in many crowded districts to below 100 in salubrious suburbs, and for 'sub-groups' in our sense the variation must have been larger still. It is already evident, in quite fragmentary calculations, that the Quakers outside London lost only about one child in ten in infancy, even in the eighteenth century. To investigate 'the reasons for the fall in infant mortality' from 1600 to 1960 requires the local and sub-group study if it is not to be based on rather general literary evidence.

It is clear, on the other hand, that all series will exhibit certain common features, and these will be as valuable as their dissimilarities. It is beyond dispute that age-specific death rates have fallen dramatically. The question is: when did this fall begin, when was it fastest, when and where did it slow down? If all England had had the death rates of London in the early eighteenth century or Liverpool in 1820, there would have been no population problem and perhaps no England. The cessation of the plague and then the smallpox on the one hand, and the influence of industrial living and working conditions, the environmental improvements of the nineteenth century, and the influence of war periods on the other, will be visible to a greater or lesser extent in all sub-groups. Whether the same will be true of natural catastrophes remains to be seen – and almost certainly the middle class and upper income groups were more or less immune against economic crises, though not perhaps against the epidemics which may have resulted from them.

Similarly, the restriction of fertility which, as we now know, has a continuous history over at least 250 years, applied sooner or later to most groups. The question of the 'why' will be more easily solved once we know the 'where' and 'when' and 'by whom'.

What are the prospects for the study of sub-groups? As far as this country is concerned, the peerage is complete. The study of other families with genealogical records has been started in places but awaits a much more massive onslaught on the records of the Society of Genealogists.[44] The Quakers are well under way, but so far as we know no other denomination has as yet begun to look at its records in this way. The material exists, for example, for the Congregationalists, though it is probably much less good than that for the Quakers.

The study of geographical isolates is less profitable in the British Isles, partly because they are hard to find. But there are many upland and coastal areas which might repay study. The Scottish possibilities are probably limited, and Wales suffers from a paucity of names from the point of view of facilitating reconstruction. An exception might be the English-speaking south of Pembrokeshire, which was in many ways a geographical and ethnic isolate until fairly recent times. Dr Rosemary Harris is at present studying the population and economy of Rathlin Island, off the north coast of Ireland, for which there are records for several hundred years, and this may yield some comparison with Arensberg and Kimball's earlier study of County Clare which, however, contained little demographic material. For the rest, the study of relatively closed populations may well be possible. A country which numbered less than ten million people on 60,000 square miles, of whom a tenth were in London and another fifth massed into urban agglomerations, will yield settlement patterns of a recognizable kind. Whether parish groups with marked social and economic characteristics survived into the era of record-keeping is yet to be discovered.

Meanwhile many other kinds of family and group statistics remain to be exploited. Each completed study can only add to our total knowledge of the past. Completeness in historical records is a welcome feature, but it is not a condition for successful exploitation. We are fortunate if we know both the age at marriage of both parents, and the number of their offspring. But records which yield only ages at marriage add to our total knowledge of the determinants of nuptiality, complete lists of children tell us about family size, and mere sequences which might lack both beginning and end can add to our investigations on birth intervals. Many series have been constructed to establish mortality patterns, based on age at death,[45] and though there are serious objections to this kind of calculation, it is possible to obtain useful approximations in this way provided the selection of deaths itself was not too biased.

Though some of Peller's work was published as early as 1943, the reconstruction of the demography of the past through the medium of records of sub-groups is little more than ten years old. Large strides in methodology have been made, and results already achieved encourage research workers to try more ambitious schemes of exploitation.

Many years ago, Gustav Schmoller suggested that the social scientist should proceed by mapping out large areas of desired information required to make and test hypotheses (the *Grundriss*). Individual pieces of research could then fill the categories in the general matrix one by one, until the whole stood revealed. This method still seems applicable in the field of demography. Each investigation of a sub-group, of whatever kind, can be used to deepen our knowledge of the whole subject. The important qualification is that one must not claim very much for each such attempt. Above all, one must be very careful to describe the group with great exactness in terms of its relationship to the whole population: in time, in space, in the social and economic hierarchy.

ACKNOWLEDGMENTS. I wish to record helpful criticisms provided by F. A. Bailey and R. T. Vann.

Notes and References

1 P. Hauser and O. D. Duncan (eds.), *The Study of Population* (Chicago 1959) pp. 93–6.
   J. Boute, *La demographie de la branche indo-pakistaine d'Afrique* (Louvain 1965).
   W. Petersen, 'The Demographic Transition in the Netherlands', *Amer. Soc. Rev.*, **25** (1960) 334.

2 This link is illustrated by the fact that some of the most important work in the field of historical demography has been undertaken by modern demographers and sociologists, and by the increasing participation of historians in the work of the International Union for the Scientific Study of Population.

3 E. A. Wrigley, 'Family Limitation in pre-Industrial England', *Econ. Hist. Rev.*, 2nd Series, **19**, 1 (1966).
   E. A. Wrigley (ed.), *Introduction to English Historical Demography* (London 1966) pp. 96ff. and Appendix pp. 269ff.

4 E. A. Wrigley (ed.) *Introduction to English Historical Demography* Chap. 2, p. 26ff.

5 J. Saville, *Rural Depopulation in England and Wales*, 1851–1951 (London 1957).

6 T. E. Smith, 'The Cocos-Keeling Islands: A Demographic Laboratory', *Population Studies*, **14**, 2 (1960).

7 J. M. Stycos, *Family and Fertility in Puerto Rico* (New York 1955)
   R. Hill, J. M. Stycos and K. Back, *The Family and Population Control* (Chapel Hill, N.C., 1959).

8 R. Freedman *et al.*, 'Fertility Trends in Taiwan, Tradition and Change', *Population Studies*, **16**, 3 (1963) 219–36.

9 For the Hutterites:
   W. A. Lessa and G. C. Myers, 'Population Dynamics of an Atoll community', *Population Studies*, **15**, 3 (1962).
   J. W. Eaton and A. J. Mayer, 'The Social Biology of very high Fertility', *Human Biology*, **25** (1953).
   J. W. Eaton and A. J. Mayer, *Man's Capacity to Reproduce, The Demography of a Unique Population* (New York 1954).
   C. Tietze, 'Reproductive Span and Rate of Reproduction among Hutterite Women', *Fertility and Sterility*, **8** (1957).
   Mindel C. Sheps, 'An Analysis of Reproductive Patterns in an American Isolate', *Population Studies*, **19**, 1 (1965).
   For the Mormons:
   W. H. Grabill, C. V. Kiser and P. K. Whelpton, *The Fertility of American Women* (New York 1958).
   For the Appalachian Fundamentalists:
   G. F. de Jong, 'Religious Fundamentalism, Socio-Economic Status and Fertility Attitudes in the Southern Appalachians', *Demography*, **2** (1965).

10 'Mennoniten', in special issue of *Archiv. für Sippenforschung* (Limburg/Lahn) **28**, 8 (November 1962)

11 Slicher van Bath *et al.*, *Voorloopige Systematische Bibliografie van de Nederlandse Demografische Geschiedenis* (Wageningen 1962), contains a number of references to material about the Jewish population of Holland as sources for demographic history. British Jewry presents particular difficulties to the demographic researcher, at least before civil registration, which were first discussed in detail by a select Committee of the House of Commons in 1833 (Evidence of Isaac Goldsmid). (BPP 1833 vol. 14.) In Germany, there was at one time a journal devoted to Jewish demography: *Zeitschrift für Statistik der Juden* (from 1923).

12 L. Henry, *Anciennes Familles Genévoises, étude demographique, XVIe – XXe siècle* (INED, Paris, 1956).

13 T. H. Hollingsworth, 'The Demography of the British Peerage', Supplement to: *Population Studies*, **18**, 2 (1964).

14 J. Boute (see Note 1).
   L. S. S. O'Mally, *Indian Caste Customs* (Cambridge 1932), for the customs of the Kulin Brahmins.

15 The question of what constitutes a 'group' for the purpose of research is constantly raised by social anthropologists. See for instance S. F. Nadel, *Foundations of Social Anthropology* (London 1951), p. 75ff. Also (ed. Gluckman) *Closed Systems and Open Minds* (Edinburgh 1964) p. 185, where the author refers back to

George Homans' *The Human Group* (1951) – a sociological work by an eminent historian of medieval England. It would appear that 'separateness' is in part physical, in part biological, in part psychological. No single definition of sub-groups can meet every case.

16 Frido Metsk, *Der Kurmaerkisch–Wendische Distrikt* (Bautzen 1965).

17 See Note 13.

18 Claude Levy and L. Henry, 'Ducs et pairs sous l'ancien régime, characteristiques demographique d'une caste', *Population*, **15**, 5 (1960).

19 L. Henry (see note 12) p. 66, note 2.

20 T. S. Ashton, *Economic History of England: The Eighteenth Century* (London 1955).

21 There are many other historical or recent studies of sub-groups illustrating one or another of the problems raised here, for example: of Ukrainians in Canada, of the Shakers and Amish people in North America, the Indians in Fiji, Jews in Australia, Chinese in Indonesia, and so on. In most cases, the authors have attempted to compare *a.* different generations of the same sub-group in the chosen locality, *b.* the sub-group with others of the same ethnic or religious affiliation in other environments, *c.* the sub-group with the host community.

22 For some recent genetical investigations of sub-groups see: A. P. Mange, 'Growth and Inbreeding of a Human Isolate', *Human Biology*, **36** (1964). J. L. Hamerton *et al.*, 'Chromosome Investigations of a small Isolated Human Population' (Tristan de Cunha), *Nature* **906** (1965) 4990. A set of definitions of what constitutes isolates can be found in: C. H. Alström and R. Lindelius, 'A Study of Population Movement of nine Swedish Sub-populations in 1800–49 from the Genetical Statistical Viewpoint.' Trns. Odelberg, supplied to *Acta Genetica et Statistica Medica*, **16** (1966). This contains a distance model which is applied to marriage horizons, and the study of offspring of these marriages. See also J. Sutter and J. M. Goux, 'L'aspect demographique des problèmes de l'isolat', *Population*, **16**, 3 (1961). For German work on isolates in relation to demographic characteristics see: D. E. C. Eversley in (ed. E. A. Wrigley) *Introduction to English Historical Demography* (London 1966) p. 73, note 42.

23 For an example of using demographic analysis in genetic work on sub-groups, see: J. Sutter and L. Tabah, 'Méthode mécanographique pour établir la généalogy d'une population. Application a l'étude des Esquimaux polaires', *Population*, **11** (1956). J. Sutter and J. M. Goux (see Note 22).

O

24 For instance:

eds. R. S. Benson *et al.*, *Descendants of Isaac and Rachel Wilson, Photographic Pedigree* (privately printed, Middlesborough, 1949) 4 vols, contains over 1,200 marriages of the descendants of a couple married in 1740, with a high degree of inter-marriage, and the majority of partners illustrated by painted or photographic portraits. These volumes form one of the principal sources for the author's present research on the Quakers. Mr M. Teitelbaum of St. Catherine's College, Oxford, has recently drawn my attention to some work in human and animal genetics which is relevant here. At his suggestion I analyzed the marriages in Benson and found that the marriages between related partners (about 60 out of more than 1200) had a significantly different sex ratio in their offspring. (Unrelated, 110 males per 100 females; related, exactly 100 per 100.) The research at Oxford had suggested that there were biological reasons for this possibility. It is too early to gauge the significance of this kind of work, but clearly the records of sub-groups can be used in this context. Compare D. R. S. Kirby, K. G. McWhirter, M. S. Teitelbaum and C. D. Darlington, 'Hypothesis – a Possible Immunological Influence on Sex Ratio', *Lancet*, 2 (1967) 139.

25 E. A. Wrigley, 'Family Limitation in pre-Industrial England', *Econ. Hist. Rev.* 2nd Series, **19**, 1 (1966).

26 But it is so recorded amongst the Quakers of some areas, notably London in the late eighteenth century, and in this case probably with a fairly high degree of accuracy since there were many good physicians amongst the Society of Friends. We have come across a number of other instances of consistent reports of the cause of death, for example, in the city of Rostock on the Baltic, starting late in the eighteenth century. It is hoped that Professor K. H. Mehlan of the University of Rostock will one day analyze these valuable records of an urban population.

27 A preliminary analysis of the occupations of males in the Society of Friends has been carried out by Mrs Jessie Dicks and Miss Kristin Wood in those Quarterly Meetings which fairly consistently report this detail in their marriage registers. This suggests an almost total absence, at least before 1837, of any common labourers. By far the largest group were the artisans, though it is not usually clear whether those described as tailors, butchers, or weavers were master tradesmen or employees. The other two substantial groups were the merchants and dealers – again with little indication in most cases whether they were in a substantial way of business or just small shopkeepers. The third large group were the yeomen and farmers, whom one may suppose to have been comfortably situated. More difficult are the 'husbandmen' – some authorities suggest that these were, socially, beneath the yeomen, but there is no consistency in this usage, and there are plenty of instances where husbandman

simply means 'tenant farmer'*. There was also a very small group of people described by their professions, or just as 'gentlemen'. All told, the Quakers seem to have included the middle classes in the widest sense, and to have been more seriously unrepresentative of the lower than of the upper strata of society.

*J.C.Atkinson, in *Notes and Queries*, 6th Series, **12**, 363, states: 'Proof that . . . down to the first half of the seventeenth century, the appellation husbandman still distinguished the man of the class next below the yeoman, and that he was literally the holder of the orthodox husband-land consisting of two ox-gangs.' (OED).

28 S. Peller in (eds. D. V. Glass and D. E. C. Eversley) 'Births and Deaths among Europe's Ruling Families since 1500', *Population in History* (London 1965).

29 See Note 28, p. 94.

30 See Note 28, p. 90.

31 L. Henry, see Note 28, p. 454.
P. Deprez, 'Demographic Development of Flanders in the Eighteenth Century', see Note 28, p. 620.

32 Age at first marriage: L. Henry, see Note 31.

33 M. K. Hopkins, 'The Age of Roman Girls at Marriage', *Population Studies*, **18**, 3 (1965).
M. K. Hopkins, 'On the probable Age Structure of the Roman Population', *Population Studies*, **19**, 2 (1966).

34 J. D. Chambers, 'Three Essays on the Population and Economy of the Midlands', see Note 28, p. 332.

35 D. V. Glass, 'A Note on the Under-Registration of Births in Britain in the Nineteenth Century', *Population Studies*, **5** (1951–2).

36 United Nations, Population Division, *Age and Sex Patterns of Mortality: Model Life Tables for Underdeveloped Countries* (New York 1955).
A. J. Coale and P. Demeny, *Regional Model Life Tables and Stable Populations* (Princeton 1966).

37 See Note 18, p. 813.

38 See Note 12, p. 55.

39 See Note 31. Unfortunately this covers a slightly different period.

40 P. Laslett in (ed. E. A. Wrigley) *Introduction to English Historical Demography* (London 1966) Chap. 5.

41 See Note 33.

42 D. V. Glass, see Note 28, pp. 229ff.

43 These figures are, of course, fictitious.

44 A new German study using the genealogical records of *bourgeois* families (*Deutshes Geschlechterbuch*) was inaugurated in 1967 under Professor W. Koellmann of Bochum.

45 See Note 33.

Age at Marriage in the
Pre-Industrial West

Dr E. A. Wrigley has observed that 'the age of men and women at first marriage (is) perhaps the most important single demographic variable in the study of pre-industrial societies.'[1] It is so because, as he noted, 'in societies in which there is little control of conception within marriage this is one of the most important variables bearing upon reproduction rates.'[2] Thus, if the age at marriage is late reproduction rates will be low, if early they will be high, and the degree to which they are early or late will help determine the rate at which a population will grow.

The importance of the age at marriage for population growth in the pre-industrial and early industrial western world has been studied in some detail by both our discussants.[3] If I might again draw on a quotation for support, Professor Habakkuk has written that 'K. H. Connell . . . ascribed the increase of the population of Ireland in the late eighteenth century to a fall in the age at marriage and I attempted to argue that the same was true of England.'[4]

The importance of this for the early economic development of the west, or more particularly of England, will, I think, be apparent to members of the conference. For if a fall in the age at marriage, leading to a rise in fertility, was the mechanism of population growth in England, we are faced with a situation very different from that in the pre-industrial countries of today. The growth of population in the currently under-developed countries is a product of a sharply declining death rate unaccompanied by a fall in the birth rate. This fall in the death rate is largely due to the impact of Western medical science, supported in some areas by large shipments of food. The United States, for example, is now said to be feeding *one* out of every *eight* Indians. Furthermore, this change in the death rate has come about largely without any social or economic changes in the pre-industrial countries that are likely to generate a greater rate of economic growth. Thus, to turn to India again, it has been suggested that the output of Indian agriculture per acre has risen only 5 per cent in the last fifty years as against 95 per cent in the United States.[5] The hindrance to economic growth caused by the rapid rise in the rate of population increase as a result of this sharp fall in the death rate is well known.

And, presumably, if a fall in the death rate were the mechanism of growth in England when its population took that decisive upward turn in the late eighteenth and early nineteenth centuries, then England too must have encountered these same demographic obstacles to economic expansion and have had an Industrial Revolution in spite of them.

But suppose the mechanism were different. Suppose the population growth was caused by a rise in the birth rate, then an entirely different prospect opens up. For, if fertility rose in late eighteenth and early nineteenth century England, this suggests first, that the birth rate was not at its physiological maximum – as it appears to be in certain under-developed countries of today, where 80 per cent of the women in the fertile age group are married and where crude birth rates are of the order of 40–50 per 1,000. If the birth rate was not at or near its physiological maximum in early eighteenth century England, this in turn suggests that it was consciously restrained either through a late age at marriage and a low incidence of marriage, or by birth control within marriage – or a combination of all three, as suggested recently by Dr Wrigley.[6] The second point to be made in this connection is that if fertility was consciously restrained then it seems fair to assume that it was so in the interests of maintaining living standards. Thirdly, if fertility rose in the late eighteenth century, then we might assume that living standards were rising – otherwise there would be no encouragement to higher fertility – which in turn suggests that *per capita* income was increasing or, in other words, that the economy was growing. Finally, if this line of reasoning is accepted, we can see population rising in response to an increase in the rate of economic growth, with demographic and economic forces in harmony, the one supporting the other. Indeed the growth of population in eighteenth century England might well have been an important aid to economic growth, providing both a rise in effective demand and an increase in the supply of labour.

Of course, a rise in fertility would increase the burden of dependency – very much so since initially all the increase would occur at the base of the population pyramid, assuming no change in age-specific death rates. If we accept, however, that living standards were in any case relatively high – since they were maintained by a controlled fertility – this increased burden could not only be borne by the working population without too much strain but also, like the 'baby boom' of the 1940s and 1950s in the USA, it could be regarded as an important stimulus to economic growth.

It is then, I suggest, important to grasp that it is not simply the growth of population which is crucial for our understanding of the first and subsequent industrial revolutions, but also the mechanism by which that growth occurred.

Our main problem in determining the age at marriage in the pre-
industrial West is a data problem. We have, as yet, very little
quantitative evidence, and the literary or non-statistical material is
usually anecdotal in form and, where it is possible to check it
against statistical evidence, often wildly inaccurate. Perhaps I might
illustrate this last point with one or two examples.

Professor Connell has argued very persuasively that the doubling in
the size of the Irish population between 1780 and 1840 was due principally to a sharp fall in the age at marriage of men and women. This
was brought about by a sharp rise in the English demand for Irish
agricultural products, particularly grain, in the closing decades of
the eighteenth century. In a country starved of capital the landlords
saw the possibilities of increasing their rent rolls by putting more labour onto their lands, so they encouraged the sub-division of hold-
ings and the colonization of the waste. The easier access to land,
necessary if one were to marry and found a family, was further
facilitated by the Irishman's willingness to live on the nutritious, if
to our delicate stomachs somewhat unpalatable, diet of 10 lb of
potatoes per head per day, and little if anything else.

The evidence for early marriage amongst the Irish at this time is
very abundant. Scarcely a single observer of the Irish rural scene
failed to mention it, and to judge by much of this evidence few
Irish men and women passed out of their teens unmarried.[7] Thus, for
instance, in a summary of oral evidence given to the Poor Inquiry
Commission in 1833, we learn that the usual age at marriage of
labourers in four of the five counties of Connaught, namely Galway,
Leitrim, Mayo and Sligo, was no later than 19 years.[8] The Commis-
sioners of the 1841 census discovered, however, from the marriage
statistics of the 1830s which they collected retrospectively, that at no
time in that decade was the age at first marriage of men in Connaught
under 25 years and in view of the way they collected their material
could well have been even later than this.[9]

The belief that the age at marriage was very low, or was falling
amongst the poorer members of society was not confined to early
nineteenth century Ireland. The same was true of Norway in the
1840s and 1850s. 'It is shocking to behold so frequently,' wrote one
clerical observer 'young people of 18–20 years marrying without the
least thought for the future.'[10] This comment appeared at a time when
less than 1 per cent of bridegrooms and less than 6 per cent of brides
were under 20 years of age.[11]

In the United States too there are scores of observations to the
effect that marriage both for men and women came early. This is
true of colonial times and well into the 1800s. Benjamin Franklin's
remark – 'with us in America marriages are generally in the morning

of life'[12] – is well known. Arthur W. Calhoun's massive three volume study, *A Social history of the American family from Colonial times to the present*, is replete with references to early marriage. 'The early Puritans', remarked Calhoun, 'married young'. Madam Knight wrote (1704) of Connecticut youth: 'They generally marry very young, the males oftener as I am told under twenty years than above. Girls often married at sixteen or under.'[13] Brickell remarked of the women of North Carolina in the early eighteenth century that 'they marry generally very young, some at thirteen or fourteen, and she that continues unmarried until twenty, is reckoned a stale maid.'[14] Calhoun gives many other references to marriages of girls at 13 or 14 years of age and of men not much older.[15]

Malthus gave the generally accepted cause and effect of this early marriage in a brief passage in the first edition of his essay on *The Principle of Population.* 'In the United States of America,' he observed, 'where the means of subsistence have been ample, the manners of the people more pure, and consequently the checks to early marriages fewer than in any of the modern states of Europe, the population has been found to double itself in twenty-five years.'[16]

Yet again what little statistical evidence we have suggests that marriage was not as early in America as contemporary observers have led us to believe, although the scraps presented in Tables 4 and 5 indicate that the age at marriage of women at least was sometimes earlier in the United States than in Western Europe.

When we leave the literary for the statistical world the problems of interpretation unfortunately come with us. For what little statistical evidence we have presents a perplexing picture. For instance, as we have no national age at marriage statistics in England until the mid nineteenth century, we must glean what we can from sources that happen to have survived. These sometimes reveal quite contrary trends. Dr Wrigley found that in the Devonshire parish of Colyton the mean age at first marriage of women moved quite markedly from 27·0 years in the late sixteenth and early seventeenth centuries to 29·6 in the period 1647–1719, to 25·1 in the years 1770–1837 (Table 1).

Dr Razell, on the other hand, drawing his evidence from various parts of England and Wales, found barely any change in the mean age at marriage of spinsters between the 1610s and the 1840s. It was constant around 24 years (Table 2). This discrepancy is obviously disturbing. If Razell is right, the view that the growth of population in eighteenth century England was due to a rise in fertility consequent upon a fall in the age at marriage must be abandoned. Only if we can generalize from Dr Wrigley's one parish sample can we salvage this explanation. But even if Dr Wrigley's figures reflect national trends in the age at first marriage of women, his figures for men must give us pause. For taken in relation to those of the women they indicate a very interesting – to modern eyes a very strange – situation.

Table 1 shows that in two of the four periods the mean age of women was higher than that of men. In the years 1647–1719 the women were on the average 1·9 years older than their husbands. More detailed tables show that the gap was even wider than this for certain sub-periods with the years 1647–1719.[17]

Table 1 is disconcerting too for the fact that the ages at marriage of the men and women do not move in step. Thus, between the first and second periods the mean age at marriage of men rises 0·5 years, that of women 2·6 years; whilst between the third and fourth periods the age at marriage of men rises by 0·8 years whereas that of women falls by 1·7 years. This lack of correlation is especially disturbing for those who support the hypothesis that the rise of England's population in the late eighteenth century was due to a rise in fertility consequent upon a fall in the age at marriage. For they generally assume that a fall in the age at marriage of men would involve a corresponding fall in the age at marriage of women. Indeed this relationship is a crucial part of the argument, for it is assumed that the changes in the economy which encouraged earlier marriage had their immediate impact on men, namely through an enlargement of employment opportunities associated with what, for want of more precise terminology, we call the Agricultural and Industrial Revolutions.[18]

The absence of the expected relationship between the age at marriage of men and women can also be seen in Table 3, which shows median ages at first marriage in Norway – at this time a pre-industrial economy – in different parts of Norway in the 1840s and 1850s. If we look at two eastern districts, we find men married earlier in Hedmark than in neighbouring Gudbrandsdalen, but women married later. In two western areas we discover that men married earlier in Søndre Sunnmøre than in Hardanger and Voss, but again women married later.

Two other features of Table 3 call for a brief comment. One is the quite considerable differences in age at marriage of both men and women in different parts of Norway. As noted earlier, Norway was still a pre-industrial economy at this time yet, for example, in the years 1841–5 women entering their first marriage were almost four years younger in Vest Finmark than in Søndre Sunnmøre, whilst an age gap of the same size separated men entering their first marriage in Hardanger and Voss from their counterparts in Vest Finmark. A second point arising out of Table 3 is that within a relatively short period of ten years the age at marriage could change by a year or more. This might be credited to changes in occupational opportunities, but in the case of the societies represented in Table 3 it seems more probably to have resulted from a shift in the age composition of the population.[19]

These two observations indicate the care that must be taken when interpreting the sort of material presented in Tables 1 and 2. For if median ages at marriage show such diversity within a single pre-industrial society and over a relatively small period of time, generalizing from the one or two isolated scraps of statistical evidence which happen to have survived or which, with much labour, we are able to construct, could well be most misleading.

If we look behind the aggregate at the differences in age at marriage between social and occupational groups we get closer to understanding the aggregates themselves. For instance, in mid nineteenth century Norway, where as we have seen earlier marriage of men in one district as compared with another did not necessarily imply earlier marriage of women, we find a corresponding difference in the marital age patterns of the two most important occupational groups, the farmers and the crofters. Thus, whereas farmers usually married quite a bit later than their labourers (that is, the crofters), the farmers' wives were younger than the crofters' wives (Table 5). To account for this difference is not easy, especially when we discover that very many farm labourers were actually younger than their wives and often quite considerably so.

At the beginning of the nineteenth century, for instance, in certain parts of Norway almost 50 per cent of the farm labourers were younger than their wives and 25 per cent were five or more years younger.[20]

To explain the marital age pattern of the farmers is not very difficult. Farmers' sons usually married farmers' daughters. The latter were sought after at an early age since their marriage portions were fixed and grew no larger with the passage of time. Often however the farmer's son would have to wait a considerable time before he could win a suitable bride or acquire a farm through inheritance or purchase.

The sons and daughters of crofters were in an entirely different situation. They left their childhood homes in their teens to live and work as unmarried servants on a farm. They aspired to a croft. The men could expect to get one from about their mid twenties, as farmers wanted men in their prime. The women in this group could rarely attract a husband through their possession of any inherited wealth. They might, however, by diligent saving hope to collect together a useful amount of clothes, bed linen, household utensils and perhaps the odd cow or a couple of sheep or goats (which their master allowed to run with his own) by their late twenties or early thirties. This would make them attractive to potential suitors.

Furthermore it appears there was a general consensus that a crofter should marry a woman his own age or rather older, especially if he himself was fortunate to get a croft at an early age, for the older woman would not only have more material possessions than the younger, but she would also, by definition, be more mature and more experienced in the multifarious activities required of a crofter's wife. This particular pattern was also reinforced both by the sex and age distribution of the farm servant population – there were both more female servants and they were on average older than the males – and by such social conventions as housing the younger female ser-vants in less accessible quarters (the main farm building as opposed to the byres or other outhouses) and by ensuring that at such social functions as dances the younger girls did not get in the way of their elder sisters.[21]

These contrasting marital age patterns appear explicable in terms of the social and economic conditions of the Norwegian countryside. At first sight, however, they do not appear so in terms of non-agricultural employment conditions. And yet, the evidence of Tables 7 and 8 suggest that the marriage patterns of the Norwegian country-side are to be found within a number of industrial and commercial occupations.

It is not, of course, difficult to account for the fact that ships' captains married later than ships' mates or that they, in turn, married later than ordinary seamen. Whether or not they sprang from the same social group, it is clear that men become ordinary seamen at an earlier age than they become ships' mates or ships' captains. In the same way we would expect sawmill foremen to be older than sawmill workers and master craftsmen than journeymen. This being so we would expect men in the more responsible or skilled positions to marry later than those who were less skilled.

The age differences between the wives of these men do not however follow the same pattern. The median age at marriage of ordinary seamen was more than four years lower than that of ships' captains, yet the wives of the latter were 0·7 years younger than those of the former. A similar discrepancy occurs in the case of sawmill workers and sawmill foremen though not in that of journeymen and master craftsmen.

Perhaps a great deal of these patterns can be explained by the fact that in the 1860s and the 1870s Norway was only just beginning to industrialize. The milieu of south-eastern Østfold (the area from which Table 8 is drawn) was still a rural one. Cottars' sons went to sea and came back to a holding, or worked for a while at some trade, or in the local sawmills. But the grip of the old forms had not been broken. By the end of the century this was much less true. A new society had by then emerged, with its own conventions about what was and what was not a suitable age at marriage. The figures in Table 9 thus appear much more 'normal' to modern eyes: the older the husband the older the wife.

These findings have implications for the general discussion of recent years on the effect of industrialization on the age at marriage in late eighteenth century England. For here it has been commonly assumed not only that the earlier a man married, the younger his wife, but also that as maximum earnings came early in the lower grade occupations that were growing so rapidly at this time, this would lower the age at marriage of men and *pari passu* that of women. At present we have little or no evidence that this actually happened in England. In view of the Norwegian material presented above, however, there is a presumption that at least in the early stage of industrialization the age at marriage of women may have altered little and, possibly, if lower class occupations increased faster than upper class ones, that the age at marriage of women may even have risen.

I have tried to argue that the age at marriage in the pre-industrial West involved a more complex set of relationships than is commonly thought, and that the transfer of contemporary assumptions on the 'normal' marital age pattern to earlier periods is unwarranted. Nothing I have said, however, destroys Wrigley's assertion of the importance of the age at marriage of men and women in our demo-graphic history. The differences in age at marriage within the pre-industrial West were obviously sufficient to explain quite considerable differences in the reproductive rates. Merely on the statistical evi-dence presented here, we see that whereas in mid nineteenth century Sunnmøre (on Norway's western coast) the median age at marriage of women was 26·7 years, among US born spinsters on America's western frontier it was only 20·0 years. Even so ages at marriage in the pre-industrial West were considerably above those in many of the currently under-developed countries and this appears to be one of the most fundamental differences between the demographic situations of the two societies. In view of the importance of these differences for economic and social advance, they appear well worth studying more deeply.

Notes and References

1 E. A. Wrigley (ed.), *An Introduction to English Historical Demography* (London 1966) p. 150.
2 E. A. Wrigley, 'Family Limitation in pre-Industrial England', *Econ. Hist. Rev.*, 2nd Series, **19**, (1966) 86.

3   H.J.Habakkuk, 'English population in the 18th century', *Econ. Hist. Rev.*, 2nd Series, **6** (1953) 117–33. 'The Economic History of Modern Britain', *Journal of Economic History*, **18** (1958) 486–501. K.H.Connell, *The Population of Ireland* 1760–1845 (Oxford, 1950).

4   H.J.Habakkuk, 'The Economic History of Modern Britain', reprinted in (eds. D.V.Glass and D.E.C.Eversley) *Population in History* (London 1965) p. 152.

5   *New Republic*, April 1967.

6   See Note 2.

7   K.H.Connell (see Note 3) pp. 51–3.

8   For further detail see Michael Drake, 'Marriage and population growth in Ireland 1750–1845', *Economic History Review*, 2nd Series, **16** (1963) 301–13.

9   See Note 8, pp. 303, 310–11.

10 Provst Bødtker, 'Om letsindige Aegteskaber blandt Landalmuen,' *Morgenbladet* (Oslo, 20 December 1850).

11 For this and further details of age at marriage in Norway see my forthcoming book *Population and Society in Norway* (Cambridge University Press).

12 Cited in Thomas P.Monahan, *The Pattern of age at marriage in the United States* Vol. 1, (Philadelphia 1951) p. 103.

13 Arthur C.Calhoun, *A Social History of the American Family from Colonial times to the present* Vol. 1. (New York 1917) p. 67.

14 J.Brickell, *Natural History of North Carolina* (Dublin 1731) cited in Calhoun (see Note 13) Vol. 1, p. 245.

15 See Note 12, p. 100.

16 Kenneth Boulding (ed.), *Thomas Robert Malthus: Population: The First Essay* (Ann Arbor 1959). pp. 7–8.

17 See Note 2, Table 2, p. 87.

18 J.T.Krause, 'Changes in English Fertility and Mortality 1781–1850, *Economic History Review*, 2nd Series **11** (1958) 67–68.

19 Michael Drake, 'The growth of Population in Norway, 1735–1855', *Scandinavian Economic History Review* **13** (1965) Table 4, p. 110.

20 Michael Drake, 'Malthus on Norway', *Population Studies* **20** (1966) 189.

21 See Note 20, pp. 190–1.

22 For the timing of the industrial revolution in Norway see Edward Bull, 'Norway: industrialisation as a factor in economic growth', *Contributions to the First International Conference of Economic History, Stockholm 1960*, (Paris–The Hague 1960) and for a detailed study of the industrialisation of Østfold his *Arbeidermiljø under det industrielle gjennombrud* (Oslo 1958).

TABLE 1 Mean and median age at first marriage in Colyton, Devon, 1560–1837[1]

Period	Men No.	Men Mean	Men Median	Women No.	Women Mean	Women Median
1560–1646	258	27·2	25·8	371	27·0	25·9
1647–1719	109	27·7	26·4	136	29·6	27·5
1720–1769	90	25·7	25·1	104	26·8	25·7
1770–1837	219	26·5	25·8	275	25·1	24·0

[1] E.A.Wrigley, 'Family Limitation in Pre-Industrial England,' *Economic History Review.* Second Series, **19**, No. 1 (April 1966), p. 86.

TABLE 2 Mean age at marriage of spinsters (England and Wales) 1615–1841[1]

Period	Region	Mean age at marriage	No. in sample
1615–1621	Wilts, Berks, Hants, Dorset	24·6	280
1662–1714	Yorkshire	23·8	7,242
1701–1736	Nottinghamshire	24·5	865
1741–1745	Surrey	24·9	333
1749–1770	Nottinghamshire	23·9	700
1796–1799	Sussex	24·1	275
1839–1841	England and Wales	24·3	14,311

[1] P.E.Razell, 'Population Change in Eighteenth Century England. A Reinterpretation,' *Economic History Review.* Second Series, **18**, No. 2 (August 1965), p. 315.

TABLE 3 Median age at first marriage (bachelors-spinsters) in certain Norwegian deaneries in the years 1841–5, 1846–50, 1851–5[1]

Deanery	No. of marriages	Male median age 1841–1845	Male median age 1846–1850	Male median age 1851–1855	Female median age 1841–1845	Female median age 1846–1850	Female median age 1851–1855
Hedmark	826	26·6	26·8	27·3	25·5	25·9	26·5
Gudbrandsdalen	1097	27·4	27·4	27·9	24·8	25·0	26·1
Hardanger and Voss	767	28·7	28·4	28·8	24·8	25·2	25·5
Søndre Sunnmøre	368	27·5	27·7	28·0	26·5	26·1	26·7
Karmsund	450	26·6	27·4	27·6	23·8	24·3	25·3
Vest Finmark	326	24·5	25·5	25·0	22·8	23·0	23·4

[1] Bishops Returns in *Folkemengdens Bevegelse Pakker,* Riksarkivet, Oslo.

TABLE 4   Median age at first marriage in certain states of US about 1850
(precise dates in brackets)[1]

State (date)	Median Age Males	Females
New York (1855)[1]	25·0	21·5
New Jersey (1848–50)[1]	24·4	21·2
Massachusetts (1850)[1]	25·2	22·5
Vermont (1858)[1]	24·6	21·4
Kentucky (1852)[1]	23·9	20·4
Wisconsin (1849–50)[2]	25·9	20·8

[1] Thomas P. Monahan, *The Pattern of Age at Marriage in the United States*
(Philadelphia, 1951) pp. 157, 161, 170, 175, 207.

[2] Calculated from entries in manuscript schedules of *United States Census:
State of Wisconsin*, 1850 (State Historical Society Library, Madison,
Wisconsin).

TABLE 5   Mean age at first marriage (bachelors-spinsters), amongst the
propertied class (overwhelmingly farmers) and the propertyless (overwhelmingly cottars) in the Norwegian dioceses of Christiania and Christian-
sands in the years 1851 and 1852[1]

	Mean Age			
	Males		Females	
Diocese	Propertied	Propertyless	Propertied	Propertyless
Christiania	29·6	28·1	26·2	26·8
Christiansands	29·8	28·4	25·5	26·6

[1] Eilert Sundt, *Om Giftermaal i Norge* (Christiania 1855), p. 197.

TABLE 6   Median age at first marriage of US born and foreign born farmers,
craftsmen and labourers in Wisconsin 1849–50[1]

		Median Age				
	No. of	US born		No. of	Foreign born	
Occupation	marriages	Males	Females	marriages	Males	Females
Farmers	373	24·8	19·8	230	27·6	21·6
Craftsmen	160	25·3	20·1	198	26·3	22·0
Labourers	71	25·2	19·7	163	26·0	21·9

[1] Calculated from manuscript schedules of *United States Census: State of
Wisconsin*, 1850. NB There was very little intermarriage between US born
and foreign born. Where intermarriage occurred the wives are classified here
according to the nationality of their husbands.

TABLE 7 Median ages at first marriage (bachelor-spinster) in certain parishes of S.E. Norway in the years 1841–60, 1861–80, 1881–1900 classified by occupation[1]

	Males			Females		
	Median Age					
Occupation	1841– 1860	1861– 1880	1881– 1900	1841– 1860	1861– 1880	1881– 1900
Farmers	27·1	28·9	29·0	24·3	25·7	25·9
Craftsmen	26·7	26·9	26·1	24·6	24·9	24·1
Labourers	26·3	25·7	25·2	24·5	24·3	24·0
Sailors	26·3	26·9	26·3	25·3	24·3	24·2

[1] Abstracted from *Parish Registers* of Glemmen, Vest-Fredrikstad, Tune and Sarpsborg (Østfold, Norway).

TABLE 8 Median age at first marriage in certain Norwegian parishes, classified by occupation in the years 1861–80.[1]

Occupation	No. of marriages	*Median Age* Males	Females
Ordinary seamen	316	25·9	24·5
Ships' mates	105	27·3	23·5
Ships' captains	69	30·1	23·8
Sawmill workers	136	24·8	24·1
Sawmill foremen	58	25·7	23·2
Journeymen	156	25·9	24·4
Master craftsmen	242	27·6	25·2

[1] Abstracted from *Parish Registers* of Glemmen, Vest- Fredrikstad, Tune and Sarpsborg (Østfold, Norway).

TABLE 9 Median age at first marriage in certain Norwegian parishes' classified by occupation, in the years 1881—1900[1]

Occupation	No. of marriages	Median Age Males	Females
Ordinary seamen	495	25·6	24·0
Ships' mates	193	27·0	24·4
Ships' captains	59	32·0	26·1
'Boom' workers	69	27·7	24·4
Quarry workers	129	26·0	24·0
Brick and tile workers	119	25·7	24·5
Timberyard workers	126	24·5	23·7
Sawmill workers	578	24·3	23·5
Factory workers	69	24·2	23·4
Journeymen	136	25·3	23·5
Master craftsmen	405	26·3	24·3

[1] Abstracted from *Parish Registers* of Glemmen, Vest - Fredrikstad, Tune and Sarpsborg (Østfold, Norway).

B. H. SLICHER VAN BATH

Contrasting Demographic Development in some Parts of the Netherlands during the Depression Period of the 17th and 18th centuries

The depression or the crisis of the seventeenth and eighteenth centuries has been much discussed in historical circles during the last fifteen years. There is the book by Abel, as early as 1935, and the articles by historians like Mousnier, Hobsbawm, Trevor-Roper, Mandrou, Lütge, Goubert, Romano, Topolski, Hroch, Petrán, Schöffer and many others.

The beginning of the recession in the seventeenth century can be placed generally between 1620 and 1630. According to Romano the economic crisis from 1619 to 1622 is the turning-point, but other historians give different years. In Spain the recession appeared soon after 1600, in Italy after 1619, in some parts of the German states very soon after the outbreak of the Thirty Years War in 1618, in others not till after 1630. The recession began in France, too, about 1630, in England and the Netherlands roughly in 1650, although sometimes the starting-point in the Netherlands has been set at 1637. The prosperous times began in England and France about 1730, in the Netherlands after 1755; in Germany the depression may have been over by 1750.

From an economic point of view the depression of the seventeenth and eighteenth centuries was bounded at one end by the price revolution of the sixteenth century and, at the other, by the mounting price levels of the eighteenth. We are hardly justified in calling it an economic crisis; it was more accurately an unusually prolonged depression that settled in western Europe, interrupted by violent fluctuations. The depression was of a far milder sort than the serious economic decline of the late Middle Ages, but its chief symptoms were the same; falling cereal prices, relatively high real wages, little reclamation activity, conversion of arable land to pasture, expansion of animal husbandry, cultivation of fodder crops and various industrial crops, a transition from agriculture to rural industry in some areas, few innovations in farming technique and little interest in questions of an agrarian nature. Even those most characteristic and distressing features of the late medieval depression, the lost villages,

P

the empty farms and neglected fields were not absent. Deserted farms were found not only in Germany, as the result of the Thirty Years War, but also in Italy, in the Campagna, south of Rome, in Tuscany, and in Spain. In 1619 there was talk in the Council of Castile of villages crumbling into ruins and of abandoned fields. During the whole of the seventeenth century there were lamentations about rural depopulation and the miserable state of agriculture.

In almost all European countries, people were sadly harassed by plague and other infectious diseases. In some of the towns afflicted by epidemics, 35 to 40 per cent of the inhabitants succumbed. It is the German historians who have placed most emphasis on the shrinkage of population during the seventeenth century. According to them, it was due, in part, to the complete depopulation of large areas of Germany, devastated by the Thirty Years War, but in other countries the population had also fallen. We have already mentioned Italy and Spain, but it may also have fallen in France, the southern Nether-lands, Sweden and Denmark. On the whole it is likely that popula-tion growth in Europe slowed down between 1650 and 1750.

What was the economic and demographic situation in the northern Netherlands, the Republic of the United Provinces, during the de-pression period ? Some economic historians supposed that England and the Dutch Republic were exceptions to the general European rule. The seventeenth century was the Dutch Golden Age, the period of the wealthy merchants and of general welfare. Nothing was known about the demographic development until research was done by the Department of Agricultural History at Wageningen. I will deal with the results of this research into population changes and economic development in the two provinces of Holland and Overijs-sel. These regions show contrasting patterns in their development : population decrease in Holland, especially north of Amsterdam, and an increase in population in the province of Overijssel, which is most striking in its eastern part, the region called Twente.

HOLLAND

The political and social commotion, which harassed the remnants of the Burgundian state after the death of Charles the Bold, did not leave the country of Holland unperturbed, and is reflected by a marked demographic decline in the last quarter of the fifteenth century. Recovery started, however, before or about 1500. Approxi-mately from this year onwards, the population continued to grow over a period of more than one and a half centuries. The only inter-ruption in this growth occurred during the seventh decade of the sixteenth century, when the military operations of the revolt against Spain took place mainly on the territory of Holland. A comparison of the population figures of 1514 and 1622 shows a growth of nearly 145 per cent, from 275,000 in 1514 to 672,000 in 1622, an enormous increase.

One of the most remarkable findings is that this numerical expansion was not caused entirely, as used to be supposed, by the many political refugees who came to the north from the Southern Low Countries after the successful revolt against Spain. In as far as the northern part of Holland is representative of the whole province, the growth in the countryside and even in the smaller towns seems to have been a little bit larger between 1514 and 1569 than between 1569 and 1622. In general the towns also had their share of the growth during the first half of the sixteenth century, but the well-known expansion of Amsterdam, Leyden, Haarlem, Delft, Rotterdam and other towns did not really start until after 1580. From a demographic point of view two reasons can be given for this fact: firstly, towards the end of the sixteenth century the countryside of Holland was becoming so over-populated that many country people could no longer make a living there and had to go to the cities; and secondly, the stream of immigrants mainly, though not exclusively, from the Southern Low Countries was directed towards the larger cities.

The excessive growth of the towns at the end of the sixteenth and the beginning of the seventeenth century far exceeded that of the countryside. Whereas in 1514 more than 46 per cent of the population of Holland lived in the towns, this percentage was 54 by 1622.

The demographic pressure in the countryside, where land was scarce, and often infertile and suitable only for extensive cattle breeding, made it necessary for an ever-increasing proportion of the population to find part-time or full-time jobs outside agriculture, shipping and fishery being the most obvious alternatives. From the places of origin of the skippers given in the Sound toll tables, some impression can be obtained of the enormous importance of shipping for large parts of the countryside of Holland. In the seventeenth century sea-fishing was looked upon as a very important, if not the most important trade in Holland.

The growing reservoir of labour and the limited natural resources made the countryside of Holland very suitable for the development of rural industries. In the beginning of the seventeenth century industries were established along the river Zaan, the most densely populated rural area of Holland.

The demographic pressure in the sixteenth century had a great deal of influence upon the rise of the ground rents. The prices of land probably rose more than those of movables. Far more trouble was now taken to protect the land against the water. The high rents and prices of land, and the relative abundance of capital compared with the possibilities of investment resulted in large-scale reclamations. Thousands of people must have earned a livelihood in these reclamations.

Detailed investigations have revealed that between 1622 and the middle of the eighteenth century important demographic changes took place. In the area north of Amsterdam the population continued to increase until *c*. 1650. After the middle of the century the population in that area began to decrease. At first the decrease was slow, but by the first half of the eighteenth century it had become catastrophic. Between 1650 and 1750 the number of inhabitants decreased from more than 200,000 to about 130,000. In large parts of North Holland the decrease even amounted to 50 per cent.

In the remaining part of Holland, south of Amsterdam, which was the largest part and where most of the inhabitants lived, the demographic development was not uniform. It can only be assumed, in the absence of more exact data, that there was an arrest, or maybe even a slight decrease in the demographic development of the countryside of this part of Holland. Also the demographic development of the towns in the southern part of Holland is still *terra incognita*. Some indications, however, enable us to trace the main lines of development with fair certainty. From the census results of 1622 and 1795 it appears that only Amsterdam, Rotterdam, The Hague and Schiedam had more inhabitants in the latter year than in 1622. All the other towns saw their population decrease, most of them even considerably. Their demographic development can be divided into three phases : 1622 – *c*. 1680 continued growth ; 1680–1750 a rapid decrease; and 1750–95 a slow decrease. The total decrease between 1680 and 1750 for the whole province of Holland may be estimated at about 100,000 persons. In 1680 the total population of Holland was about 883,000 and in 1750 about 783,000 persons.

The causes of the decrease are not yet clear. It may have been caused by a lower average number of children per marriage, a higher age at marriage and an increase of celibacy. Perhaps this may explain the very remarkable stagnation and lessening of the Protestant denominations during the eighteenth century, while on the contrary the Roman Catholics increased, or decreased to a lesser extent.

The demographic development after 1680, and in the north after 1650, clearly shows that, in the second half of the seventeenth century, the economic trend in Holland must have taken an unfavourable turn. This has, however, not yet been confirmed by research in economic history. It will therefore be necessary to employ new material in future investigations into the development after 1650.

Meanwhile it can already be stated that the excessive tax burden was probably a main cause of the economic decline. The government was not able to adapt the tax rates to the falling price tendency, so that taxes were accounting for an increasing proportion of the pro- duction costs. This must have influenced wages unfavourably which, in its turn, cannot have been without effect upon the competitive position of Dutch products and services. Owing to the frequent wars in the second half of the seventeenth century the government had to contract many big loans, and a large revenue was therefore needed for interests and discharges. As a result, the tax burden had to be increased, just at a time when the economic situation asked for the opposite policy. To make matters worse agriculture, which was still very important in Holland, was struck by heavy blows. Summarizing, it may be stated that the economic regression or stagnation in seventeenth century Europe did not leave Holland unperturbed.

OVERIJSSEL

Overijssel suffered considerably as a result of the Eighty Years War (1568–1648); for many years there was fierce fighting, particularly in the eastern part of the province. The country districts were plundered and laid ransom by either side. At this period a good many persons emigrated from these districts to Amsterdam and other towns in Holland.

When peace was restored a very remarkable development occurred, particularly during the period from 1675 to 1764. There was a sur- prisingly rapid increase of the total population of Overijssel from 71,000 in 1675 to 132,000 in 1764. Closer inspection reveals great regional differences, the most noticeable being the rapid increase in population in Twente, especially between 1675 and 1748. The growth occurred chiefly in the rural areas and hamlets during the first period, from 1675 to 1723. During the second period, from 1723 to 1748, the increase was most striking in the villages and the Twente towns. The increase in population in Twente is paralleled by the increase in the adjoining German districts, the bishoprics of Münster and Osnabrück. The increase is remarkable, the more so as it occurred contrary to the general trend in western Europe. The increase in population in Salland, the western parts of the province, is far less spectacular but much more regular. This area is very similar to the Veluwe on the other side of the river Ijssel. In the north of the province, the Land of Vollenhove, the population even declined in some towns and villages on the Zuider Zee coast. With respect to those areas situated along the Zuider Zee, a precisely similar develop- ment is found in Holland and Friesland.

The rapid increase in population between 1675 and 1748 was due to the excess of births over deaths, as is shown by the large number of children.

The pattern undergoes a complete change during the second half of the eighteenth century; in many parts of Overijssel the population remained stationary or even declined. This is in great contrast to some other Dutch provinces, where this was a period of slight recovery.

Some historians, for example in England, connect the growth of population in the eighteenth century with improvements in nutrition, clothing, housing and medical care. In Overijssel such improvements were still unknown at the end of the seventeenth century. Here the important factor was that the post-war recovery and the higher level of economic development of Holland afforded more economic possibilities. After the war, in the first instance the agricultural potentialities were exploited; the abandoned farms and fields were resettled again. The population growth that had already begun in this way, could continue as a result of the development of the textile industry. When the latter had difficulties to contend with after 1750, the termination of population growth coincided with the economic recession. At the same time epidemics occurred far more frequently. The general state of health of the population must have deteriorated at this period owing to the extreme poverty and the resultant meagre diet and malnutrition.

As a result of the low cereal prices, the period from 1675 to 1755 was not a prosperous one for agriculture. There were few possibilities for land clearance because the wastelands were used as a source of heather sods and humus for the arable lands (turf-manuring). Owing to the taxes, which fell particularly heavily on agriculture prior to 1760, the low prices of corn and the ruinous results of cattle diseases, there was no inducement to the reclamation of land and establishment of new farms. This was why the expansion of arable land did not keep pace with the increase in population.

Overijssel became dependent on cereals imported from other areas, not only in order to supply the towns with food, but also to supply the villages and the rural districts. Nor did the livestock population increase in proportion to the growth of the human population. As a result of this backward situation in agriculture, there was insufficient corn and animal protein available to the population, and this had an adverse effect on their health. The cottage weavers of Almelo were said to be weak and lacking in energy. Conditions were aggrava-ted by the poor housing in towns and rural areas where people lived in turf huts, sheds, bakehouses, and pigsties. Many new houses had a surface area of $4 \times 4 \cdot 5$ yards, the height being about 6 feet. House-building also lagged behind the increase in population.

In the livestock-raising districts in particular, farming suffered great losses owing to the three periods of cattle-plague. But these cattle-plagues did not lead to any structural changes in agriculture; there was no transition from livestock farming to arable farming. After the cattle-plague disasters a surprisingly quick recovery was made.

In Twente it was the textile industry that relieved the burden of over-population during the period of agricultural recession. At first the cottage weavers lived among the farmers, in the neighbourhood of the farms. Eventually they broke away from this environment and became professional weavers, most of whom settled in a number of villages and towns. This meant an increase in their cost of living; they were no longer able to share in the output of the farm but were obliged to subsist on expensive imported food. The various wars fought between 1688 and 1748 were exceptionally favourable for the Twente textile industry. After 1750 the period of prosperity was over. There was keen competition from Scotland, Ireland, and especially Silesia, where the linen was produced more cheaply. The consequent depression in the textile industry resulted in universal poverty.

In the Land of Vollenhove a small number of people were engaged in livestock farming. In this area peat excavation was an important form of employment. The transportation of peat led to a great expansion of shipping. The latter also resulted in the rise of many other branches of industry such as ship-building, sail-making, rope-making, shoe-manufacturing and bakery. But like gold-digging, peat-digging only brings temporary prosperity in its wake. Once the peat has been removed all that remains is lakes and ponds. Part of this district, which provided no further livelihood, was abandoned by the population who were attracted by fresh possibilities in the peat of Friesland and Drenthe.

From the social viewpoint, the period from 1675 to 1758 was marked by the decline in the importance of the nobility. The *bourgeois* group increased, and this benefited a group of higher middle classes rather than the ruling patricians in the towns. So the supremacy of the nobility and city patricians was broken. The upper middle classes in the three main towns acted as money-lenders to the nobility, giving mortgages on the castles, and even becoming their new inhabitants.

In addition to the more marked differentiation in the middle class, the rise of a rural and industrial proletariat can be observed. The phenomenon of differentiation occurred especially in the social stratification of rural society. The number of cottars increased in the arable districts, and these were followed by squatters and day labourers. It is these groups that grew most rapidly, whereas the number of bigger farms remained practically unchanged.

In the livestock districts there was no increase in the number of either farmers or cottars, although there were many day labourers and servants living off the premises. The farms of livestock farmers were usually relatively extensive. These farms required a great deal of capital; the farmer had to be in a position to keep a considerable population of livestock. As a result the social gap between the farmers on the one hand and the cottars, day labourers, and servants on the other was very large.

For some decades after 1760 Overijssel underwent a serious indus-trial crisis. Both the textile industry and the peat-digging industry encountered difficulties. Since these industries were predominant, this was a severe blow to the economy. The steadily increasing price of cereals after 1755 led to further rises in the cost of living, but wages did not rise, so that real income constantly dwindled. Owing to a change in the fiscal system, as a result of which the highest tax incidence was shifted from agriculture to excise, the condition of the lowest strata of the population was further aggravated. Since the excise was levied on the principal foodstuffs it was this section that proportionally had the heaviest tax burden to bear. There was a threat of famine in 1772, and some years later riots broke out at Enschede, a textile town. An accompanying feature of the universal poverty was the high consumption of brandy. The yield from excise levied on strong alcoholic drink had become one of the province's chief sources of revenue – 15 per cent of the total tax yield during the period from 1770 to 1790.

Agriculture benefited by the higher cereal prices from 1755 on-ward. They were particularly favourable for self-employed small-holders. Since agriculture afforded more possibilities than industry there was a return to agriculture in certain industrial districts. Buckwheat had become an important new food crop. Although certainly known in Overijssel from the end of the fifteenth century, it was not cultivated on a large scale until the eighteenth and nine-teenth centuries. An even greater change was brought about by potato cultivation. The rapid growth of this form of cultivation was no doubt due to the continually rising prices of cereals. As early as 1781 potatoes had become the staple diet of the poor of Almelo. Weavers' families had two meals of potatoes a day.

The increase in the amount of property declared for the purpose of property tax remained well below the increase in population. The increase in the number of paupers unable to pay the poll-tax was far greater than the population increase. In some places in Twente in 1764 paupers accounted for 50 to 60 per cent of the population.

As a consequence of the population increase not only were the housing conditions exceptionally bad, but also medical care was on an insignificant scale, and the same was true of spiritual care and education. There was only one doctor for nearly 4,000 inhabitants, one midwife for nearly 8,000, one teacher in 1,000, one Protestant clergyman in 1,600 and one Roman Catholic priest in 4,300 inhabitants.

THE GENERAL PATTERN

By comparing and combining the data recorded for the various regions we obtain the following broad outline for the Netherlands as a whole. The period from 1650 to 1750 is characterized by stagnation and decline in the towns and rural areas engaged in shipping trade, certain industries and livestock farming (North Holland and the Zuider Zee areas of both Friesland and Overijssel). There is a moderate growth in the bailiwick of Bois-le-Duc (Northern Brabant), the sandy regions of Friesland and the Veluwe; a considerable growth in Overijssel, especially in Twente. In Overijssel and the Veluwe such means of livelihood as the textile industry, peat-digging, paper-making and the cultivation and processing of tobacco, were developed side-by-side with traditional agriculture, probably under the favourable conditions of a lower level of costs. These economic activities were still in a comparatively flourishing state at this period of stagnating economic growth and were able to provide work for the growing population.

The general pattern during the depression period of the seventeenth and eighteenth centuries is the coincidence of the economic recession with a population decrease. The findings for the province of Holland are in conformity with the general development in western Europe. The population increase in Overijssel is remarkable as it occurred contrary to the general trend, although the phenomenon of a rapid growth of population in rural districts in the seventeenth and eighteenth centuries may also be observed in some other countries. In Brandenburg-Prussia it was very considerable between 1688 and 1770, the peak coming between 1740 and 1770, after which there was a slackening off. In Alsace the most rapid increase was between 1720 and 1750, the downswing beginning in the second half of the century. As in Twente, the growth of population in Maine (France) coincides with the progress in the textile industry. Here there was a considerable increase between 1698 and 1761. When the industry declined between 1763 and 1803 the population also decreased in a number of villages. The population growth in the bishoprics of Münster and Osnabrück has already been mentioned, but the exact data of the increase are still unknown.

The depression period is characterized by a general trend of falling prices, especially grain prices. The significance of grain prices is often overrated. The curve of those prices should be considered in the same way as a temperature curve. A thermometer does not indicate the nature of the disease but only its presence ; in the same way, high or low grain prices give us no clue as to the underlying causes of this development. To get a picture of the changes in agricultural output and consumption, prices should not be studied absolutely but rather in the framework of the development of the ratios between different categories of prices : between prices of grain and of dairy produce ; between prices of grain and of industrial crops ; between prices of grain or agricultural produce in general and those of industrial products ; between prices of grain or agricultural produce and wages or incomes. The changes affecting the price ratios do not explain anything by themselves but give us important information on socio-economic changes.

A study of the available material on prices demonstrated that the ratio between the prices of grain, other commodities, and wages was unfavourable at the end of the Middle Ages and in the seventeenth and the first half of the eighteenth century. The periods of low grain prices were those of agricultural regression. It should be kept in mind, however, that the term 'agricultural' is used here in a limited sense and refers only to grain growing. Though not entirely correct, such an identification of grain growing with farming at large is justified by the paramountcy of grain in the agriculture of those times. When speaking of the depression of the seventeenth century, one is in fact referring to the grain crisis, a period character- ized by an unfavourable ratio between grain, on the one hand, and other goods and wages, on the other. This by no means precludes prosperity in other sectors of economic life. We can observe the creation of rural industries, particularly the textile industry during the depression period. Grain is used for industrial purposes in breweries, distilleries, starch manufacture, and so on. During the period of agricultural setback more industrial crops were grown, such as flax, hemp, hops, oil-seeds, woad, and madder, often at the expense of the production of grain.

Some historians are of the opinion that one can follow the trend of demographic developments from the price lists of grain. They have, however, lost sight of the fact that the grain prices in them- selves are not the determinant, but the ratio between the grain prices and wages or earnings. A change in these ratios does not affect each professional group or class in the same way, since what means profit to some is a loss to others. Precisely because the various social groups react differently, one ought to investigate the relative importance of each of these groups and the way in which they react to economic changes.

Usually, the transition from boom to depression and the reverse are not clearly defined. Nor does the crisis affect all countries at the same time. It is rather a question of a critical situation arising in different areas at different times from different causes, and which may eventually lead to a crisis. The movement may spread from one area to the next. Urbanized areas with a diversified economy resist longer than those which produce hardly anything but raw materials. The causes of the depression may be demographic, monetary, political-economic or just political.

The period of economic progress in Overijssel is found to coincide with that of the increase in population. The same applies to the period of economic stagnation or setback in Holland and the *decrease* in population. The starting point in Overijssel was the post-war recovery and the exploitation of agricultural potentialities; the rise of the rural textile industry was a second stage, favoured by the general depression. Holland was affected by the depression rather late. The decrease in transportation of corn through the Sound after 1650, perhaps a consequence of the rising production of foodstuffs in western and southern Europe, together with the stagnation of demographic development in many other countries, may have caused a decline in foreign trade, export industry, shipping and all the branches of industry connected with it, such as ship-building, sail-making, rope-making, etc.

In the case of economic growth as well as depression a reinforcing secondary effect sets in. Economic progress leads to more marriages at an earlier age and consequently to a higher birth rate. The depression resulted in the postponement of marriages and a greater celibacy, thereby leading to a decline or stagnation of the birth rate.

#
Bibliography

B. H. Slicher van Bath, 'Die europäischen Agrarverhältnisse im 17. und in der ersten Hälfte des 18. Jahrhunderts', *A.A.G. Bijdragen* **13** (1965) pp. 134–148.

B. H. Slicher van Bath, *The agrarian history of Western Europe, A.D. 500–1850* (London 1963).

J. A. Faber, H. K. Roessingh, B. H. Slicher van Bath, A. M. van der Woude and H. J. van Xanten, 'Population changes and economic developments in the Netherlands: a historical survey', *A.A.G. Bijdragen*, **12** (1965) pp. 47–113 (On Holland, A. M. van der Woude, pp. 50–62; on Overijssel, B. H. Slicher van Bath, pp. 72–89).

B. H. Slicher van Bath, *Een samenleving onder spanning. Geschiedenis van het platteland in Overijssel* (Assen 1957).

B. H. Slicher van Bath, 'Les problèmes fondamentaux de la société pré-industrielle en Europe occidentale. Une orientation et un programme', *A.A.G. Bijdragen* **12** (1965) pp. 3–46.

Comments

Professor Habakkuk

I have first some minor points to make on Dr Eversley's paper. The first concerns the use of sub-groups, and it is the same point that arises on Mr Hollingsworth's work on the peerage. I will state it first in respect of the peerage. The problem is this : in respect of what is the peerage a homogeneous group ? Almost implicit in the choice of the peerage is the notion that it is, in some sense, a socially homo-geneous group. But, of course, additions to the peerage are partly the result of a highly random influence, the whims of the sovereign (or the whims of the Prime Minister) and at least on one occasion in the eighteenth century the influx of new creations was sufficiently large, one might suspect, to be of possible statistical significance. One of the many interesting conclusions, which as I remember it Dr Hollingsworth suggests, is the very curious relaxation of controls on birth within marriage among peerage families within the later eighteenth century. Most of the influences which might be supposed to lead to such a relaxation do not seem very obviously to apply to the peerage : it is possible, of course, that the greater availability of posts for the children of peers in the late eighteenth century lessened the need for controls on births, but the possibility is rather remote. Nor is it very likely that improved nutrition had an effect on the rate of conception or the abortion rate in the families of peers. One is therefore led to speculate that it is just possible that the social com-position of the peerage had changed as a result of new creations, and it would be very interesting to see whether the old creations and the new creations do really have different patterns. Most of the new creations were from quite long-established landed families, but they were on the whole of a rather different social group from the older peerage, and there might be an explanation in this fact. I think, too, that it is possible, although this is even more of a speculation, that the rate of accession of younger sons to the titles may have an effect.

Whether similar considerations apply to other sub-groups I do not know. I would expect from just general knowledge that the Quakers were, at the time, a remarkably consistent social group ; but if one were able to study, for example, the demographic history of Presbyterians between 1650 and 1750, if by happy chance they had left the sort of records which the Quakers had left, we would, I feel, meet the problem of the homogeneity of the group in quite an acute form. One would not know how far one's results were results relating to a change in the demographic habits of a social group whose composition remained the same, and how far one was really measuring a change in the social composition of this particular sub-group.

Now still on the field of minor points, I do not want to start an argument about English population in the later eighteenth, early nineteenth centuries, but I think there are two suggestions I would like to make. The first is about mortality. It seems to me that the evidence for the view that a really large and persistent decline in mortality set in, in the later eighteenth century, is still uncertain. If one looks at Finlaison's tables (I find them very difficult to interpret and I think it is very difficult to reconstruct the methods he used) which analyze the expectation of life, the mortality experience, of the holders of government annuities, it is evident that he thought, when he wrote in 1829, that they showed no perceptible increase in the expectation of life of males over the period in which they dealt, which is broadly speaking the century before the 1820s. His calculations do not, of course, include the first five years of life because of the conditions of the annuities, and they do not exclude the possibility that there was a dramatic improvement in infant mortality, or mortality in the early years of life, but the apparent absence of an increase in expectation of life above the age of five is curious, and I wish that the statistical demographers would look again at Finlaison's material and recalculate his figures. Secondly, as to the causes of the decline in mortality, assuming now that there *was* a significant decline, I am not certain that we can rule out causes which you can call medical, in the way in which McKeown and Brown argued. The fact that they were medical men naturally gave their opinions on medical matters peculiarly great weight, but I think it is clear from Mr Razell's work that they too readily dismissed the possibility that inoculation was a significant factor in causing the fall in mortality; and I wonder whether possibly the same is not true of the treatment of certain of the other medical improvements of the eighteenth century. I think that one of the general arguments urged against the importance of medical improvements is of very limited force, namely that these improvements were concentrated in towns and that what one must look for is an influence which affects very large masses of population and therefore, since the urban population in England was really very small, improvements affecting the towns cannot have had a very wide demographic impact. I think that this argument is open to the objection that if towns were in fact centres of infection, if they had some crucial role in the spread of epidemics, then medical improvements in the towns might have been capable of having very wide-ranging effects upon mortality.

So much for the specific points. I now want to consider a more general point, and to refer mainly to Professor Slicher van Bath's paper. It seems to me, considering the work of the historical demographers from the point of view of a customer – an economic historian interested primarily in the relations of the population growth and the economy – that there are two broad ways of looking at the history of European population and the economy. You can first of all suppose that there was a self-adjusting mechanism of the sort that Malthus had in mind. According to this view, the population adapted its rate of growth to its capacity to support population at some conventional standard of living; the social controls by which this adaptation was made partly operated on the age of marriage, partly on the level of nuptiality, and partly on fertility within marriage. But these were controls operating on the birth rate side, and when these were ineffective, when they failed to prevent population over-shooting the mark, then Nature audited her accounts in red, and there was a rise in the death rate induced by deficiency of food or by economic circumstances. One could argue about the relative significance in different periods of one or other parts of this mechanism, but this is a sort of self-adjusting mechanism of the sort which Malthus described. On the other hand, one can adopt a quite different line of approach and regard population growth as dominated by independent changes in mortality due to fluctuations in the incidence of diseases, for reasons which have little, if anything, to do with the economic capacity of the economy to support population, for example outbreaks of great epidemics, like the bubonic plague, or medical improvements, like inoculation, which are not in a very close sense related to the capacity of the economy in question. Of course, these are two extreme views and no doubt in any given situation elements of both mechanisms are present; but I think that it is unlikely that the balance of truth lies half way between them. Which way of looking at things one adopts in one's initial examination of the facts, which preference one has, does, I think, determine the nature of the questions one asks. If one adopted the first line of approach in relation to England, one would say that up to the mid seventeenth century there were social controls on the rate of population growth, but that they did not prevent population growing in excess of the ability of the economy to support population growth. Therefore, sometime after the middle of the century, if one were to generalize from Dr Wrigley's study of Colyton (I am sure that the author of the article would not, but since I am not responsible for the work, I am sure he would not object to my being rash with his material), population growth was checked and there was a reinforcement of social controls, a rising age of marriage among women, perhaps reinforced by controls on births within marriage.

Then, when the economic base increased for quite independent reasons in the late eighteenth century, the restraints on marriage were relaxed and relatively rapid population growth was resumed. On this version of events, one could fit a population into the industrial revolution by emphasizing the period when there was only a very slow population growth between the 1650s and 1740s. Here was a period, one could say, when output was increasing in a place of virtually stationary population, at rising incomes per head, and this really was the beginning of the movement of sustained economic growth leading to the Industrial Revolution. On this view, the economic historian is led naturally to concentrate on the forces, independent of population change, which increased the economic base. On the second way of looking at things, one would say that early periods of population growth had been checked by purely fortuitous increases in mortality, the plague in the fourteenth and fifteenth centuries, the spread of smallpox in the seventeenth century, the plague of London, and so forth. When these causes of high mortality disappeared, or were reduced for non-economic reasons, population growth resumed something like its former rate. And on this view of things, one would be naturally led, I think, to inquire into the ways in which the growth of population stimulated economic growth.

Professor Slicher van Bath, it seems to me, although his paper is cautious and scholarly, does really opt for the first type of interpretation, for an interpretation which gives primary importance to economic factors. Take his explanation of why population declined in Holland, and why it increased in Overijssel. Although the increase in Overijssel is partly the result of a fortuitous fact, war, the war operates by increasing the opportunities for establishing new households and encouraging marriage; and it is via the age of marriage and possibly via nuptiality that the process is initiated. In the same way it seems to me that, in his account, the decline of population in the province of Holland is very directly related to a decline of economic opportunities which is set in motion for independent reasons. It is difficult for someone not familiar with the Dutch literature to assess this hypothesis, because one does not know in these cases how far one is measuring the different rates of natural increase and how far internal migration is part of the explanation. This was one of the questions I think I have to ask Professor Slicher van Bath. How far were these very dramatic falls in the population of certain parts of the province of Holland the result of a fall in the rate of natural increase, and how far were they merely the result of a movement of population from regions of declining economic opportunity to regions where opportunities were better. It seems to me that Dutch historians in general, and I should say the same is true of the older German demographic historians, tend to interpret population movements in terms of some sort of equilibrating mechanism, whereas in England the tendency, in earlier days at least, was to think very largely of external factors affecting the death rate.

Turning now to Drake's paper, it raises I think two questions. First of all, what change in the age of marriage occurred in 'pre-industrial' societies of the kind we are interested in ? Secondly, what sort of change would be significant for our purpose ? When I first started, the only figures I could find on the age at marriage came from Nottingham, and there was no doubt a temptation ten or fifteen years ago to suppose that Nottingham and England were broadly identical. So far as the Nottinghamshire evidence goes, the marriage licences for the eighteenth century do show a fall in the age at first marriage of both men and women, and, happily, women normally married younger than men. Now, looking at the table which Dr Drake has produced, I see that the sort of assumptions I made about age at marriage were excessively simple-minded, and what I am trying to decide now is how embarrassed I should be by his tables. What one is really trying to get at is the amount of a woman's child-bearing period spent in marriage. I am not excessively worried by his Table 3 because, although there are variations between the male median age and the female median age between one part of the country and another, they do both move in the same direction. (I can quite see that if you aggregated them, and spoke about all the areas together, you might get some very curious results.) But I am much more worried by the fact that, in two of the periods, the male and female age at marriage move in opposite directions. This I think makes it very much more difficult to calculate the changes in the proportion of women's child-bearing age spent in marriage. The second question is what sort of change in age at marriage would be significant. When people marry earlier they have, other things being equal, longer in the child-bearing years. Moreover, some people marry at earlier ages, who, if they postponed, would have died before marriage. Then, thirdly, the fall in the age at marriage shortens the intervals between the generations, so that, even if the same number of children are born per family, more children are born per unit of time. These are the sort of effects which I am sure demographers would find it very easy to take account of in a model, into which you could feed various assumptions about the orders of magnitude and the variables. I cannot perform this task myself, but one can take the Dunlop figures to which Professor Connell has referred, and do a piece of simple speculative arithmetic. Professor Connell

Q

argued, on the basis of Dunlop's figures, that a year's change in the age of marriage of a woman made a difference of something of the order of one third of a child to the family. On the assumption of Gregory King that the number of births per every married woman in the later seventeenth century was 4·6, and taking a generation as 25 years, a fall of a year in the age at marriage would cause a rise in the annual rate of population growth of a little under 0·3 per cent. This is an extremely rough calculation but it suggests that, so far as the orders of magnitude are concerned, even a year's fall in the age at marriage *could* have made a significant contribution to the increase in the rate of population growth that took place in the late eighteenth and early nineteenth centuries. Whether, in point of fact, it did so can only be decided by further research into the age at marriage, but, meanwhile, I should like to make a plea to those who are expert in the construction and manipulation of models to devise, for the purposes of demographic historians, a more sophisticated measure of the effects, on varying assumptions, of given changes in the age at marriage.

General Discussion

W. Brand, W. Brass, C. Clark, M. Drake, D. C. Eversley, E. Grebenik,
H. J. Habakkuk, T. H. Hollingsworth, R. Illsley, P. Laslett,
B. H. Slicher van Bath, and E. A. Wrigley

The discussion of these papers is being presented as if they all took place in one session, whereas in fact Drake's paper was presented separately. For a number of reasons the time available for discussion at that session was short, and a good deal was taken up by an extended comment which unfortunately we are not able to reproduce here. As a result the report of the discussion on Drake's paper is extremely brief. On the other two papers the discussion was very vigorous and many points were given and taken in swift debate. In editing the discussion, therefore, it has been reduced to three main sections in order to summarize it reasonably succinctly. These are as follows:

1. An extended discussion arising from reference to the work of McKeown and Brown on the one hand and Razell on the other. The well-known debate on the influence of medical improvements on population in the nineteenth century was continued with particular reference to the effects of smallpox inoculation.

2. Discussion arising out of Habakkuk's comments on homogeneity and the peerage.

3. The consideration of detailed points in van Bath's paper with particular reference to the effects of migration.

Throughout, a recurring theme was the difficulty of handling historical data and the problem of its precise interpretation.

1. Eversley started the ball rolling by referring to Razell's work, while making it clear that he had not intended by his paper to start a discussion on the fall of mortality in the nineteenth century. Any reference to this was largely by way of background. Nevertheless, he pointed out that Razell took the evidence of the smallpox inoculators themselves at its face value, and this did not seem scientific to him. Also against Razell's argument was the fact that in other countries, Denmark in particular, the inoculators were at work, and Danish historians on the whole do not believe that this was an important cause in the decline of mortality. Furthermore there was evidence of a change in the virulence of the smallpox organism which was quite autonomous but contemporaneous with other changes; for instance there is data indicating a decline in death from smallpox even in

areas where there is no evidence of inoculation. In any event, if mortality did fall this would have very important consequences for fertility, and simply to argue that mortality falls were the most important cause of the rise in population would not rule out that family size became larger or that effective fertility became greater. The debate was really one of priorities, whether the chicken came before the egg. Eversley himself no longer felt prepared to make generalizations in this area until a good deal more evidence was available.

Drake referred to a recent article by Sigsworth in which he took up the points made by McKeown and Brown, among others, to the effect that people entering eighteenth- and nineteenth-century hospitals could be fairly sure of dying, even if not from the disease with which they entered hospital. The celebrated remarks by Florence Nightingale which seem to support this statement were backed up by evidence she produced for mortality in London hospitals in the nineteenth century. This evidence, however, had been found to be faulty as what she had done effectively was to take all the deaths in a year against the number of patients in the hospitals at any one moment! For other reasons some of the assertions about the mortality in the eighteenth- and nineteenth-century hospitals appear open to question, and Sigsworth had examined the local hospital in York in the eighteenth century. He found quite high percentages of people discharged from hospital, some of them undoubtedly to die outside, but others apparently cured; the idea that going to hospital effectively meant that the patient died was not supported by these figures. Drake also mentioned that the Dublin lying-in hospital in the 1750s had records showing over 20 per cent of the live births dying before they left hospital, but by the mid 1780s this figure had been reduced to 5 per cent. Other articles in local journals on the Manchester Royal hospital and elsewhere have also suggested that hospitals were not as poor as McKeown and Brown had suggested. Although Drake agreed that Razell made too much of his material on inoculation, one of his colleagues had been examining local material in Dorset through parish records, and found that in the late 1780s a remarkable amount of money was spent on inoculation by parish authorities. Admittedly this might have been totally thrown away, but it was striking as they were paying something like 5s. per head for inoculation at that time. When one considers that the rate for mass inoculation today is still something of this order, the fact that local authorities were prepared to pay out such large sums of money on many inoculations suggests that they must have had some effect at least on the incidence of smallpox. Brass stated that he had in the past done expenditure surveys in Africa, and felt that the amount of money spent should not be taken as a measure of effective-ness. The amount of money spent in Africa on inoculations is very large, but he did not feel that this had a great deal to do with the reduction of mortality there. This was largely because the number of deaths caused by diseases for which inoculation is of any use is comparatively small. This point supported a remark by Grebenik to the effect that only a small percentage of deaths in the period covered by McKeown and Brown was due to smallpox – at any rate according to their article. There was some discussion as to the accuracy of this figure which, as Habakkuk pointed out, was based on the Bills of Mortality which may very well not apply to the country as a whole.

Drake pointed out that the Swedish material suggests that in bad years smallpox epidemics could cause up to 25–30 per cent of the total deaths in that year, but these large epidemics tended to be followed by periods of comparative absence of the disease, which averaged out the effects. The Swedish figures also indicate that when smallpox went down measles went up. The effects did not entirely balance but, assuming correct diagnosis, the number of deaths due to measles between the 1780s and 1820s did rise very substantially as smallpox apparently disappeared. Brass pointed out that there are very complex interrelationships between some of the infectious diseases which are not particularly well understood, but the really important point had been mentioned earlier and this is the variation in virulence of all the infectious diseases. It is a very difficult feature to assess, but it is known to happen and does so rather frequently.

Eversley recounted that he once asked for help from the Institute of Tropical Medicine in Hamburg which specializes in smallpox, and was asked to which type of smallpox he was referring. This he admitted left him somewhat at a loss, and they then pointed out that they knew of four entirely different strains of virus in Germany in the eighteenth century, each with its own pattern both of virulence and of age incidence. As a result, knowledge of the type of smallpox involved was essential because assessing the effects of inoculation or vaccination would depend entirely on the strain present. From the figures he had been able to give them, the impression of the Institute was certainly that different kinds of smallpox were involved, and that the great epidemic at the end of the seventeenth century was almost certainly different from later ones both in age incidence and in virulence. When Razell's statement that inoculation did not begin seriously until after the time of the great epidemics is taken in con-nection with the possibility that smallpox was, by then, less danger-ous the problem becomes extremely complex. Any attempt to take the matter further requires the distribution of deaths by age, season, and territory, which is only available for limited groups. In the case of the London Quakers, for instance, deaths were recorded consistently from 1660 onwards, and Eversley felt the cause of death recorded was likely to be reasonably accurate as they had many good physicians amongst them. The Quakers were among the early experimenters with inoculations and it is true that smallpox was not a major cause of death. Nevertheless the infant mortality among the London Quakers was extremely high and remained extremely high. This was caused by diseases variously described as convulsions, fevers, and so on. This small piece of evidence suggests that dealing with smallpox is not likely to have been a major factor in getting down infant mortality whatever it may have done for adults. Finally, he pointed out that if inoculation was so effective, and was widely known to be so, it was difficult to explain why the work of Jenner caused so much interest at the beginning of the nineteenth century. Habakkuk claimed that this was, at least to some extent, because Jenner went to great lengths to advertise himself and promote his methods. There was, after all, considerable argument between those believing in inoculation and in vaccination. Furthermore he did not think that it was fair to say that Razell relied entirely on the figures in contemporary pamphlets written by the inoculators. The Poor Law material in the Midlands, for example, shows quite clearly that whenever there was a rumour of a smallpox epidemic in the neighbourhood, the Poor Law authorities vaccinated the entire population. He felt the cost was nearer to 1s. or 1s. 6d. a head than 5s., but certainly mass inoculation took place, and although the effect on mortality is debatable, the inoculation of large numbers of the population seems beyond doubt.

It was suggested at this point by Laslett that, if virulence can change in an autonomous and biologically controlled way, it supports Habakkuk's second model of change (referring to non-economic factors) rather than the models depending essentially on economic factors. Habakkuk replied that this did not necessarily arise as he was not really convinced that there was evidence that the virulence of the disease declined in the eighteenth century. The only detailed study of case fatality (by Blake in Boston) suggested that the case fatality among cases of natural smallpox seems to rise. Hollingsworth claimed that it certainly did rise in the seventeenth century, and this is presumably why it was not considered a very serious disease before the mid seventeenth century, and he saw no reason why it should not rise in Boston and England at the same time. Laslett replied that he was not necessarily referring only to smallpox. The argument can apply to all those infectious diseases which affect the young. If these diseases can change their virulence in a way which is largely biological and not attributable to social behaviour this in fact provided evidence for Habukkuk's second model. Wrigley pointed out that in fact there is a link between changes of this sort and general socio-economic change in that the chance of contracting a disease is very often a function of the density of the settlement in which one lives.

At this point Hollingsworth focused on the question of the accuracy of data. He pointed out that the data for this period may be all wrong. A study in England in the 1960s had shown by careful post-mortem examinations that something like 45 per cent of the causes of death shown on death certificates were in fact incorrect. This casts very great doubt on figures for deaths in 1760. Drake felt that comparison was not very fair as the nature of death had changed. Infectious diseases are hardly important at all today compared with a hundred years ago and this makes diagnosis very much more difficult. Hollingsworth, while agreeing with this, claimed that the real cause of the discrepancy lay in the motives of the man signing the death certificate. As he put it; 'The medical practitioner signing the death certificate is not in fact a man who is interested in historical demography.' He felt it was absolutely basic to this kind of work to consider very carefully the probable motives of the man compiling the document. The possible errors that can creep in in this way are very much larger than possible errors from any other sources one can think of. Eversley suggested that as far as causes of death were concerned, historical demographers should make a sharp distinction between diagnoses like smallpox, of which there was little doubt, and things like convulsions, or fever, or ague, which could be one thing or another. He claimed, in other words, that in the early records smallpox could be fairly accurately identified. Certainly, as far as degenerative diseases were concerned, he agreed that the early records were quite unreliable and suggested that this was true even today. Grebenik argued that to say that people who died with a rash were necessarily correctly diagnosed seemed rather question-able. Habakkuk remarked that not only were other rashes sometimes put down as smallpox but also there is a type of smallpox which operates so rapidly that no typical rash occurs and death may be put down to convulsions. Brass objected that these cases could not represent a very large proportion of the total recorded smallpox deaths.

There was also some interesting general discussion on the inter-pretation of statistical evidence, arising from a comment by Hollings-worth to the effect that there was a sharp reduction in infant mortality at one time during the eighteenth century. This fall, he said, seemed to him something most likely to have actually happened, in the sense that it seemed probable for other reasons. This point of view was countered by the argument that it was a matter of *fact* whether it did or did not, but Hollingsworth and some others felt that this was too simple a solution to a complex problem. They believed that there was such a thing as a probability of belief in the information and that this is the fact which is often in doubt; whether the event alleged to have happened did in fact occur, even if the evidence suggests it may have done. Hollingsworth went on to suggest that he felt this fall in infant mortality was to be accepted, partly because the great magnitude of the drop as shown in the statistics made it more likely to have occurred. He put the view that the drop which occurred was from about 70 per cent to about 20 per cent, and even if the figures were inaccurate and instead of this it went from 60 per cent to 20 per cent it did not really affect the argument, whereas if one reduced smallpox deaths by 10 per cent the entire incidence had disappeared. The opponents of this position felt that if the data were questionable the mere size of the effect could not really be taken into account as adding validity.

2. Eversley, in an initial reply to Habakkuk, suggested that the question of homogeneity with regard to the peerage was not of the first importance. To him homogeneity was something more biologi- cal than sociological. He would not feel that any group of people in an advanced Western society were ever homogeneous in any sense of the word. The term was a relative one meaning capable of being identified as being the same in respect of certain characteristics. If by this one meant were they all the same sort of people then of course the answer was no. Neither dukes nor Quakers nor any other group could properly be homogeneous. Two things may be homogeneous with respect to one variable but not with respect to all variables, and this could not be something one aimed at or ever claimed. Habakkuk came back to say that this was an important specific point. He was trying to suggest that some of the sub-groups may be heterogeneous in respect of a variable which was highly relevant to demographic behaviour. He gave an extreme example, suggesting that if George III in 1784 had created a hundred brewers as peers, then to ignore this fact in the analysis of changing fertility patterns would merely reflect the policy of George III in respect of the peerages, and an initial difference between the habits of brewers and the peers who already existed. Whereas this was an absurd example, the case of the Presbyterians would not be, and he suggested that there had been a great change between 1650 and 1750 in the social and economic groups from which this religious group was drawn. He admitted that the peerage presented an easier problem because one could see when new creations were made. But unless one had very detailed figures

about newcomers to a sect it must remain very difficult to know how its social and economic composition was changing with time.

Hollingsworth was asked at this point to make a few comments about the facts as he knew them for the peerage. Turning first to the 1784 creations he suggested that they were not really very numerous, but it happened to be the case that for about 50 years before there had been very few creations indeed and this had exaggerated their importance. Many of the people created peers in 1784 already had peerages of some kind and they could not really be counted. The group as a whole spread over a considerable age range and therefore affected different cohorts although they were created at the same time, and as they were presumably from very much the same social groups anyway the effect of the creations would be very slight. But he suspected a very much more marked effect would be obtained in 1603 and the years following when there was a very large increase in the peerage. The numbers were doubled in the reign of James I and this would have made a very considerable difference, as they could not all have been the same as the older families. In reply to a question from Laslett, Hollingsworth said that he had not tried to assess the effect of the influx on demographic data but that it could be done. The material was all on cards but would take considerable time to analyze. Pressed further by Laslett, he said that he had not done this work at the time because it seemed to him on the whole less interesting than the general trend, and one could not do every- thing at once. He said that purely subjective impressions indicated that there was a tendency for people who were created peers to have been previously married, and married rather late in life. Very few people were created peers before marriage, and later married. Furthermore, in order to be created a peer very young, one had virtually, as he put it, to be the illegitimate son of a King or for that matter a legitimate one! But, even allowing for this, he would imagine differences between created and hereditary peers were not a very marked factor. He suspected the age of marriage might be about five years older for created peers than for hereditary peers. Wrigley asked whether it was not true that the fertility change ante-dated the creations. Hollingsworth agreed with this, remarking that the change actually occurred at a time when there was an attempt to limit the peerage altogether.

3. The discussion on van Bath's paper was of a rather technical kind. Clark wondered to what extent the decline in population growth in parts of the Netherlands and the continuing increase in other parts could be due to migration. He suggested that there was evidence that before the late seventeenth century there was considerable

immigration into agricultural land by Danes, Germans and Poles, and he suggested that there might have been a check to this immigration in the late seventeenth and early eighteenth centuries for one reason or another. Furthermore there must have been migration from some parts of the Netherlands as many people went to South Africa and America in this period. Clark asked whether any estimate could be made of the rates of emigration or immigration. A rather more difficult hypothesis to investigate was whether there was a change in the age at marriage of Dutchmen at this time. Brand supported Clark by pointing out that the rise in population in Holland between 1514 and 1622, referred to by van Bath as very large, was in fact by modern standards very small, being an increase of only 1 per cent per annum, and the same thing would hold for the increase in Overijssel between 1675 and 1764. This could be the differential between the birth rate and the death rate, but he felt the figures were so small that they could be due to internal migration. If internal migration were taking place then it could be that the whole question of increases in nuptiality and fertility would not arise.

Van Bath replied that the work on parish registers which would provide the necessary background was still in progress and so very little could be said at this time. It was known that the age of marriage was later in the eighteenth century than in the seventeenth century as far as Amsterdam was concerned. This was also possibly true for Friesland, but for Overijssel and Veluwe there was no information. As far as migration was concerned this was also a very difficult question to answer. It was known that people from the north were going to Amsterdam at this time and that there was a decrease in population in Holland while the towns of Amsterdam, Rotterdam and The Hague increased slowly. A comment from the floor indicated that emigration to South Africa could not be very important statistically as the entire population of the Cape about 1730 was only about 2,000. Van Bath said that the immigration from the south and Germany was mainly before 1650, and thereafter some Huguenots came to the Netherlands, but not in such great numbers. He agreed that it was possible that the check to immigration did partly explain the check to the population. Certainly in Amsterdam there was very considerable immigration until the 1650s. He also took up Brand's comment, suggesting that the increase might not be very large in modern terms but historically it was of great importance. The economic potential of many provinces was very small, especially in the sandy regions. In these areas there were very considerable stretches of common land which were of great importance for farming. The size of arable land might have been about 10 to 15 acres per farm, but there was a system of turf manuring whereby sods were taken from the common land which then subsequently had to recover. Thus the common land had to be perhaps six times as large as each farm in order to continue this kind of agriculture. Brand, however, pointed out that he was not so much concerned with the question of whether the increase was large or not, but simply that whereas van Bath emphasized the increase in nuptiality, and thus the increase in the number of children, he wondered whether the rise could not simply be caused by a decline in the death rate and a small migration surplus. Van Bath replied that it was known that in Overijssel families still had very large numbers of children in the eighteenth century and that there was not much immigration into Overijssel apart from entrepreneurs for the mining industry, for instance from Czechoslovakia.

Turning finally to Drake's paper, the time available for comments was very short. Illsley pointed out that there was a possible danger in the use of occupational material in this kind of study. For example, Drake spoke about differences between ordinary seamen's mates and ships' captains, and between sawmill workers and foremen. Illsley's own work analyzed in this way could suggest that railway engine drivers never had first babies and never got married early whereas railway firemen had first babies but never had second or third babies! In other words a great deal of care had to be taken to make certain that one knew the extent to which the occupations were interchangeable. Thus if, in fact, the ships' captains had formerly been ships' mates or ordinary seamen, and only became captains by the time they were thirty, then clearly the age of marriage of men who are already ships' captains cannot be before thirty.

Clark provided a contribution which makes a fitting close to this report, as it leaves the population growth controversy very much alive. Owing to its complexity it is reproduced in a revised form supplied by him. Clark claims that a demographic model gives us fairly good grounds for believing that falling mortality accounted for the observed increase of the rate of population growth in England in the late eighteenth and early nineteenth centuries, without our needing to formulate any hypotheses about changes in age at marriage, or changes in marital fertility. In this model, the known Swedish mortality rates are assumed to be applicable to England and Wales, and the 1851 proportions married at given ages to be approximately applicable to the eighteenth century. The model predicts very closely the observed rates of population growth as shown in the accompanying table.

Demographic model of the eighteenth and early nineteenth centuries population growth in England

Age-group	Female survivors of 1,000 total births based on Swedish mortality of: 1757–63[1]	Female survivors of 1,000 total births based on Swedish mortality of: 1816–40	Expected[2] % married, not widowed	Marital[3] specific fertility	Specific fertility, all women[4]	Offspring survival rates of: 1757–63	Offspring survival rates of: 1816–40
15–19	1448	1731	2	0·43	0·01	14	17
20–4	1391	1683	30	0·43	0·13	181	219
25–9	1338	1627	60	0·41	0·25	334	406
30–4	1247	1558	70	0·37	0·26	324	405
35–9	1202	1487	75	0·30	0·22	265	327
40–4	1130	1400	70	0·15	0·10	113	140
45–9	1049	1308	65	0·02	0·01	10	13
Total fertility					4·90		
Gross reproduction rate					2·38		
Net reproduction rate						1·241	1·527
Average length of generation years						31·6	31·7
Average rate of population growth per cent per year						0·7	1·4

[1] Only general survival rate given : ratios of female to general rate assumed the same as in 1816–40.

[2] Based on 1851 data for England and Wales, but raised slightly because of eighteenth century rates of male emigration having probably been lower than nineteenth century.

[3] Henry's general estimate for eighteenth and nineteenth century Europe (15–19 added).

[4] Product of two previous columns.